The Lawsuit Lottery

The Lawsuit Lottery

Only the Lawyers Win

Jeffrey O'Connell

THE FREE PRESS
A Division of Macmillan Publishing Co., Inc.
NEW YORK

Collier Macmillan Publishers
LONDON

TO TOM AND ANNIE
ever perceptive and zestful

The Free Press
A Division of Macmillan Publishing Co., Inc.
866 Third Avenue, New York, N.Y. 10022

Collier Macmillan Canada, Ltd.

Library of Congress Catalog Card Number: 79-7579

Printed in the United States of America

printing number

1 2 3 4 5 6 7 8 9 10

Library of Congress Cataloging in Publication Data

O'Connell, Jeffrey.
  The lawsuit lottery.

  Includes bibliographical references and index.
    1. Accident law--United States. 2. Actions and
defenses--United States. 3. Insurance, Accident--
United States. I. Title.
KF1250.02   346'.73'032   79-7579
ISBN 0-02-923280-5

Copyright Acknowledgments

Contents

Preface

AMERICANS HAVE ALWAYS been drawn to the subject of jury trials with a mixture of fascination and anxiety. Because of detective stories in both print and visual media, we often tend to associate the jury process with criminal trials. But in real life Americans are much more likely to get involved in civil trials, which, for the most part in our society, mean accident cases. This book is an attempt to describe the fascination of such lawsuits—and fascinating they can be, with an often classic confrontation between lonely, frightened, needy victims, represented by colorful, even flamboyant ethnic plaintiffs' lawyers, against huge, sophisticated, impersonal insurance companies, represented by sleek, WASP corporate lawyers. All this is played out before impressionable jurors. But in the course of immersion in the fascination of trial by modern combat, the reader will come to appreciate the frustration—dwarfing the fascination—of a lawsuit lottery as a means of deciding who is to be paid after accidents. For this reason, in the second part of the book I propose a much less frustrating—if perhaps less fascinating—means of compensating accident victims without further injuring them through the cut and thrust of litigation. In other words, I aim toward an ideal where the only litigation that most of us will ever have to endure will be watching Perry Mason do battle with fictional criminals.

Acknowledgments

I AM INDEBTED to the John Simon Guggenheim Memorial Foundation: I have twice been awarded a Guggenheim Fellowhip and that encouragement—intellectual as well as financial—means much to me.

I am also grateful to my research assistants for their help: former and present University of Illinois law students John Forhan, Janet Beck, Joseph Switzer, and Byron Matten. I am also grateful for the editorial help of Robert Wallace and George Rowland of The Free Press; manuscript editor Norman Sloan; my brother, Thomas E. O'Connell, President of Bellevue Community College, Bellevue, Washington; his wife, Anne Ludlum O'Connell; and my wife, Virginia Kearns O'Connell.

On formulating some aspects of my proposal for reform contained in this book, I benefited greatly from discussions with Robert Martin of the Wichita, Kansas bar.

Thanks are due to Nancy Baker and Judith Edwards for their expert and patient secretarial assistance.

Portions of Part II of the book, dealing with a solution to the accident law mess, appeared in more technical form in the *University of Cincinnati Law Review*, the *University of Illinois Law Forum*, the *Michigan Law Review*, the *Nebraska Law Review*, the *Texas Law Review* and the *Washington University Law Quarterly*, from all of which permission to use such material in altered form is gratefully acknowledged.

The Lawsuit Lottery

Part I
The Fascination and Frustrations of Accident Litigation

1

Blind Man's Buff

After now some dozen years of experience [as a judge] I must say that as a litigant I should dread a lawsuit beyond almost anything else short of sickness and death.

—LEARNED HAND[1]

THE JURY HAD BEEN DELIBERATING for ten hours, following an eight-day trial. The case concerned Jimmy Farrell, who had been born prematurely in Holy Cross Hospital, Silver Spring, Maryland, on October 12, 1969, and shortly afterward developed a rare disease called RLF (retrolental fibroplasia) that left him blind. Jimmy and his parents sued the hospital along with two attending doctors, asking for $3.5 million based on supposed negligence in administering an excessive amount of oxygen to the infant during incubator maintenance. In response to the suit, the hospital's attorneys eventually offered $85,000 in settlement. By the time the trial started—six years later—the parties were still about $400,000 apart. Jimmy Farrell's team of three lawyers was demanding $650,000, and the hospital's team of three lawyers limited their highest offer to $250,000. After ten days of trial, the hospital had raised its offer to $425,000 and the plaintiffs had lowered their demand to $600,000.

At 11:40 A.M., July 30, 1976, a member of the jury knocked on the locked door of the jury room to signal that a verdict had been reached. Hearing that a decision was imminent, the lawyers on the two sides, fearing an adverse verdict for opposite reasons, decided to

3

make one more strenuous effort to settle. Meeting in the judge's chambers, within minutes they arrived at a compromise figure of $500,000. Shortly before noon, Judge Phillip M. Fairbanks of the Montgomery, Maryland, County Circuit Court announced the settlement and then dismissed the jury. As attorneys for both sides stood outside the courtroom shaking hands with the jurors—six men and six women—the word quickly spread: It was a defense verdict. The jurors had been about to exonerate the hospital and doctors and award Jimmy Farrell and his parents nothing. Split 10-2 in favor of the hospital as it began its deliberations, the jury had spent ten hours considering voluminous hospital records and the testimony of four doctors, as well as that of Jimmy's parents.[2]

Not long before, about 200 miles north, a jury in New York City had been considering the similar case of Gail Kalmowitz. She, too, had sued two doctors and the hospital where she was born, alleging that her almost complete blindness had been caused by RLF, in turn caused by excessive administration of oxygen at her premature birth. Here, too, after a lengthy trial, moments before the jury was to announce its verdict, lawyers on both sides—also fearful for opposite reasons of the jury's decision—scrambled to reach a settlement. In this case, they arrived at a figure of $165,000. Moments later the jury revealed that it had been ready to make an award of $900,000. Members of the jury and Gail, by then twenty-two years old, wept in the corridor of the Brooklyn Superior Courthouse after the jurors told her she had forfeited $735,000 by her settlement. "You shouldn't have done it," tearful jurors told her. "You should have gone all the way. Our hearts were with you."[3]

But the jury decision against Jimmy Farrell lends considerable support to the wisdom of Gail Kalmowitz's mistaken (in hindsight) decision. Her later remarks reveal the agony of her choice: "Because of the problems of discrimination against handicapped people, you just want the money in case you can't get a job. I was afraid I would lose everything and wind up with nothing. I think I made a wise decision. Everybody said, 'You've got it won,' but I wasn't sure. [The other side] said they definitely would have appealed and there's a chance I would have lost it all." Just before agreeing to the settlement she told her lawyer, "I've been unlucky my whole life. I'm just afraid I'll be unlucky again."[4]

Why such different jury decisions in two cases on essentially the same facts? The answer reveals a great deal about the capricious nature of our legal system as it applies to personal injury cases.

It is now generally accepted that oxygen in high concentrations is a cause of RLF in premature infants, but in 1952, at the time of Miss Kalmowitz's birth, such dangers from oxygen therapy were by no means definitely established. As science writer Lawrence Altman has pointed out,[5] in the early 1950s there was great confusion as to the cause of RLF. It had rarely occurred before 1942, when Dr. Theodore L. Terry, a Boston ophthalmologist, drew attention to it and its apparent connections to prematurity. Before long RLF was recognized as the prime cause of infantile blindness and was also seen as the leading complication from premature birth. It was even suspected as an innate condition of prematurity, long overlooked because previously so few premature babies had survived at all.

In Altman's words, "a frenzy of research" was undertaken to establish the cause of RLF and to stop an epidemic that was all the more infuriating because it broke out so capriciously—varying in crazy patterns from hospital to hospital and city to city, with no cases in some places and many in others. Among the almost maddening variables:

RLF seemed to strike only premature infants, sparing those fully developed.

The eyes of afflicted children were normal at birth but became scarred after several weeks.

The disease occurred with disproportionate frequency in the most modern hospitals with the best pediatric equipment and techniques.

Perhaps, it was hypothesized, well-trained pediatricians were somehow treating premature babies in a damaging way. Was infants' biochemistry being undermined by elements in new infant formulas that caused a new metabolic disorder?

Altman recounts how the medical journals in 1953 reported on research possibly implicating many different physical, chemical, and microbiological factors as the cause of RLF. A lack of certain vitamins? Cow's milk? Too much potassium chloride, sodium chloride and other electrolytes, the effects of which on human physiology were by no means yet fully appreciated? According to one researcher, a possible cause was body temperatures that were too low. Other studies implicated light.

While research and studies continued, doctors tried almost everything—patches over the eyes of the newborn, vitamins, new formulas, and so forth. But the epidemic raged on.

As Altman describes it, a few experts experienced in international comparative techniques began to point to the greater use of oxygen for premature babies in America than in Europe. Could *that* explain it? But how could *oxygen* be guilty? Oxygen was life-*giving*. It constituted one-fifth of the earth's atmosphere. True, some studies in the early 1950s had tried to implicate oxygen, but others had concluded that too little—not too much—oxygen caused RLF.

Note the dilemma of the doctor accused of negligence. Each month dozens of medical journals publish numerous articles reporting on research of a technical nature, often conflicting in their conclusions. Hypotheses are advanced; inconclusive tests are reported; advocates urge their solutions. How much evidence of danger is needed before a doctor will withhold a treatment like oxygen and perhaps risk killing an infant? By 1956, after carefully controlled experiments in a cooperative study among eighteen hospitals sponsored by the National Institutes of Health, confirmation of oxygen's role in causing RLF was finally available. But the results of that study were not available until three years after Gail Kalmowitz's birth; in fact, the study itself was not even begun until three months after her birth.

And yet a skillful lawyer, using hindsight, could sway a jury into condemning doctors who failed to heed early warnings. What is a doctor to say when confronted on cross-examination with those earliest studies in reputable medical journals implicating oxygen? That he hadn't read them? That he had read them but ignored them? That they seemed inconclusive? Maybe a group of his peers at a pediatrics convention would sympathize with such understandable confusion, but think of the reception such testimony would meet in a courtroom where a blind girl sits as living testimony to the consequences of ignoring those studies.

It is ironic that Gail Kalmowitz's doctors, using oxygen before its side effects were well established, were judged negligent by a jury, whereas Jimmy Farrell's doctors were exonerated by a jury for using the same technique in 1969, years after the dangers were apparently conclusively established. How can that be explained? After it was discovered that some infants' eyes were more sensitive than others to high doses of oxygen therapy, oxygen concentrations in incubators were lowered to what were then thought to be less toxic levels. Incidents of RLF correspondingly declined. But according to some evidence, lowering oxygen concentrations to prevent relatively rare occurrences of blindness was accompanied by an increase in mental retardation in premature infants deprived of oxygen. Apparently the choice for the physician was less oxygen to prevent blindness at the risk of mental retardation—if in fact the infant survived at all without the extra oxygen.[6] It was such evidence that swayed the jurors in Jimmy Farrell's case.[7]

In both Gail Kalmowitz's case and Jimmy Farrell's, *everybody* was guessing—the doctors at birth, expert witnesses on the stand, jurors in deliberating, and claimants and their lawyers and doctors and their lawyers in negotiating a settlement.

2

The Underworld of Tort

UNDER THE COMMON LAW "tort"* or fault-finding system, after an accident involving Smith and Jones, Smith can be paid only by claiming against Jones and proving Jones's conduct or product faulty and himself free from fault, or at least comparatively so. Because Smith is an "innocent" party claiming against a "wrongdoer," Smith is paid not only for his economic loss, largely comprising medical expenses and wage loss, but for the monetary value of his pain and suffering as well.

The operation of the tort system is akin to a lottery. Most crucial criteria for payment are largely controlled by chance: (1) whether one is "lucky" enough to be injured by someone whose conduct or product can be proved faulty; (2) whether that party's insurance limits or assets are sufficient to promise an award or settlement commensurate with losses and expenses; (3) whether one's own innocence of faulty conduct can be proved; and (4) whether one has the good fortune to retain a lawyer who can exploit all the variables before an impressionable jury, including graphically portraying whatever pain one has suffered. Small wonder that for those significantly injured in traffic accidents, 55 percent get absolutely nothing from the tort liability system.[1] For injuries from malfunctioning

*Derived from the Latin *tortus,* "twisted." Thus a tort is conduct that is crooked, not straight. Similarly "wrong" is derived from "wrung." W. Prosser, *Law of Torts,* 4th ed. (1971), p. 2.

8

products[2] or medical malpractice[3] the percentage of those paid from liability insurance is far less. But while many, especially among the more seriously injured, go unpaid, many others, especially among the less seriously injured, are overpaid.[4] Moreover, any payment to anyone is usually long delayed.[5] And far too much is spent on insurance overhead and lawyers' fees.[6] Indeed, the biggest irony of the tort liability system is the degree to which it has come to reward the supposedly supporting players—in this case lawyers and increasingly, as we shall see, certain doctors—rather than compensate accident victims.

Other features exacerbate the common law tort liability system. For example, no deduction is made in a settlement or verdict when the victim has already been paid for his losses by his own health insurance or sick leave. Such compensation is said to come from a collateral source—collateral to the defendant, that is—and hence the term "collateral source rule" for such nondeduction. As a result, the tort liability system often transfers money, when it does so at all, in a hugely inefficient way: to pay for losses already paid for by other insurance coverage! This wastefulness originated in an age when there were relatively few collateral sources available to accident victims. In that earlier age it was deemed unjust to allow a "wrongdoer" to benefit from the foresight of his victim by subtracting from what was owed the benefits the victim had prudently purchased for himself. But the rule has long made no sense: Collateral sources have grown exponentially, and most tort suits stem not from any malefic wrongdoing but from relatively neutral acts of carelessness. To allow individuals to be paid twice for their losses obviously gives incentives to incur extra medical expenses or to incur work loss in hopes of, in effect, drawing two paychecks for not working. The folly of such insurance practices stands out in contrast to the rigid rules in fire insurance against overinsuring.

Nor is the situation improved by the fact that the value of pain and suffering for a tort claim is often measured—at least roughly—by the size of the victim's medical bills, which, at least for smaller losses, are being paid mostly by Blue Cross and Blue Shield. For many claims, then, for every dollar of Blue Cross's money the accident victim can manage to spend, he will get back from his tort claim that dollar of medical expenses *plus* two or three more dollars for his pain and suffering. A lawyer will therefore see to it that his client is sent to a cooperative doctor who won't spare the treatment (paid for out of an impersonal health insurance pool), and the "buildup" is

on. Keep in mind how hard it is to detect such practices. The patient
has, after all, been in an accident and may welcome the comfort of
diathermy or some other medical attention. Who is to deny his needs
when ordered by a reputable doctor? And if one doctor won't coop-
erate (by giving people more treatment than they need, and lining his
own pockets in the bargain), the lawyer can easily find another who
will. Orthopedic specialists and others specializing in accident victims may rely on referrals from lawyers for a good portion of their
practice.

Such conduct is all the more common in view of the general economics of the medical profession. Many doctors are financially dependent on treating people who don't need treatment. Not long ago
a young internist (who prefers to remain anonymous) expounded on
medical billing practices. Like all private practitioners, he faces considerable overhead in the form of rent, telephone, nurse's salary,
laboratory fees, malpractice insurance, and other expenses. His
monthly expenses in 1977 came to about $4,000, against income in
fees of only $3,800 in January, $3,900 in February, and $5,500 in
March. So pressed was he that he was forced to go to a bank for a
loan to tide him over. According to the doctor, "The way to overcome this [is] to increase business in some way, and the way to do
that, I found, is to suggest to patients that they come in for an annual physical examination." Not that he felt that they absolutely
needed it. "A doctor has to do this sort of thing in order to provide a
base income, so that he can continue to take care of his patients. Not
every patient is going to be sick, not every patient is going to have a
medical problem that warrants a complete physical, but in a way
that's sort of the dues of the population to their doctor." Not only
are the fees for the physicals a money-maker, but physicals lead to
lab tests, and the doctor is allowed 50 percent of the lab costs for
himself, so that if the lab charge is $2 the doctor gets to add $1 on.
The doctor denied that he would simply make up a diagnosis in conjunction with the physical so that his patients could collect from
their insurance companies for the physical and lab work. But he admitted: "I'll be very general and vague in my description of the
problem, such as weakness and fatigue, which justifies doing certain
blood tests. Chest discomfort of any sort justifies doing an electro-
cardiogram." Almost anything goes, as long as it doesn't actually
harm the patient (such as needless X-rays—but here this doctor is
probably being more fastidious than many of his peers). "The pie
can be cut up in so many ways—the pie being the fund of money to

pay for professional medical care—and everybody is fighting for their share of the pie. So, do you use frugality with insurance companies . . . when everybody else is not being frugal? Then you're the guy who doesn't make it financially. I mean, why should I go broke and not take my share of the pie? That's our retainer. That's what keeps us going. . . . I don't believe anybody in medicine takes care of 100 percent sick people. You gotta take care of healthy people if you want to make a living."[7]

Well, given that climate, what a boon to the medical profession are accident victims with tort claims, where health insurance is usually applicable without much if any deductible and where, far from costing anyone anything, a patient can wring *further* profit from every dollar charged by the "buildup" of medical bills to enhance the value of the pain and suffering claim. Of all the insane incentives to increase medical costs needlessly in our society, none are so rampant as the rules governing compensation of accident victims. As the writer Martin Mayer has put it, the "money in personal injury lawsuits has corrupted two professions."[8]

Indeed, the money is sometimes a little too easy. After an auto accident in 1969, Mrs. Lydia Jiminez of Perth Amboy, New Jersey, was referred by the Woodbridge, New Jersey, law firm of Rabb and Zeitler, specializing in personal insurance cases, to a physician for treatment of a back injury. After she complained of feeling "very nervous," her lawyers sent her to a Dr. Herbert Boehm for neuropsychiatric treatment twice a week. Testifying before the New Jersey State Commission of Investigation, Mrs. Jiminez said, "He locked me up in a small closet with a heat lamp and a pair of dark glasses." After six visits she informed the doctor that she could perform the treatment on herself just as well at home and never came back. Even so, Dr. Boehm submitted a bill for $630 to Rabb and Zeitler, for allegedly treating Mrs. Jiminez thirty-nine times. Mr. and Mrs. Antonio Elias of Newark had a similar experience with Dr. Boehm; they testified that they too had gone to Dr. Boehm, in their case "eight or nine times," principally for heat therapy for their headaches and "tension." According to the couple, treatment of each of them consisted largely of ten minutes of therapy under a heat lamp. But, according to the couple, Dr. Boehm billed them for sixteen visits, in addition to charging them for the administration of "analgesics, tranquilizers, and reassurance." In point of fact, however, Mrs. Elias had never taken any tranquilizers because of her pregnancy at the time.[9]

If those eligible for payment from fault-finding claims are a small percentage of accident victims, they still constitute a large number of people. So lucrative is this money tree of accident claims that it has led, as every schoolchild now knows, to widespread ambulance-chasing all over the country. According to one Chicago newspaper, "Ambulance-chasing is one of the safest and most lucrative rackets in America." But, unlike "dope, gambling and prostitution . . . it is all but unpunishable."[10] People involved in accidents have often unwittingly stumbled onto a very substantial asset, one that can be pumped up to a lot of money with a minimum of risk and effort on their part. But the typical accident victim may have no idea about translating that asset into cash, nor may he know that his claim can be worth four or five times the amount of his medical bills, or even more. Furthermore, accident victims may be frightened or at least uncomfortable about dealing with lawyers. Lawyers, in turn, are prevented under their canons of ethics from soliciting clients, that is, seeking out accident victims and alerting them to the riches that may await them. But lawyers are very aware that insurance companies, not being law firms, are not constrained from having their adjusters get to the victim and buy up the claim for what may be a fraction of its value. How many accident victims will suspect—especially if the adjuster misleads them about it—that they are entitled to be paid all over again for items already defrayed by their own insurance? What is to prevent an insurance adjuster from telling a claimant that payment by one insurance company bars payment by another? After all, that makes more sense than the law as it is written. And how many accident victims suspect that they may be entitled to three, five, or even ten times their medical bills for pain and suffering? Indeed, according to one survey only about 28 percent of accident victims who eventually were paid from the other driver's insurance company knew at the time of the accident about being paid for pain and suffering.[11] Keep in mind that the insurance adjuster is dealing, in the case of a liability claim, not with one of his own insureds but with a stranger, indeed an adversary party—an "enemy," if you will. Thus, insurers often get away with paying only the claimant's out-of-pocket losses, with nothing for (1) pain and suffering or (2) losses already compensated by other insurance, despite the claimant's common law entitlement to both. One can cite many cases where adjusters have taken egregious advantage of hapless accident victims, getting them to sign releases for a relative pittance.[12] And one can cite even worse: A five-year-old boy, Ernest Gene Gunn, was seriously injured by the negligent driving of one John J. Washek.

An adjuster from Washek's insurance company visited the boy's mother shortly after the accident, telling her that she needn't retain an attorney because the company would make a settlement as soon as the boy was finished with doctor's care. If at that point Mrs. Gunn was not satisfied, he told her, she could hire an attorney and file suit. The boy was sufficiently injured to require a doctor's care for about two years. At the end of that period, Mrs. Gunn tried repeatedly to reach the insurance company adjuster but without success. Finally she hired a lawyer who promptly filed suit, but to no avail, because the insurance company successfully pleaded a two-year statute of limitations![13]

Knowing all this, plaintiffs' attorneys are frantic to join the chase, and the canons of ethics be damned. If lawyers are prevented from using CB radios and rushing to the scene of an accident in person, they are not averse to maintaining contacts among those whose job it is to reach the scene, or who at least learn of an accident shortly after it happens: ambulance drivers, interns, hospital orderlies, nurses, policemen, tow truck operators, garage mechanics. In a metropolitan area, a lawyer may pay such a surrogate "chaser" a minimum of $100 to $150 "a head" for sending claimants to him; for a really big case, a chaser may himself charge a contingent fee, usually one-third of the lawyer's third. If the case is big enough, the chaser may ask for bids.[14] According to a 1971 Philadelphia investigation, chasers were being paid $150 when the claimant was signed up, as a draw against 10 percent of the lawyer's fee.[15] Chasers can be either amateurs, such as former clients occasionally referring a case, or highly disciplined, full-time "professionals." Charles Kelson, formerly chief investigator for the Los Angeles District Attorney's Insurance Fraud Division, describes some of the techniques of one operator:

> We had this hot-shot lawyer in Los Angeles who had 50 employees, his own building and was taking in $4 million a year in personal injury cases. Through his ambulance-chasers he got several thousand cases a year. He'd tell the client he'd be handling him on a percentage or contingent fee basis. That is, the lawyer would get a third of the settlement and the client two-thirds. Yet somehow in the typical case involving a settlement of about $1,800, the client would end up with only [$200–$300].[16]

The lawyer accomplished this by deducting imaginary or grossly inflated expenses. In one $3,050 settlement, the client got only $285. Although the lawyer was finally disbarred, Kelson states that similar practices are still going on: "We've recently indicted 40 other lawyers on ambulance-chasing. Most of their clients were being cheated the same old way."[17]

As the legal sociologist Jerome Carlin has described it, some highly successful personal injury lawyers are totally dependent on "highly organized methods of solicitation, cooperating with chasers" whose business it is to locate and approach the potentially lucrative case. Armed with retainer contracts in blank, chasers develop elaborate and effective procedures to win the race to those with promising claims, using their contacts with police, especially accident squads, and with interns, doctors, nurses, and ambulance drivers. Certain hospitals are "controlled" by certain chasers. Carlin says that such a chaser's lawyer may be able to make a million a year or more from "his" hospital. Any other personal injury lawyer who attempts to find potential clients there will find himself escorted out by the police and perhaps prosecuted for unethical practices![18]

The *Northwestern University Law Review* described the situation in Chicago as "an exciting version of cops and robbers which might be called 'ambulance chasers and insurance adjusters.' "[19] Adjusters, trying to get a settlement, and chasers, trying to sign up the victim for their lawyers, work frantically, using stratagems and spoiler tactics, even to the point of climbing hospital fire escapes or otherwise sneaking into hospital rooms to a patient's bedside as soon as he has recovered sufficiently to write his name. Nor is all this limited to penny-ante cases and operators. The scramble after a major air crash is dizzying. Prestigious personal injury lawyers—protesting that they themselves do not solicit cases, but rather get them on referral from the victims' family lawyers—complain that their rivals stalk hospital corridors in an effort to reach crash survivors or relatives of dead victims. One lawyer bitterly tells of a rival who sent Christmas hams to relatives of those killed in a chartered aircraft accident.[20] According to knowledgeable observers in Chicago, almost every lawyer makes "some kind" of payment to people who bring in business. A claims supervisor of one insurance company asserts that "a large percentage of the legal representation of personal injury clients in Chicago is got by unethical means. . . . If the police are called to the scene of an accident, there is no forseeable chance but that an active and vigorous solicitation will follow. Corrupt politicians are on the payroll of chasers."[21]

Because chasing involves breaches of professional ethics—and, indeed, of the law—it is bound to be pervaded by corrupt elements. Chasers often will have criminal records. Sometimes they even take over a lawyer, putting pressure on him, sending him an increasing volume of questionable cases, and increasing their demands up to 40 or 50 percent of the lawyer's fee.[22]

John Gregory Dunne, in his marvelously evocative novel *True Confessions,* captures the ugly interaction of accident claims and the underworld. In the novel, set in the 1940s in Los Angeles, Tom Spellacy, a cynical, corrupt detective, is investigating the murder of a young prostitute, Lois Fazenda, who has been killed and then brutally dismembered. In the course of his search for the murderer, Spellacy interviews "Brenda," a madam. They discuss the fact that Lois Fazenda had worked for the "Protectors of the Poor," a charitable organization specializing in aiding accident victims, mainly Mexicans, by handing out candy, cigarettes, and religious tokens such as rosary beads. The madam reveals that some of her "girls" used to work for the Protectors.

He stared sharply at her, wondering what whores were doing working for a Catholic charity. "Doing mission work?"

"Rubbing up against guys. Flashing their tits, too, you want to know the honest truth. I bet she was very good rubbing up against guys, that girl."

"Why would she want to do that?"

"To make the guy feel good, I guess. You're all broken up, it must make you feel good, looking down a girl's dress."

"I bet it would at that."

"That's when she flashes the insurance form at him, Tom. 'Sign this, I'll get you a lawyer who'll sue the bastard who hit you.' "

It was slowly beginning to come clear. No wonder whores were volunteers. "I bet there's lawyers who'd pay for a form like that."

"Fifty bucks each, I hear," Brenda said. "Maybe more."

"And the wetback, I bet he never sees the insurance settlement."

"There's a lot of expenses involved, Tom."

"Ambulance chasing is what you'd call it, you want to put a dirty name to it."

"If you want to put a dirty name to it," Brenda said. . . . "It's worth a fortune. They can't complain, the wetbacks, they don't get their money, because they're illegals, most of them."

"And if they do bitch. . . ."

"They can always get hit by another car. . . . When's the last time Robbery–Homicide broke its hump for a dead Mex?"[23]

It turns out that the mastermind behind the scheme is Jack Amsterdam, an underworld figure who has become a pillar of the Catholic Church. He has used as a front Monsignor Ruben Aguilar, "seventy-nine years old and an IQ to match," as Spellacy characterizes him. Amsterdam convinces the gullible monsignor that what the Mexicans at County General Hospital need is people to give them attention: speaking to them in Spanish, along with handing out candy and religious items—something that Anglos, indifferent to Mexicans, won't do. Spellacy reconstructs the scheme:

> If there was one way to get Ruben Aguilar's attention, that was it. Anglos not caring about Mexicans. A tax-exempt charity. Just the thing. You head the charity, Monsignor, I'll get the tax exemption. That was the way Jack operated. The Protectors of the Poor. It would take Ruben Aguilar to come up with a name like that. Or Monsignor Amigo, as the newspapers called him. What a shill. All the volunteers were Jack's people. And the towing companies and ambulance services and body shops and auto-wrecking yards that supplied the Protectors with the names of Mexican accident victims were all paid off by Jack for just that information.[24]

Repeatedly over the past few years, grand jury investigations in major cities have turned up extensive accident rings, including doctors, lawyers, private investigators, and policemen acting as "runners" or chasers, who direct accident victims to particular lawyers and get kickbacks in return. Such rings involve not only padding of chased claims but even multimillion-dollar rackets that go far beyond padding to fabrication of personal injury claims stemming from accidents that in fact involve only property damage. Furthermore, not only are medical bills padded and fictitiously created, but accidents themselves are fabricated in the scramble for tort liability insurance dollars! Unscrupulous lawyers will hire two or three people to stage an accident between two cars at enough velocity to damage fenders in such a way as to make personal injury a plausible outcome. A cooperative doctor then helps the lawyer file a personal injury claim for a whiplash injury to one of the participants in the front car against the driver of the rear car, the latter being well covered by a liability insurance policy taken out in preparation for the "event." The claimant does his part by feigning injury and getting admitted to a hospital.[25] One of the biggest fraud rings was led by a 250-pound Chicagoan, LeRoy (Big Red) Anderson. His group staged auto accidents from Buffalo to San Diego, collecting a total of $500,000 from some five hundred collisions. Several members of the gang would cruise around a city until they spotted a likely victim.

The driver would then swerve abruptly in front of the victim's car and stop quickly, causing the victim to plow into the rear of the ring's car. Under the usual rule that the rear car is to blame, the gang members were regularly able to collect for car damage and "whiplash" injuries.[26] Recently Charles G. Ward, Midwest Regional Director of the Insurance Crime Prevention Institute, charged that doctors and lawyers are commonly the "masterminds behind schemes to stage phony accidents and inflate or falsify outright medical bills or other claims." In April 1978, he stated, four Kansas City, Missouri, physicians and lawyers were indicted for hiring "runners" and "bird dogs" to solicit accident victims or to pose as victims themselves in a $2.5-million insurance fraud case.[27]

The variations of the swindle, worked by either loners or teams, are endless. In the summer of 1975, a bicyclist was struck by a rented car on a New Jersey highway. It was scarcely a typical accident. After falling off his bicycle, the cyclist unwrapped a vial of his own blood, which he then poured on the ground. Next he reached into a bag he had brought along and took out chips of glass, which he spread around. Then the cyclist and his accomplice, the driver of a rented car, went to a nearby house. There, after spraying himself with a local anesthetic, the cyclist cut himself with a razor blade on the arm, leg, cheek, and forehead. Next he broke off two of his teeth with a pair of pliers. Then he checked into a local hospital. It was his fifteenth automobile-related accident within two years, for which his total payments had exceeded $30,000.[28]

W. S. Stead, a well-groomed personnel officer with a large corporation, has a lucrative sideline which has netted him about $60,000 over the past few years. *Wall Street Journal* reporter Hal Lancaster described how he does it (Stead is a pseudonym adopted from a passenger on the *Titanic):*

> Is there a grape on the floor of a supermarket? Mr. Stead will slip on it in front of a horde of witnesses and suffer lumbosacral strain: a generous check from the store chain's insurer alleviates it. Is there a distracted mother with a station wagon full of kids on the Santa Monica Freeway? Mr. Stead will abruptly change lanes and swerve in front of her, trying to induce a rear-end collision. A mild collision, of course, but his whiplash injury is just terrible.
>
> . . . But Stead is careful to get corroboration for his claim, sometimes from a cooperative doctor. After one staged pratfall, he says, he saw this physician: the latter gave no treatment and never saw the

"victim" again, but presented him with a bill for a whopping $800. To Mr. Stead, this was not highway robbery: both he and the insurer knew that if the case came to trial and the insurer lost, the jury would be likely to make a pain-and-suffering award based on a multiple of the doctor's bill. The more the doctor charged, the larger the likely award. The insurer coughed up $8,000 in an out-of-court settlement.[29]

In an Eastern city not long ago five people filed forty claims in a three-year period, all complaining that the bread they had eaten contained glass, causing lacerations to their mouths and stomachs. Actually, they themselves had inserted fine glass from light bulbs into the bread, rebaked the loaves to cover the holes, and then sued.[30]

Insurance companies insist that they are losing billions of dollars annually on fraudulent claims—costs that they insist they must pass on to other insurance buyers. The companies estimate that 10 percent of all automobile claims are fake, at a cost of about $1.5 billion a year.[31]

Although it is true that insurance fraud is common in many kinds of claims—health insurance, burglary, fire—liability insurance claims are uniquely susceptible to fraud for several reasons. You are claiming not against your own insurance company but a stranger's. Even more important, damages for pain and suffering, coupled with payment of any amounts already paid for from other forms of insurance, give liability claims a multiplier effect that is really staggering. Indeed, so tempting is it that not only the charlatan but even the legitimate and conscientious sufferer is beguiled by the system into presenting fattened claims. A lawyer will feel that his biggest weapon against an insurance company is the company's fear of the uncertain extent of its "exposure," the company's term for the ultimate worth of the injury and therefore its cost. Once the condition of the victim is stabilized, the lawyer has reason to believe the insurance claims manager, knowing the limit of what he has to fear, will harden his bargaining position. But if the lawyer can keep his client incurring medical bills (paid from his client's health insurance), he increases not only the value of his claim before a jury but also the pressure on the insurance company to buy the claim before it balloons much higher. Insurers, on the other hand, face so much padding and fudging—not to say outright chicanery and dishonesty—and so much legitimate uncertainty, even where no questionable practices are present, concerning whether the claimant's conduct is faulty and in establishing the monetary value of the claimant's nonmonetary loss, that they feel compelled to bargain with flinty-eyed determination. Thus claims managers, lawyers on both sides, and doctors are caught in a vicious cycle, given the nightmare of uncertainty of the insured event under common law tort liability.

The problems are further aggravated by the practice of the single lump-sum payment, dictated by the common law system. In other words, nothing is paid periodically as losses accrue; only at the end of the entire claims process is payment made. So an insurance company, understandably, will use the fact of the months' or years' delay before trial to try to force the claimant and his lawyer to accept much less than a jury might award simply in order to settle the matter and perhaps get badly needed cash to cover wage loss and medical expenses not being reimbursed from other sources. This lump-sum method stands in contrast to many other forms of insurance, such as health insurance, which are paid periodically as bills become due. In addition, the common law system of one lump-sum payment means that in the event of serious injury, where losses may continue beyond the date of settlement or verdict, predictions must be ventured on the extent of the injury into the future. This leads to a further bitter and often counterproductive battle between plaintiff and defendant, with the plaintiff's doctor grossly exaggerating the aftereffects of the injury and the insurance company doctor just as grossly disparaging them—and the jury, "twelve people of average ignorance," as one wit called them, left in the middle trying to decide which doctor is exaggerating less. (One sometimes gets the impression that in an amputation case, the plaintiff's doctor will predict that the amputation will spread, while the insurance company doctor is confident that the limb will grow back.) Keep in mind that once damages are settled by either agreement or verdict, the amount determined cannot be changed, even if it turns out, in light of the patient's subsequent condition, to be either pathetically inadequate or wildly overgenerous.

The result is a system that, even in the hands of legitimate professionals, ends up injuring the injured while supposedly trying to help them. It has always been axiomatic in medical circles that promptness is essential to good medical treatment of trauma. The victim must be made to put the accident behind him, especially if rehabilitation is needed. In the words of a member of the American College of Surgeons' Committee on Trauma, "Rehabilitation should commence on the day of injury and be continued until the limit of im-

provement is reached."[32] Personal injury lawyers expertly and efficiently foster exactly the opposite attitude. Consider the following
advice American trial lawyers give to their injury victim clients:

INSTRUCTIONS TO CLIENTS
"MY DAY"

1. "MY DAY"—We have talked to you about "My Day" when
   you were in the office. We would like you to start keeping a
   diary at once. This record will be very valuable throughout your
   case. *It will be kept strictly confidential.*
2. HOW THESE INJURIES HAVE AFFECTED YOUR LIFE—
   We call it "My Day" because we want you to take a normal day,
   from the time you get up until the time you go to bed, and explain in detail how this occurrence has changed your life. For example, the way you put on your clothes, the way you get in and
   out of bed, the way you take a bath, etc. By your life, we mean
   your work, your playtime, your hobbies, your life as a husband
   or as a wife, etc. This includes your disposition, your personality, your nervousness, etc. We need to know how your injury has
   affected the marital relations between you and your spouse.
3. YOUR PAIN AND SUFFERING—We want a description of
   your pain, both at the scene of the occurrence and at all times
   thereafter. We want to know whether or not it is a shooting
   pain, throbbing pain, etc. We want your words and not anyone
   else's.
4. START AT YOUR HEAD WHEN RECORDING YOUR
   COMPLAINTS AND INJURIES—A good rule to follow in order to remember all of your problems is to start at your head
   and, in detail, go down through all parts of your body, moving
   from your head, neck, shoulders, etc. Explain in detail any
   problem that you have with each part of the body. Also, give
   details with regard to the medications you are taking and what
   they are for, if you know.
5. DON'T USE THE WORDS "I CAN'T"—Please do not use the
   words "I can't," because "can't" means physical impossibility.
   For example, you can't use your left hand, if you haven't got
   one. Don't say "I can't do it," "I don't do it," "I never do it."
   We would prefer you would use such words as "I am not able to
   do it as well" or some other words meaning the same thing. You
   should always work toward the idea that "I am trying and I will
   continue to try to do more things." Everyone will admire you
   more if you try. In regard to your activities such as your house-

work, your yardwork, your work at the office or factory, you should detail what things you are not able to do as well as before.

6. "MY DAY" WITNESSES—We would like for you to contact your friends, neighbors, associates at work, etc., and on a separate sheet of paper for each witness give us his name, address and telephone number. Have each describe, or you describe in detail, on a separate sheet of paper what he or she knows about how this injury has changed your life. For example, your neighbor might tell about how you are not able to work as much around the house, or your friends could tell how you don't bowl now, or you don't engage in some other type of hobby. It is better if these witnesses are not your relatives. It is all right if they are your friends, because they would be more likely to have observed you. *It is impossible to be too detailed.*

7. LOSS OF WAGES OR LOSS OF POTENTIAL INCOME— One of the major aspects of your case may be loss of income or potential income. We will need a copy of your union contract showing wage rates, copies of your W-2 forms and your income tax returns for at least the last five years. Please obtain from your employer the exact days you missed from work because of this accident and the amount of money you would have made if you would have been working these days. If this injury has prevented you from being advanced in your employment or has prevented you from obtaining employment, please give us the names, addresses and telephone numbers of witnesses who can prove this for you. We would also like to know in detail what services you have been prevented from performing around the house, such as supervision of the children.

8. QUESTIONS OR HELP IN ANSWERING YOUR "MY DAY"—If you need any help in keeping your records, please call this office for an appointment. *Do not come in without an appointment.*

9. USE YOUR IMAGINATION—You know your own life better than we do. Use your imagination and go into all aspects of your life. Explain to us, in the greatest detail possible, how this occurrence has affected your life.[33]

Given the purposes of the tort liability system, lawyers cannot be blamed for thus advising their clients. But many in the medical profession are understandably shocked by a system that, contrary to all medical wisdom, encourages accident victims to preserve, hug, and indeed nurture and memorialize every twinge and hurt from an accident. According, once again, to the same member of the Committee on Trauma, "Many a temporary partial disability has become a permanent partial or even permanent total [disability] because emphasis was placed entirely on the legal rather than the medical facet of the problem."[34] John Nemiah, writing in, of all places, the magazine of the American Trial Lawyers' Association, has stated:

> It should be appreciated by all concerned that the adversary nature of a tort [claim] subsequent to injury heightens the patient's sense of grievance, entitlement to redress, and revenge—which tends to foster his aggressive drive and to shift his attention away from the goals of rehabilitation and eventual regained independence.

> [I]t should be recognized that the delays so frequently encountered in settling personal injury litigation tend to keep the patient trapped for months, even years, in a limbo of indecision and idleness in which dependency needs are fostered. During this time, it frequently becomes so pointless to try to work toward rehabilitation that, practically, the patient remains an invalid until legal elements emanating from his injury are resolved.[35]

But, as indicated above, by the time the legal proceedings are concluded it may be simply too late to start on rehabilitation. What a tragedy that accident law forces accident victims into "the schizophrenic choice between 'recovery' in the medical sense and 'recovery' in the legal sense," in the words of Law Professor Alfred Conard of the University of Michigan.[36]

And so the occasional accident victim who makes it through the labyrinth of tort liability, with all its emotional and technical vicissitudes, often ends up defeated even when he wins. He wins the legal battle but loses the war he should have been fighting for maximum physical and psychological recovery. He will be left not only with the injuries and suffering that compensation is designed to ameliorate but with the distinct possibility of a condition aggravated by focus on legal rather than medical recovery.

Furthermore, any large award made in one lump sum can easily be dissipated in frivolous expenditures and luxuries, rather than spent on sensible substitutes for the losses caused by accidents. Paternalistic as it may sound, putting the burden on the accident victim of wise investment and providential management of tens or hundreds of thousands of dollars seems needlessly risky. A study some years ago of 1,700 accident compensation victims to find how they disposed of their lump-sum settlement payments concluded that the disposition of such sums "is not generally such as to offer assurance of a stable substitute for the loss of wages incurred in the severe and fatal injuries."[37]

Trial lawyers and other exponents of the tort system are fond of defending it on the grounds that, by focusing on unsafe conduct, tort law succeeds in deterring such conduct. But the experience under no-fault auto insurance does not seem to bear out the tort liability system's deterrent effect. To cite a United States Department of Transportation study:

> Prior to the adoption of no-fault [auto] laws and some actual experience with the operating results, some observers argued that change to a . . . no-fault system would remove accountability for accident fault and thereby increase driver carelessness and the likelihood of highway traffic accidents. In other words, it was argued, there would be "havoc in the streets." Factual evidence that conclusively proves or dispels this theory does not exist, but traditional safety statistics give no credence to this argument. Indeed, looking at accident rates over the 1970–75 period for each of the 16 no-fault states, no discernible jump in accident frequency following the institution of these states' no-fault laws can be found. In fact, the accident rate trend for each state generally follows the gradual downward aggregate trends for the U.S. as a whole, as well as those trends for the U.S. urban highway and the U.S. rural highway accident rates.[38]

Product liability law, too, seems to have little deterrent effect. Studies conducted for the National Product Safety Commission seem to demonstate how ineffectively the present common law system deters the manufacturing of unsafe machinery, given the law's unpredictable, dilatory, and cumbersome operation.[39]

The first such study was done by William Whitford, a University of Wisconsin law professor, who was commissioned to conduct an empirical study to assess the impact of product liability litigation on the decisions of manufacturers regarding the design of their products. Professor Whitford concludes that product liability litigation usually has minimal direct impact on product design. He suggests three explanations for his conclusions. First, the time period between the occurrence of the injury and the final outcome of the litigation often exceeds five years. Because product designs often change at shorter intervals, litigation usually involves a discontinued design. Second, many manufacturers isolate themselves from product liability claims by funneling all claims to their insurers and thereafter largely ignoring them even to the point, on occasion, of not inform-

ing themselves of the final outcome of claims. Litigation is unlikely
to affect design decisions of such manufacturers. Finally, a majority
of rotary mower manufacturers, in an industry plagued by litigation,
fail to keep abreast of litigation involving other rotary mower manufacturers, indicating a general lack of concern.[40]

A further reason, incidentally, behind the indifference of industry and its engineers to the lessons of tort liability is that they have
reason to view common law litigation as a circus—crude, emotional,
unscientific, and therefore scarcely able to teach anything to scientists about their profession or trade.

A study by former Pennsylvania Insurance Commissioner Herbert Denenberg, then of the Wharton School of the University of
Pennsylvania, indicated how seldom insurance companies writing
product liability coverage encourage manufacturers to concern
themselves with safety. Denenberg points out that the insurance industry is in a strategically perfect place to promote safety. "Insurance industry opportunity and insurance industry self-interest for
loss prevention should blend into a near perfect picture."[41] But in
surveying product liability insurance companies, agents, brokers,
and insureds, Professor Denenberg laments that even the billion-dol-
lar companies did not consult their records to discern principles for
preventing future product liability claims. He found that insurance
companies generally did not calculate the payoff for loss prevention
service. Many insurance executives were ignorant of the costs of the
loss prevention programs that they administered. Insurers admitted
that they do not compete for the best engineering and loss prevention
personnel. Denenberg noted a rather negative reaction throughout
industry to the utility of loss prevention services: 62 percent of a
sample of corporations on the "Fortune 500" list stated that their insurers did not make an important contribution, by loss prevention
advice, to an overall product liability safety effort.[42]

These responses are not simply a result of ineptitude on the part
of the insurance industry, as Professor Denenberg is inclined to suggest. Rather, the problems of measuring the achievement of safety
against the size and structure of liability insurance premiums and experience are extraordinarily frustrating.[43]

Still another study, by the federal government's Interagency Task
Force on Product Liability, found that the effect on insurance premiums of insurers' safety inspections and services "is not well defined, nor are the benefits associated with implementation of improved manufacturing procedures necessarily reflected by fewer

claims or reduced settlements."[44] Indeed, according to the report, although it sees some attempts at improvement being made, "most
premiums for product liability coverage are determined quite subjec-
tively by individual insurance companies."[45]

The lack of a deterrent effect for product liability is mirrored in
medical malpractice insurance. According to the Special Advisory
Panel on Medical Malpractice of New York State:

> *There is no ready evidence that the distribution of the economic
> burden* [of medical malpractice premiums] *is rationally related to
> the objective of the tort system to deter negligent practice.* Unless
> there are major differences in loss experience with regard to medical
> malpractice suits, each physician pays the same premium as his spe-
> cialist colleague, with the neurosurgeons and orthopoedic surgeons
> paying the highest rate and the general practitioners and the pathol-
> ogists paying the lowest. Thus, because specialists applying the most
> advanced procedures developed by medical science run the highest
> risk of an adverse medical result, they, also, regardless of compe-
> tence, bear the highest financial risk of medical malpractice due to
> negligence. This may be a logical insurance approach, but it is at
> variance with our other systems for accessing quality of care
> through specialty board examinations and peer reviews. [Emphasis
> in original.][46]

In medical malpractice cases too one finds proud professionals,
offended by the tawdry techniques of courtroom theatrics, unlikely in the extreme to accept lessons from "unwashed" jurors—
or, if you will, jurors washed in what professionals view as the unscientific emotional bathos of common law trials. There is considerable
evidence that malpractice litigation not only fails to deter unsafe
conduct but encourages it. According to one authority, for example,
a study of 570 children consecutively admitted to a hospital emergency room for head trauma showed that the "treatment of only one
was altered as a result of the skull X-rays taken."[47] The costs en-
tailed in such apparently needless use of X-rays are indicated by an
estimate that "one of every 3 X-rays taken in the U.S. was for legal
reasons. Since X-rays cost American families about $3 billion an-
nually . . . the public spends $1 billion a year on medically useless
films. This is not to mention the hazard of exposing people to excess
radiation."[48]

Personal injury lawyers themselves see little real malpractice in
medical malpractice cases that justifies disciplinary action. According to the New York State Medical Malpractice Report, "Plaintiffs'

attorneys have not made a practice of reporting themselves, or advising potential clients to report, incidents of alleged malpractice to either the appropriate professional societies or state agencies, even if the damages were not worth pursuing."[49]

This tends to confirm a very significant point: Very rarely are personal injuries inflicted by conduct that is morally reprehensible or heinous. Overwhelmingly accidents are just that—"accidents," morally neutral and actuarially inevitable. All the less reason to govern payments therefore by an accusatory, investigatory, adversary process. Ray Gambino, a professor of pathology at one of the most eminent medical schools in the country, the College of Physicians and Surgeons of Columbia University, has described a "serious error" for which he was responsible: In asking how anyone could make such a mistake he indicates that the following case history "will tell something about the genesis of [medical] error":

> As a resident in pathology I had to take night call for emergency lab tests. Late one night I set up a crossmatch, and I typed a patient as group O. At 2 A.M. I was awakened to release the blood for that patient. I gave a unit of blood to the nurse who looked at the bottle and signed our blood-bank register. The transfusion was started by a resident who also looked at the bottle of blood and presumably at the attached requisition slip. An hour later I was awakened by a call from the nurse on the floor. She said the patient had some chills. I mumbled something to the effect that febrile reactions were not uncommon and proceeded to fall back to sleep.
>
> As I was dozing off I suddenly saw, in my mind's eye, a picture of a bottle of blood with a faint pale-yellow "A" inscribed on the label. I leaped out of bed and ran to the nursing station. The unit of blood was nearly completely transfused. I was too late.
>
> The requisition slip was marked "O" and the bottle was marked "A." Three people had looked at that bottle and all three of us failed to notice the discrepancy. Fortunately the patient had a low anti-A titer and the only complaint he ever had was mild chills.
>
> Why didn't I see that I was selecting the wrong bottle? A change in labeling was partly responsible. That week our regional blood bank had adopted the new national standards for colorcoding, sizing and shape of identification labels on units of blood. The new "A" labels were very different from the old labels. Furthermore, the printing was so poor that the yellow "A" was nearly invisible.
>
> A time of change is a dangerous time because habits are hard to break.

"You can't depend, says Dr. Gambino, "upon written instructions or on unfamiliar color coding." Note, he says, that in this case of the wrong blood, "more than one person was involved, so there isn't any safety in numbers. Error is also more likely to occur when you are tired, rushed or overworked."[50]

In other words, most errors—by doctors or others—are very human; "accidents" in every sense of the word. That this is so is confirmed by the application of the law to more serious errors. In the event of heinous conduct by a defendant, the law allows a judge or jury to impose "punitive" damages, payment over and above that necessary to reimburse a claimant for his actual losses. In other words, additional payment exacted from the wrongdoer to punish him. But in fact punitive damages, though often sued for in personal injury cases, are *rarely* exacted. As Tom Davis, the president of the Trial Lawyers Association, has admitted:

> [A U.S. House subcommittee] report states that according to the Insurance Services Office, there was only one instance where punitive damages were actually awarded out of 24,000 claims closed during an eight and a half month period ending March 15, 1977. Another study for the Interagency Task Force on Products Liability found only three reported appellate cases upholding punitive damages in the last ten years.[51]

Similarly, former Trial Lawyers' Association President Robert Cartwright of California agrees that punitive damages are not assessed very often in product liability cases. If the trial verdict is appealed by the product manufacturer, he says, the punitive damage award is usually thrown out by the appellate court. Thus, he asserted in a speech to a West Coast product liability seminar, the total amount of punitive damages actually paid by product manufacturers is very low.[52]

The reasons punitive damages are often asked for although very rarely exacted are illustrative of the manipulative, deceptive, subterranean world of tort litigation. Plaintiffs' lawyers request them for four reasons: (1) to inflame the jury against the defendant by the very terms of the accusation, regardless of whether the defendant's conduct in fact justifies the accusation; (2) to widen the plaintiff's scope of pretrial inquiry in questioning the defendant and searching his records, supposedly to aid the plaintiff in proving the heinous conduct of the defendant but in fact simply to cast a wider net gener-

ally; (3) to get evidence of the defendant's income and net worth
before the jury, supposedly to help it decide how big a verdict will
"punish" him, but in fact to implant the idea of the defendant's
wealth; (4) to divide the defendant and his insurer, inasmuch as punitive damages are often not covered by insurance. The insured then
becomes more anxious to have the insurance company settle the
claim within the limits of insurance coverage that will compensate
the plaintiff only for his actual losses. That way, assessment of punitive damages against the insured alone is simply cut off by the fact of
settlement. As a further result of the possible conflict of interest between the defendant insured and his insurer as to settlement, with
some of a possible verdict covered by insurance and some not, the insurer becomes anxious about *its* possible liability for a verdict in excess of insurance limits if it is held to have violated its duty to its insured in failing to settle.[53] The net result is thought to be a greater
proclivity on the part of both the defendant and his insurance company to settle.

In sum, the tort system, with its unique standards of "fault" and
"pain and suffering," in the words of a report of the New York
State Insurance Department, offers "rich rewards to the claimant
who will lie, the attorney who will inflame, the adjuster who will
chisel and the insurance company which will stall or intermediate."[54]
Daniel P. Moynihan has put it this way:

> [T]he victim has every reason to exaggerate his losses. It is some
> other person's insurance company that must pay. The company has
> every reason to resist. It is somebody else's customer who is making
> the claim. Delay, fraud, contentiousness are maximized, and in the
> process the system becomes grossly inefficient and expensive.[55]

3

The Tricks—and Tragedies—of the Trade

PHILIP CORBOY IS a silver-haired, jut-jawed, fifty-three-year-old Irish–American lawyer, erect and trim. Practicing in Chicago, he is one of the most successful plaintiffs' personal injury lawyers in the United States, earning a million dollars or more annually. His posh office, decorated with Picasso lithographs and Steuben glass figurines, overlooks the Daley Municipal Center in Chicago, the scene of many of his courtroom victories.[1]

Max Wildman, also a Chicago lawyer, is on the other side of the fence, earning a six-figure income, representing many of America's largest insurance and industrial firms in personal injury cases brought against them by Corboy and his fellow plaintiffs' lawyers.

The style, techniques, and tactics of the two adversaries present a fascinating contrast:

Representing big, prosperous clients against badly injured individual accident victims, Wildman is at great pains to play down his own affluence and authority. In court he wears a baggy tweed jacket with elbow patches and badly frayed sleeves. His shoes are scuffed, and one of them is coming apart at the seam. He carries a battered briefcase. He carefully avoids smoking his custom-made cigars in front of the jury and makes a point during trial of eating in the courtroom cafeteria, where the jurors eat, rather than at his usual luncheon place, the baronial University Club. Speaking of such poses he asks with a smile, "Why should the other side have a monopoly on sympathy?"[2]

Corby, on the other hand, representing the lone injured individual, lets his client's pathetic conditions (heightened, as we shall see, by Corboy's careful tutoring) speak for itself and goes out of his way to suggest his own personal majesty. He owns two dozen custom-made $400 suits, along with thirty pairs of elegant shoes. As the *Chicago Tribune*'s Jack Star has observed, "Corboy would never be caught wearing a brown watchband with a blue jacket—he owns 10 watches that match appropriate costumes."[3] Corboy brings his own lectern to court (or rather one of the seven lawyers he employs as assistants lugs it there on his shoulder as they both walk across the street to the courtroom). Corboy is careful to stand behind it while questioning witnesses and during arguments. During a closing argument he will pull it over to face the jury. The lectern, says Corboy, is a "credibility device," endowing him with the authority of a university professor or minister.[4]

For both Corboy and Wildman, jury selection is all-important, but they naturally seek diametrically opposite goals. "It isn't enough to get jurors who will find the defendant liable," Corboy says, "they must also be willing to give the plaintiff big money."[5] Aiming at that goal, Corboy rejects retired people because, living on fixed incomes, they are "too tight with a buck." By the same token, he welcomes blacks and Jews because "they have tasted discrimination and therefore tend to identify with the underdog plaintiff." Similarly he warms to blue-collar workers, because, as Corboy told the *Wall Street Journal*'s Jonathan Laing, "they empathize more with victims because their own bodies are their livelihood."[6] But no rule is sacrosanct: "Do you think I would take a Jewish man who earned his living by listening to complaints all day in a department store? Never! He would be too inured to trouble. For the same reason I would never take a black nurse who had become accustomed to the pain her patients suffer. She might take my client's pain for granted."[7]

Wildman's ideal jurors are often the opposite of Corboy's. "You have to find people able to resist the natural impulse to give the plaintiff the moon," he says, "and that's not easy." Wildman welcomes retired people living on fixed incomes and older blue-collar and middle-management workers. "They are accustomed to shifting for themselves, and are usually conservative with awards." Wildman also avoids younger jurors because of what he calls their "tendency to have a social-worker, do-gooder mentality." On the other hand, in his jury selection Wildman will often seek racial and class variety in order to sow dissension. As he puts it, "a disunified jury rarely grants large awards."[8]

In the courtroom Corboy is careful to have his young associate (the one who carries his lectern through the Chicago streets for him) sit with the spectators, not at the counsel table. That way, his associate will be ready to help, but the jury doesn't get the impression that the plaintiff has a cadre of high-priced lawyers.[9]

Wildman too is very conscious of who is at the counsel table with him. In his case, although he invariably represents large insurance companies or corporations, he makes a point of having a humble employee (or "goat," in his term) sit with him. At one trial, Wildman was defending Coath & Gross, Incorporated, a Chicago building contractor, in a $1.2-million suit brought by the widow and three small children of a young elevator mechanic's helper who was working below when a one-ton elevator fell four stories and crushed him. At Wildman's side throughout the trial, dressed in his work clothes, was the defendant company's general superintendent at the accident site. Such a "goat" is essential, in Wildman's view, in personalizing the defense. The superintendent's presence was meant to counteract, at least in part, the dead man's attractive twenty-seven-year-old widow, who sat primly at the plaintiff's counsel table throughout the trial, and her three young children, who were called before the jury. Wildman's only witness in the case was his "goat," and in an emotional closing argument Wildman went out of his way to suggest that it was the superintendent—rather than Coath & Gross, Incorporated—who was being accused of responsibility for the death. According to Wildman, "I want to create the impression with the jury that the goat's head is on the block, so that when they retire to the jury room to decide the case, their sympathy for the plaintiff will be offset by their concern over the fate of the goat."[10]

As can be seen, for all their differences in approach, Corboy and Wildman are quite similar. Each is very careful and studied in what he does before the jury. Says Wildman, "Everything I do in front of a jury, whether done in court, during recesses, or in the corridors outside court, is calculated to create an impression with them. The facial expression, the physical gesture, the mannerism are often more important than what a lawyer actually says."[11] As if to illustrate Wildman's point, Corboy, for example, is careful to wave away the glass of ice water the bailiff pours for all trial lawyers. "The jury doesn't have water to drink, so why should I?" he asks.[12]

Each goes to elaborate lengths in thinking through his tactics and stratagems. But they label them differently. "Please don't call them tricks," says Corboy.[13] Wildman is less reticent: "You can put on the strongest case in the world, but if you don't use your ingenuity and pull tricks you'll get murdered by the jury anyway."[14] Corboy thoroughly questions every witness the night before he or she is to testify. In his view, it's imperative that both he and the witness clearly understand what the testimony will be. The witness will even be escorted across the street to examine the empty courtroom to lessen any apprehension of the unknown. But scripts are carefully avoided. "A jury will suspect the testimony is phony," Corboy says.[15]

Corboy is careful to space his medical witnesses, trying to call at least one a day. He explains, "I like to keep the jurors reminded of the hurt my client has suffered, but I don't want to overwhelm them with half-dozen doctors, one after another."[16]

Similarly, Corboy usually will not permit his client to come to court except on the day he gives his testimony. In one case, the entrance of his client, blinded by the accident, was staged for maximum impact on the jury. Two weeks after the trial began the jury got its first view of the victim when the doors of the court swung open and Corboy's client, wearing dark glasses, led by his twenty-eight-year-old son and a seeing-eye dog, entered the room. Says Corboy, "a jury should not be allowed to become too familiar with a client—sitting in the same room with him for several weeks conditions the jury to live with the plaintiff's infirmities and to accept them. I don't want my client to be a friend of the jury, but an abstraction."[17]

Wildman admits to going much farther with his "tricks": "In this day of consumerism and distrust of the establishment, a lawyer defending corporations doesn't have a hell of a lot going for him, so he has to make his breaks."[18] In the *Wall Street Journal*, Jonathan Laing wrote:

> In one trial in which Mr. Wildman's client was charged with negligence by a middle-aged businessman whose wife died in an auto wreck, he had his attractive blond secretary come into the courtroom at the end of the trial and sit next to the widower. Following Mr. Wildman's instructions, she asked the man an innocent question, smiled, patted his hand and quickly left. "Just one look at the cold expressions on the lady jurors' faces was enough to tell me that we were home free," Mr. Wildman recalls with a smile. "When the jury came back with a [verdict against him] the plaintiff's lawyer

never knew what hit him. You see, the entire interchange took place
while he was facing the jury in the midst of his closing argument."[19]

Nor is such a tactic an isolated example: At the trial against Coath &
Gross concerning the elevator accident, Wildman arranged for a
claims supervisor of Liberty Mutual Insurance (his client) to stay in
the courtroom during the entire trial and chat in a friendly way with
the widow in front of the jury whenever her lawyer wasn't there, to
suggest to the jury that she had a boyfriend.

Perhaps it should not altogether surprise us that a reputable defense lawyer's trickery should rise to such repugnant levels. As I put
it in an earlier comment on this phenomenon:

> Although it is hard to justify trickery, one can perhaps better under-
> stand the pressures that lead to such practices by understanding the
> unique nature of personal injury cases, as a class, in engendering
> one-sided emotional appeal. Personal injury cases often pit a lonely,
> needy, pathetic injured person against a large, wealthy impersonal
> corporate institution (either an insurance company or a large self-in-
> suring corporation). No other class of cases, not even criminal
> cases, so uniquely, as a general proposition, involves this one-sided
> aspect. In criminal cases, it is true, the defendants are lonely, often
> pathetic people facing a large impersonal institution—the state, but
> the state also has emotional appeal on its side. The individual de-
> fendant is charged with a criminal, often a heinous, act. Not only
> emotional outrage against him but also sympathy for his alleged vic-
> tim can be exploited. In criminal cases, then, it is often the prosecu-
> tion—the representative of the large, impersonal, institutionalized
> party—which can appeal more to emotion than can the opposing
> side. And the mutual possibility of exploiting sympathy often leads
> to mutual restraint on each side for fear of retaliatory exploitation.
>
> The same *mutual* possibility of emotional appeal exists for other
> classes of cases in which human factors are intense, such as divorce
> or child custody cases. But in personal injury cases there is no such
> possibility of even-sided emotional appeal. The most the victim is
> usually guilty of is carelessness—scarcely very heinous. So the plain-
> tiff can indulge in appeals to emotion with relatively little fear of be-
> ing checked, because, as Wildman indicates, for the defendant to
> keep objecting to the plaintiff's emotional evidence of, say, the na-
> ture and gravity of his injury is to risk appearing heartless or "in-
> souciant." As a result, personal injury cases become uniquely emo-
> tional affairs, with the restrained and frustrated defendant often
> turning to trickery. In sum, all litigation is subject to some irration-

al, emotional appeal, but personal injury cases seem unique in the strength of that appeal.[20]

Consider the following examples of tricks, ranging from the trivial to the unconscionable (although it is no easy matter to judge what is trivial, considering the stakes involved in personal injury litigation):

When opposing counsel in cross-examination was really beginning to hurt the defense, Charles Pipkin, a Dallas insurance lawyer, would cause a whole file of papers to fall on the floor and scatter in all directions. Down on his hands and knees, Pipkin would apologize to the judge, but it would be five minutes before things calmed down and opposing counsel could get the witness back to the crucial point, if at all.[21]

Joseph Goulden tells of a lawyer who sets his alarm pocket watch to go off when it will disrupt the opposing counsel's closing argument to the jury.[22]

Max Wildman routinely relies on semantic trickery. "Take the word 'accident,' which is at the bedrock of all tort litigation," he says. "To a lawyer it means an occurrence, while to the layman sitting on a jury it means a mishap where no one is at fault. I can't tell you how many cases I've won exploiting that confusion in meaning."[23]

In his defense of Coath & Gross in the elevator accident case referred to earlier, Wildman maintained that Westinghouse Electric Corporation's elevator division was not only as responsible as his client, Coath & Gross, from a legal point of view, for guaranteeing the safety of the elevator, but that Westinghouse had improperly installed the unit, thereby causing the accident. Rationalizing this contention, Wildman admitted, "The argument was partly sophistry, but I was trying to plant enough doubts in the jurors' minds on the liability question to keep down the size of the verdict."[24]

At a recent annual meeting of the American College of Legal Medicine, Dr. Samuel D. Rehm, a doctor and a lawyer, as well as a lecturer at the Baylor College of Medicine and a licensee of the National Board of Medical Examiners, said the following: "Medical textbooks in various jurisdictions have various evidentiary standing. But the best way to hurt [a medical] expert, particularly a pathologist, is to look in a textbook, get [him] involved in a very technical discussion about the chemistry, about how the values are obtained,

and then use out-of-context statements. Unless the physician is totally prepared, you're going to destroy him."[25]

Rehm asked, "If you have a prestigious expert on the other side
of the case, how do you handle him?" The first thing is to stipulate—in other words concede—his qualifications as an expert, presumably to save time but actually to keep the jury from hearing how
qualified he really is. "Now, hopefully the other side is going to let
you get by with that. The best thing to do is keep the guy's expertise
out of the minds of the jury. If [a highly qualified] expert . . . gets up
there and 30 minutes later he says, 'and then I got my M.D. degree,'
you are pretty well hooked, because they're going to listen to him."[26]
Rehm told the seminar participants: "Now, I'm not telling you all
these bad things because I want you to go out and do them. But I hope
by knowing what the sins are, those of you who function as witnesses
will avoid these traps. Don't let the lawyer push you out there onto
the limb. Don't let him force you into out-of-context statements.
And don't ever let him stipulate to your qualifications."[27]

Speaking at the same meeting of the American College of Legal
Medicine, Richard Abbuhl, another doctor who is also a partner in a
Phoenix, Arizona, law firm, stated, "We defense lawyers have ortho-
pedists that we use most frequently, and we usually pick an ortho-
pedist who is conservative—not dishonest, but he has conservative
opinions. We know who these people are in town. They've testified
hundreds of times. We know some of them don't believe in pain. It
never existed. This is probably a guy who gets his leg shot off and
crawls down off the mountain, if he acts the way he talks in
court."[28]

To illustrate the necessity for a doctor–expert witness to shave his
testimony in the interests of partisanship, Abbuhl told the following
story:

> An orthopedist was testifying in a case I was representing. This fel-
> low is absolutely 100 percent straight. His idea was you give the sci-
> entific facts, the truth, and he's a reasonably good witness. He testi-
> fied, yes, he thought there was disability, and, yes, certainly she had
> pain from this. And then he was asked, "Well, there aren't too
> many positive physical findings in this case." "Yes, there are some,
> but not very many." And the other lawyer says, "You're taking
> what she says in her history to a large extent and using that in your
> diagnosis. Isn't that true?" "Yes." "And if her history were differ-
> ent, if in fact she didn't have pain, then you wouldn't be of that

opinion?'' "Yes, that's true." "Well, can you be absolutely sure
that she's telling you the truth?" "No," he said. "There's a possibility," he said, "that she's lying." "Yes, that's possible. I happen
to take what she says. I don't think so, but it's possible."

The other fellow gets up and he comes out and very convincingly
tells the jury that he thinks that this gal isn't telling the truth and
blah, blah, blah. Now you've got a jury faced with someone who is
being not an advocate, he's calling the shots just as he sees them,
and he's up against a defense attorney who *is* an advocate. He believes in his position, he's not lying, but he is forceful, he is convincing that jury. And that, in my opinion, does not help to get a good
result.[29]

Where justice goes astray, in my opinion, is where you get a plaintiff's physician who says, for instance, "Now this lady is hurt worse
than anybody I've ever seen before," and the defense lawyer gets up
with his physician, and he's straight. That doesn't do justice, but
that's our system.

This is why I urge my medical experts to be advocates in court
and I tell them why. I tell them that if you play it straight and you
don't go an extra step to convince the jury of what you believe, what
you find on your examination, and sort of take the part of your patient, then you are doing your patient a disservice, because I can assure you that the other side is going to actively recite their position,
and you're not going to come out very well. Now if that's being an
advocate in court, then I suggest that your doctors be advocates in
order to do justice.[30]

Responding to Abbuhl, Cyril H. Wecht, another doctor–lawyer,
said, "Whether the [medical expert] should be an advocate or not as
Dick [Abbuhl] has talked about is a philosophical discussion and
probably a semantic one. But certainly he should not be *made* to
look like one."[31]

Continuing the discussion, Walter Ward, a Miami lawyer–doctor, practicing full-time law, stated, "This advocacy problem is, of
course, one that we all face very often. It seems to me that the resolution, at least in my personal experience has been if you have a good
case, the facts are with you, then what you need is a good cold expert
who will get there and tell the truth and can withstand any sort of on-
slaught. You need an advocate when your case is weak and you have
to have someone make up for that which you lack in your own abilities or else in the fact situation with which you are faced."[32]

Lawyers will sometimes try subliminal suggestions: On December 7, 1973, Rosemarie Gilborges, a sixteen-year-old girl, was totally

disabled when an automobile driven by a classmate, Linda Giannini, in which Rosemarie was a passenger collided with a truck driven by John Wallace. The accident occurred while Rosemarie and her classmates were returning from a trip sponsored by the Maple Shade High School for a class in which the girls were students. As a result, suit was instituted on Rosemarie's behalf not only against the two drivers but against the Board of Education of the Maple Shade Township. The jury at trial returned a $1-million verdict against the two drivers and the Board of Education.

Shortly after winning his million-dollar verdict, the plaintiff's lawyer was called on to give a lecture at a seminar for fellow attorneys. In the course of it he said, "[S]omewhere in the back of my brain I knew that somewhere somebody on that jury had read about a million-dollar verdict for somebody else, somewhere else." In his closing argument he had said:

> Dr. James [one of the plaintiff's expert witnesses] said there were seven million nerve cells in each hemisphere of the brain, and as a result of this accident various nerve cells in her brain have been irreparably damaged.
>
> I don't know how much each brain cell is worth. I don't know how much each sigh is worth, each cry is worth, each laugh is worth.

In his lecture, he advised his fellow lawyers:

> Now, after talking about the injuries, I got into the real loss, the loss that you have to evaluate. The real loss in my mind is astronomical. And again you use words—like astronomical. You use words like "big case." You use phrases like "the millions of ways that she won't be able to talk or the millions of"—yeah, I know, but you see it all boils down to being able to get them to empathize with this girl in terms which they can then translate into dollars and cents. . . .
>
> [T]he really significant injury was the fact that the girl could not do the *millions* of things *and again I used the word as much as I could*—the *millions* of things that she could do if she had not been injured in this accident. [Emphasis added]

But in this case the lawyer, for all his boasting of his slippery skill, had gone too far. The township appealed, and part of the appellate court's opinion reads as follows:

> It is the established law of this State that counsel may not state to a jury in opening or closing [remarks to the jury] his belief as to the pecuniary value or price of pain and suffering per hour, per day or per week since suggestions by counsel constitute an unwarranted

intrusion into the domain of the jury and import into the trial elements of sheer speculation on a matter which by universal understanding is not susceptible of evaluation on any such basis.

In the course of his closing argument, the girl's lawyer had mentioned numbers again when he had stated:

How do you compensate somebody for pain and suffering? If you go to a movie, you pay three dollars or four dollars or five dollars for two hours of enjoyment. How much is one hour of pain and suffering worth? You have to decide that. That's the big thing. That's the thing that's going to make your figure, if you do give it, reasonable and adequate compensation, if you do give her what's truly what she should receive for what she's gone through and will go through in the future.

The appellate court reversed the award of damages of $1 million and ordered a new trial to correct the amount of damages, citing the improper argument of counsel and also citing his seminar lecture, the terms of which had been brought to its attention by the Board of Education. Referring especially to the argument concerning the price of movie tickets, the court said his language was "an oblique but nevertheless transparent attempt to circumvent" the prohibition against such per-unit-of-time arguments stated under the law in question. "It would equate the price per hour for pain and suffering to the cost of admission to a movie." (Note the fairly typical duration of this personal injury case: The accident took place on December 7, 1973; the complaint was filed on January 15, 1974, with an amended complaint adding the Board of Education on October 23, 1974; the two-week trial was held from June 18 to July 3, 1975; the appellate argument was on May 24, 1977, and the decision was handed down on September 22, 1977—ordering a new trial!)[33]

On January 30, 1968, Michael Squalls drove his car through a boulevard stop sign at an intersection in Los Angeles, striking a vehicle driven by Carmella Cook. Cook's car, in turn, was forced into a car being driven by Walter Richardson, also occupied by his wife, Florence. As a result of the collision, Richardson's car went out of control and struck an adjoining gas station. Both the Richardsons sustained very severe injuries. Although Squalls was clearly uninsured, the Richardsons' insurer, Employers Liability Assurance Corporation, refused to accept the convincing evidence of that fact and therefore refused to pay on the Richardson's uninsured motorist coverage (under which the injured party's own insurance company agrees to pay him if he has a valid claim against an uninsured motorist). The Richardsons brought suit against Employers not only for their actual losses but for punitive and emotional damages stemming from the insurer's refusal to pay.

During the trial, the Richardsons' lawyers had carefully placed on the counsel table in front of his seat a Xerox copy of a newspaper article with this headline: "Didn't Settle in Policy Limits; OK Mental Suffering Award." The article was placed on the counsel table during the second day of the trial, prior to the court's reconvening for the afternoon session while the jurors were returning to the jury room following the noon recess. It remained on the table after the jurors were in the jury box. At the trial the jury rendered a verdict for $75,000 and $100,000 in favor of Walter and Florence Richardson respectively, amounts considerably in excess of the uninsured motorist policy limits of $10,000 apiece, and based on the refusal of Employers Assurance Company to settle in good faith. The insurance company appealed, alleging, among other things, improper conduct by plaintiffs' counsel. Using exhausive measurements of the headline and the distances between counsel's table and the jury box, the appellate court had no trouble concluding that "the headline was clearly legible." The court went on to state that counsel for plaintiffs "denied any intentional wrongdoing, stating that [the Xeroxed article] was only one of the numerous documents and files he had on the counsel table, and that 'the document . . . is a case citation which I have used along with other citations to discuss jury instructions . . . and other leading points.'" He later stated that it was an article from a legal newspaper on the *Crisci* v. *Security Insurance* case, an earlier California case authorizing damages for mental suffering when an insurer has unreasonably refused to settle a case. The court said:

> This excuse is incredible. [The Crisci case] was decided over three years before trial of this action. The decision covers eight pages in the official reports. The [Xeroxed] article appears on one sheet only; although not in the record, it would appear to be only a synopsis at most, a poor source of information for the purposes advanced by counsel. We cannot help but conclude that the article with prominent headlines was exposed for the purpose of influencing the jury. No one knows whether any jurors saw the headlines, and if so, what, if any effect they had on the jury in its deliberations. It would appear from the size of the verdicts that the headlines might have influenced the jury.

The Appellate Court thereupon reversed judgment and called for a new trial on the issue of damages.[34]

It is true that in both this case and the one discussed immediately preceding it, the illicit conduct of the lawyers resulted in a reversal of the trial court's decision in his favor. But to the extent that the trickery helped gain a verdict in the first place—with the realization that it might or might not be appealed and with the certainty that any verdict can be used as a lever in bargaining over settlement pending appeal—a lawyer could well conclude that such tricks are worth a try.

In a mock trial based on an actual case against a wealthy defendant named Thomas Covington III, who had allegedly allowed a fire on his property to spread to a neighbor's land, Philip Corboy, representing the neighbor, kept referring to the defendant as "Mr. Covington the Third" and to Covington's habit of practicing golf on his property. His obvious purpose was to inject irrelevant but probably influential class bias into members of a jury panel who lacked aristocratic names and pastimes.[35]

Joseph Goulden cites a similar ploy by Franklin Jones, Jr., a Texas personal injury lawyer. Jones was representing a man who was injured when the car he was driving hit the defendant's stray horse on the highway at night. In its pretrial preparation, Jones's firm, Jones, Jones, and Baldwin, had photographs taken of the wealthy defendant's property, showing his estate stretching over prime land just north of Dallas. While looking over the pictures, Goulden remarked that the jury "might get the idea that a man who owned that much land in the north Dallas suburbs is rather wealthy and capable of paying off a citizen who ran into a horse." Baldwin, Jones's partner, smiled impishly: "Well, now that you come to mention it—"[36]

Overlapping with such "tricks" are the many subtle ways lawyers on both sides—as suggested earlier—can inject emotional and jury appeal into a case. Some further examples are instructive:

In representing Patty Hearst, F. Lee Bailey personally went shopping with her and selected oversize clothes to lessen her glamour and make her appear more pathetic. (Although Bailey was representing a defendant in a criminal case, the same tactics would also be applied to a plaintiff in a personal injury case.) According to an article in the *New York Times* headed "Defense Is Changing Image of Miss Hearst," Bailey and his associate, J. Albert Johnson, "talked to her endlessly, won her confidence and . . . have put together an emotional and factual scenario [for the jury]."[37]

In a case concerning an eye injury, counsel had a mother remove her young daughter's glass eye in front of the jury. In another case involving injury to a leg, counsel had the plaintiff show the numbness of her leg by sticking pins into it.

Out-of-town lawyers—especially from big cities—will often make sure to retain a local lawyer to sit at the counsel table with them, not because they really need their aid but rather to counter jury prejudice against strangers. Opposing counsel will miss no opportunity to call attention to any "big-city lawyer" or "out-of-state lawyer." In one Illinois medical malpractice trial in Peoria, defense counsel in his closing argument characterized the plaintiffs' lawyer as a "slick attorney from Chicago" and a "slick hired hand." In addition he characterized plaintiffs' medical expert as the lawyer's "sidekick" and "right-hand man." The appellate court opinion in the case noted:

> Defense counsel claimed that plaintiffs' counsel "manufactured" evidence, had a "wild imagination," and was not worthy of the jury's trust. He further stated that plaintiffs' counsel was the "captain of [the] ship" who was "piloting" the testimony of plaintiffs' expert witness. In addition, defense counsel compared the relationship between plaintiffs' counsel and his expert witness as that existing between the "Cisco Kid and Poncho" and "Matt Dillon and Chester." The expert was characterized as a "professional witness" who carries a "shiny black leather bag" containing instruments that "have never been used."

The defense lawyer's remarks were held on appeal to constitute reversible error, but the important point is that the lawyer thought he could get away with such remarks and indeed won a trial verdict, in the appellate court's opinion, in part based on those remarks. Had the court not believed so it would not have reversed. And having thus obtained the verdict, the lawyer could at least bargain on the basis of it concerning an appeal or, as he did, take a chance on getting his verdict upheld on appeal. Of course, trial judges are supposed to stop this kind of unfair language and tactics but, as this case illustrates, they often neglect to do so. In the heat of battle it is not always easy to separate the unfair from the fair. The timing of this case is again interesting. The alleged malpractice occurred on August 24, 1970; the appellate court opinion was handed down six years later, on April 26, 1976 remanding the case for a new trial![38]

Joseph Goulden illustrates how lawyers attack "foreign" expert witnesses with a Texas case involving a young worker's loss of his hands, allegedly caused by a defect in a press brake manufactured by the defendant, the Verson Allsteel Press Company. Verson's chief defense lawyer, Tom Alexander, cross-examined the plaintiff's expert witnesses, Paul F. Youngdahl, a mechanical engineer from Palo Alto, California, and Richard Fox, an engineering professor from Case Western Reserve University in Cleveland. Alexander tried to depict them as professional witnesses, ready to testify to anything for a fee. He expressed surprise that Fox had appeared as a witness at 138 personal injury cases in five years. He was amazed that Youngdahl had not even visited the Tyler, Texas, plant where the accident took place during his "investigation" of the accident:

YOUNGDAHL: It was not important to reach an opinion about this Verson Press Brake.
ALEXANDER: Well, sir, I wasn't talking about reaching an opinion. Actually, you reach your opinion in many, many cases right off the bat, don't you? These people know where to hunt for somebody to say a machine is defective.

An objection by plaintiff's counsel was sustained. Alexander then asked how many cases Youngdahl had appeared in during the last year. "Perhaps fifty in the past year, in one way or another," Youngdahl replied. Alexander quickly came back: "Will you be surprised to know that's more cases than I have, and law is my full-time occupation?" The judge cut off Alexander even before an objection was made, asserting the point was "immaterial and irrelevant." Alexander pressed on, asking Youngdahl, "You would imagine that there are quite a few [engineers] closer to Marshall, Texas [the site of the trial], than Palo Alto, California, who are qualified engineers and who have actually had experience with presses?" In his closing argument, Alexander was even tougher. Fox, he said, "has appeared as an expert witness on plastic toy horses, on bicycle seats, on Exercycles, on tailgate accidents, automobile accidents, every kind. Whenever anybody has any kind of an injury, Mr. Fox is willing to show up."[39]

An expert witness—doctor, engineer, or whatever—will often be picked not so much for his expertise as for his appearance and his ability to woo and win a jury. Also crucial will be his ability to reduce technical matters to simple terms appropriate to the jury's level of understanding. Increasingly, medical malpractice and product liability trials are dominated by theatrically professional expert witnesses who do little else but tour the country testifying in case after case, usually for only one side, with skillful and often slanted partisanship. Indeed, nothing has led to the rise of medical malpractice and product liability suits more than the availability of such a pool of expert witnesses whose availability is advertised to plaintiffs' lawyers in legal journals. Legal scholars have recently urged that such experts be retained and paid on a contingent fee basis, thus enabling them, along with plaintiffs' lawyers, to have a stake in plaintiffs' cases. The safeguard against abuse, it is argued, is that opposing counsel can bring this fact out on cross-examination. But that simply adds another subtle and emotional variable into the jury's already imposing task of deciding technical matters based on diametrically opposing opinions from warring experts.

One exceptionally scholarly, soft-spoken personal injury lawyer, prominent for his technical writings on tort law, mentioned to me that he succeeds as a trial lawyer because of his brains and hard work but knows he will never achieve the success of a Belli or a Corboy. Personal injury trial work, he says, involves a sixth sense, an intuitive "feel" of the emotion in a courtroom, which transcends logic and legal research. The really big stars are those who have that sensitivity to an extraordinary degree, and no years can ever really teach it. It is similar to a natural stage actor's ability to feel an audience's response at the most subtle levels.

I recall working as a young lawyer in the 1950s on a case under James St. Clair, already a leading trial lawyer in Boston and later Richard Nixon's Watergate counsel. We were taking a deposition in a case concerning a plastics manufacturer whose product had allegedly flaked and cracked. The manufacturer had entered a claim for payment for the goods, and a counterclaim demanded payment for damages caused by their supposed defect. I spent many hours studying the chemical properties of the product and talking with potential witnesses. St. Clair, busy with many other cases, had not yet had much time to focus on the matter. During this particular deposition of an opposing chemist, St. Clair ranged far and wide with endless probing. That puzzled me, because, despite my homework, I did not yet understand much about plastics, and I knew St. Clair at that point understood even less. (By the time of the trial he would usually be more than caught up.) I still had not grasped where St. Clair had been going in his questions when we left after several hours. I asked him directly what he was up to. "That guy is a phony," said St. Clair flatly and with suppressed emotion. "And the jury is going to see he's a phony when I go after him in court with all that ammunition we'll get from that transcript.'' Well, if the witness was a phony I certainly hadn't sensed it, but I knew right away that it was St. Clair's uncanny intuition on such matters that our client was paying for, not my research on law and chemistry. Incidentally, I never got to find out whether St. Clair's intuition was right in this instance, because the case was settled, but I did realize it was his ability to sense the emotional flow in a courtroom—and to anticipate what could govern that flow—that gained him such respect as a trial lawyer.

The personal injury courtroom as a cockfighting pit is illustrated by a mock trial based on an actual case before practicing lawyers at the University of Michigan's continuing legal education advocacy seminar. The case was based on an accident wherein Isaak Hert was injured when his car collided with a city car owned by the City of Brush Arbor and driven by Carlton Abernathy, manager of the city's Water Department. Hert alleged that Abernathy had run a stop sign and included the city as a defendant, on the assumption that Abernathy was acting within the scope of his duties as a city employee. At the time of the accident, Abernathy, a married man, was returning from a noonday visit to the home of his personal secretary, twenty-seven-year-old Louise Miller. A snoopy neighbor of Miss Miller's had provided information as to Abernathy's daytime and occasional all night visits to Miss Miller. The cross-examination of Abernathy by Hert's lawyer, Joseph Kelner, a leading New York City personal injury lawyer, went as follows:

Q. All right, Mr. Abernathy, you were bound for lunch, is that right?

A. Well, no. I was going out to take these records out to Mrs. Miller.

Q. You were going to take the records over to Louise, is that right?

A. Mrs. Miller, yes.

Q. All right. You never called this girl Louise, did you?

A. I never called her Louise? Yes, sure I called her Louise.

Q. Sure you did. As a matter of fact, this wasn't the first time you had taken records out to her apartment, was it, in the middle of the day?

A. No.

Q. As a matter of fact, how old is Louise?

A. Well, I think she's around 26, 27.

Q. How old are you, sir?

A. I'm, let's see, about 45.

Q. How long has she been working for you?

A. [Five years.]

Q. And for how long has this changeover in your procedures and your office machines and your bookkeeping system been proceeding, so that you have been taking records out to her? In the middle of the day, I mean.

A. Well, for three or four years, whenever we got behind.

Q. Approximately two or three times a week, on average, is that a fair estimate?

A. Well, she wasn't sick that often, no.

Q. I see. This day she had a cold, is that right?

A. A bad cold, yes.

Q. You weren't afraid about contracting her cold, were you, sir?

A. Oh, yes, I was. I'm allergic to penicillin; I was very careful.

Q. And you didn't come close to her at all. Did she have a cold two or three times a week for the last few months before this day?

A. No. And I wouldn't say I went out two or three times a week.

Q. Did you ever visit her to comfort her and give her the benefit of your companionship and society in evening hours, at any time?

MR. SHEPHERD [defense counsel]: Excuse me. Wait a minute. Wait a minute. That has nothing to do with this lawsuit. I object to it. It's wholly immaterial.

He is trying to create some inference here that has nothing whatever to do with this lawsuit, and I object to it. And on behalf of Mrs. Abernathy, I resent it.

MR. KELNER: May I reply to it, sir?

THE COURT: A brief response.

MR. KELNER: My response, sir, is that it is pertinent—

MR. SHEPHERD (Interposing): This is [to be] outside the hearing of the jury, I assume? . . .

THE COURT: I think the first objection having been made in the presence of the jury, it is only fair for a response to be made in the jury's presence, as well.

MR. KELNER: Thank you very kindly, your Honor.

MR. SHEPHERD: Note my objection, sir.

THE COURT: Let's hear this briefly.

MR. KELNER: Sir, it is relevant and material, and certainly pertinent to show the frame of mind that this gentleman was in at the time of this impact with my client's automobile, to go into his temperament, to his mentality, to his physical and mental capacity with regard to his ability to drive an automobile at that time; and, sir, I submit this is vital and relevant evidence.

THE COURT: You needn't reply. The objection is sustained. The evidence is remote and prejudicial. Its probative value on the issue of the case, the negligence of this driver, is slight; its tendency to prejudice is great.

The jury is now instructed to disregard this exchange, and also to disregard evidence which has entered the record prior hereto concerning this witness' relationship with said Louise.

MR. SHEPERD: Thank you.

MR. KELNER: Your Honor—

MR. SHEPHERD (Interposing): At the request of the Court, I would like to add just one phrase to the statement, to say: If any.

MR. KELNER: Your Honor is being very gracious and impartial, and I accept your ruling without reservation.

Q. (By Mr. Kelner, continuing): However, sir, I'm interested in knowing whether you had anything to drink during this little siesta where you were working with Louise?

MR. SHEPHERD: I object to the form of that question, for the same reason that the Court just sustained the objection.

THE COURT: The word "siesta" is a loaded word.

MR. KELNER: Very well, sir.

Q. (By Mr. Kelner, continuing): This "working" session with Louise, did you have any alcoholic beverages there during this period from when you arrived shortly after eleven A.M. until you left, I think you have said, about two P.M.?

A. I just had some of my good Brush Arbor water, with a little chlorine on the side.

Q. You were there for approximately two hours and twenty or two hours and fifteen minutes, is that a fair estimate?

A. Oh, I don't think that's fair. I don't think I was there that long.

Q. During all that time you were working hard, is that right?

A. No, not all the time. I might have talked with her. She had a cold. I tried to be a considerate employer.

Q. And for two hours you were consoling the young woman, were you?

A. Not the whole two hours. But good secretaries are harder to get than good mayors.

Q. Mr. Abernathy, is it a fair statement to say that you worked continuously for at least two hours there, or were you just chatting and consoling her during two hours, during a business day, when you were on the City payroll, with the taxpayers footing the bill for your time? Yes or no?

A. In my opinion, it was all work.

Q. All work. All right.

A. Whether I was consoling or whether I was showing her forms.

Q. And this was a frequent pattern of work with you, going there in midday, is that right sir?

A. Not a pattern, I wouldn't say. Occasionally.

Q. Well, did you have lunch there?

A. I don't remember.

Q. As a matter of fact, there are a lot of things you don't remember about this entire sequence of events, is that a fair statement?

A. Well, it happened a couple of years ago. That is a fair statement.

Q. As a matter of fact, sir, when you got out of there, is it a fair statement to say that you were tired? Yes or no, please.

A. I don't remember being particularly tired, no.[40]

Speaking in a critique of Kelner's cross-examination, Andrew Watson, a nonlawyer who, as a psychiatrist, teaches at the University of Michigan Law School, stated as follows:

I'm always very worried—in fact, I can tell you that before I ever began to participate in these Advocacy Institutes, I faced a serious moral problem in myself. I was very uneasy about turning over the secrets of the mind to loyal opposition. I know what lawyers do sometimes, and this distresses me when they are just plain, downright mean to witnesses, and so forth, and do things that are not good for the person at all, and are probably of very questionable value to the case, so that I was very reluctant to get involved in these things at first.

Now, I thought that the way [the judge] handled the psychological undercurrents was beautiful, and I wish all judges did that.

He immediately began to respond to the cover messages that counsel were throwing out, and this is the only way I know that you can control this type of activity.

[I]n communication terms this is where most of the significant messages come from, these innuendoes, and if, indeed, you wish to run a trial without prejudice, there is no alternative but to

have the judge swiftly move in as [the judge] did in this demonstra-
tion. I wish we could train all the judiciary to that, that taut kind of
running of the Courts in relation to these questions.

Responding, Kelner said to the audience of lawyers:

First we are indulging in psychology in the questions of whether
lawyers who try cases for many years have a different slant than a
psychologist like Dr. Watson. And I am not going to engage in an
open quarrel with anyone. But as I saw this case, there are three
principal areas of attack for the plaintiff's lawyer to undermine this
defendant.

First, he is lewd, lecherous and lascivious. Just looking at the
man you can tell that. He's been engaging in a meretricious relationship, and as an advocate who lives in the jungle of the court battles,
down in the cockpit, if I've got this kind of material and it's relevant
and material . . . I would have [argued with the judge to use it].

On the relevancy of this testimony, here's a man who has been
locked up with a beautiful young woman for two hours and, as we
say in New York, where we are suing divorce cases as I did years
ago, if a man and a young woman are frequenting with each other
and socializing under such circumstances, it is presumed that they
are not there to say their Pater Nosters.

Now, here's a man whose physical and mental capacities were an
issue with regard to distraction, fatigue, and his physical capacities
certainly were on the block, as far as I was concerned, and so it was
my judgment, and still is, and no one has persuaded me differently,
in spite of the niceties and delicacies about not wanting to make a
martyr out of this evil-looking witness, that [in an actual case] I
would have done what I did, and there isn't a person in this Courtroom sitting on a jury who would have had any doubt that this man
was not himself after getting out of this little siesta after two hours
with this beautiful, charming girl.

Kelner cited as his second and third areas of attack evidence of Mr.
Abernathy's epilepsy and his propensity to fail to stop at the accident intersection. He continued:

And so from every standpoint, the psychology was to give this jury
bits and pieces of evidence to sample and taste the morsels, whether
it was the epilepsy, whether it was the Louise situation, whether it
was the accident itself. My experience, as an advocate for some 29
years, tells me that, I don't know which of these jurors is going to
like to taste this, that, or the other bit or sample of the evidence, but
when they get it all together, the conglomeration is enough to cook

out the verdict I want. We had enough to say, and I say here and now we killed him dead; he's dead, we won our case.[41]

As was illustrated by the two cases of plaintiffs who sued for blindness caused by too much oxygen administered at birth (pp. 3–7), the risks of personal injury cases are such that even while the jury is deliberating, frantic efforts at settlement continue. Not always, though, will a lawyer leave such matters to chance. Joseph Dahl Gamail of Houston, Texas, age fity-three, has won more than twenty-five verdicts and settlements of a million dollars or more in his career. For many years, Gamail would routinely take the same seat in the empty jury box of one courtroom after the jury had retired to deliberate. Gamail appeared to be simply resting after the strain of his labors. But Texas District Court Judge William Blanton finally figured out that Gamail was using that particular chair to "rest" because from that spot he could hear jurors deliberating in the nearby jury rooms. With what he could pick up from his eavesdropping, Gamail was able to decide whether to press for or refuse settlement. "We put felt padding on the door," Judge Blanton says.[42]

In *My Life in Court*, the famous trial lawyer Louis Nizer wrote a chapter entitled "Life and Limb: Two Cases of Negligence," which graphically portrays the tension and tremendous uncertainty of personal injury litigation. The first case he describes illustrates how even a lawyer of legendary skills who is quite certain of a trial's outcome can trip himself up. Nizer's second case illustrates how exhaustingly nerve-racking most cases can be when, as so often happens, the potential outcome is difficult to ascertain.

In the first case he describes, Nizer represented the husband and child of a young woman who had died in childbirth. She entered the hospital at 3 P.M. on July 13. Her only previous child, it is important to note, had been delivered by Caesarian section by the same doctor attending her this time. Both children were in a transverse position in the womb. On direct examination, the doctor testified to *his* version of the events surrounding the tragedy: By 5 P.M. on the day she entered the hospital, the mother was experiencing false labor pains, and by the morning of July 14 real labor pains had begun. The amount of pain was normal, and there was no indication that a second Caesarian section would be needed. The patient slept well that night. On the morning of July 15 the woman's condition was good, and by 11:30 A.M. the membrane had ruptured. Pain was normal and birth was expected at approximately 2:30 that afternoon. The doctor left the hospital but at 1:30 P.M. received an emergency call and returned. The mother was ready to deliver and was in a state of collapse. After delivery, despite efforts to resuscitate the child, it died. The mother died at 3 P.M. The doctor's further testimony stated that the mother's heart had suffered an acute dilation; he explained that when one of the heart's four chambers dilates, blood is drawn away from the rest of the body. This, he stated, killed the child. The mother's cause of death was listed on the death certificate by the doctor as chronic myocarditis, a heart condition. In anticipation of plaintiff's theory, the doctor also testified that there was no rupture of the uterus.

Plaintiff's expert was a recent medical school graduate who had never delivered a baby, but he was also the only doctor Nizer could get who would testify on behalf of the plaintiff. Although such testimony would be sufficient to prevent an early dismissal of the case, Nizer was aware that his young and obviously inexperienced "expert" simply would not be able to carry the day. The only possible way to win the case would be to extract crucial admissions from the defendant doctor himself on cross-examination.

When the time came to cross-examine the doctor, Nizer first forced him to admit that he really didn't know how the woman rested during the night of July 14. The doctor was further maneuvered into admitting that the woman was in acute pain from the moment she entered the delivery room at 3 P.M. on July 13 until the moment she died at 3 P.M. on July 15. There was no mistaking the impression that these admissions had left upon the jury: The poor woman had lain in harrowing pain for forty-eight hours, struggling in the delivery room to give birth to her child.

And what had the doctor done for her? On cross-examination he stated that he had examined her at 5 P.M., some two hours after she entered the hospital, and again at 9 A.M. on the second day, July 14. The doctor was immediately contradicted by plaintiff's counsel and had to admit that, as a matter of fact, he did not examine the woman the second time until 4 P.M. on July 14. Although the doctor tried to explain that he had not understood the question, it was apparent that his credibility was failing.

The next line of questioning by plaintiff's counsel was directed squarely at establishing that the real reason for the mother's death was a ruptured uterus caused by the fact that her pelvis was too small to pass the baby, not a heart condition, as the doctor had contended. Nizer first maneuvered the doctor into admitting that the woman's pelvic measurements were abnormally small. This alerted the doctor to the ultimate goal of the cross-examination, and he firmly settled in for the fight. The questioning continued:

Q. Now, as a matter of fact, doctor, it was because you knew that this woman was small that you performed the first Caesarean operation, wasn't it?

A. It was not.

Q. Well now, let us look into that. You say that the reason you performed the first Caesarean operation was that the child was in a transverse position, is that your testimony?

A. Yes, sir.

Q. Where the child is in a transverse position, if the measurements are normal, there is no indication for a Caesarean operation, is there?

A. No sir, not— That can't be answered yes or no.

Q. Can't it?

A. No, sir.

Q. Let me put it again to you. Where the measurements of a woman are normal, but the child happens to be in a transverse position, then an operation is not necessary, is it?

A. Not automatically, no sir.

Q. As a matter of fact, the transverse position, doctor, is a very unusual situation, isn't it?

A. It is, yes, sir.

Q. Would you say that less than one-half of one per cent of the cases are transverse position

A. Yes, sir.

Q. So that the very fact that a child is in a transverse position is in itself some indication of an abnormality, isn't it?

A. Yes, sir.

Q. Now isn't one of the leading abnormalities for transverse position the small size of the pelvis?

Q. No, sir.

Q. You now testify the smallness of the woman . . . is not a contributory factor to the transverse position?

A. It may be, but it is not the most prominent.

Q. Well, let us not quarrel about whether it is the most prominent. It is one—

[Opposing] Counsel: I object to those comments on his testimony.

Court: I will sustain the objection. The jury will disregard it.

Q. Is it a contributory factor towards a transverse position of the child that the woman is built small?

A. In some cases.

Q. In the case of a woman who is giving birth to a first child, what do you call it—primipara?

A. Primipara.

Q. That is a medical word meaning the first baby?

A. Yes, sir.

Q. In the case of a woman who is giving birth to her first child, where there is a transverse position . . . doesn't that indicate a pelvic contraction?

A. No, sir.

Q. And doesn't that indicate such a pelvic contraction as indicates necessity of a Caesarean operation?

A. No, sir.

Q. . . . Doctor, would you consider Professor Franklin S. Newell, Professor of Clinical Obstetrics at Harvard University, an authority on the subject of obstetrics?

A. Yes, sir.

Q. You have undoubtedly heard of Newell's famous book, called *Caesarean Section, Gynecological and Obstetrical Monographs*?

A. Yes, sir.

Q. Let me read this sentence from that book to you: "Transverse presentations in primipara . . . are an indication of sufficient pelvic contraction to warrant the assumption that Caesarean section is probably the best method of delivery." Do you disagree with that, doctor?

A. That is a matter of opinion.

"Apparently," Nizer later wrote, "he had remembered the admonition of his counsel, 'If in trouble, remember your best shield is that you exercised your honest judgment.' "

Q. First I ask you whether you disagree with it?

A. Yes.

Q. You disagree with Professor Newell on that?

A. Yes.

Q. But although you disagree with him, you did perform a Caesarean section?

A. After giving the patient time enough to see that she would not deliver herself.

Q. Well, you found it necessary finally, didn't you?
A. I did.
Q. To that extent, Professor Newell seems to be right, doesn't he?
A. He does.

This was a crucial admission. As Nizer later described it, the doctor

> . . . had performed a Caesarean on this woman the first time she gave birth. The child had lain in transverse position. This indicated a small pelvic region. If her measurements had been normal, she might still have given birth naturally despite the transverse position. He gave her time to deliver the baby normally. He found she could not, and performed a Caesarean section. Was this not conclusive proof that her bone structure would never permit her to bear a child without a Caesarean? Why had he on the second occasion let her struggle for forty-eight hours to deliver a child that could not possibly pass out her narrow pelvic structure?

In further pursuit of this point, the doctor admitted that he performed no version extraction, a method of turning the baby while it is inside the womb in order to alleviate the abnormal transverse position of the child. The following exchange then took place:

Q. Well, when do you consider a transverse position so dangerous that a Caesarean section must be performed and version extraction impossible?
A. If there was a contracted pelvis.
Q. In other words, when there is a contracted pelvis and you have a transverse position, then you must perform a Caesarean, is that right? Isn't that what you have just said, doctor?
A. Yes.
Q. And in this woman's case there was a transverse position and you performed a Caesarean, didn't you?
A. Yes, sir.

A fatal admision, it would seem.

After this the doctor repeatedly was caught contradicting himself. He steadfastly contended that the woman's heart condition had nothing to do with his decision not to perform a Caesarean section but was contradicted by the fact that in a prior suit to collect his fee he had stated that he did not perform a Caesarean because the condition of her heart was so bad that her system could not stand the sur-

gery. (The reason for the change, no doubt, stemmed from the fact
that many noted authorities state that when a woman suffers from a
heart condition, the risks associated with delivery by Caesarean section are less than those associated with normal delivery.) The doctor
also stated that the patient was in a state of collapse at the time he arrived back at the hospital, but again Nizer showed that he had testified differently in the former proceeding.

In his discussion of this case, dependent as he was on cross-examination, Nizer emphasizes the pitfalls it entails for *both* sides. Essentially, he says, cross-examination is a means of "forcing the witness to
abandon his prepared positions and improvise under circumstances
of stress." But to succeed the lawyer needs "resourceful techniques"
and "an agile mind." The witness needs them too. Nizer writes:

> That is why injustice can occur in the court. There is no scientific
> yardstick for the truth's evaluation. If the lawyer, as Benjamin
> Franklin once said, is not glorious because he has not been labor-
> ious, or if in his duel with the dragon, his sword is not skillfully
> wielded, the truth may never come to light. This is what makes al-
> most any trial more fascinating and breathless than the most elabo-
> rate creation of the fiction writer. It is genuine contest, suspenseful
> because the outcome is uncertain. . . . The judge or jury make an af-
> firmative contribution to the exciting drama, by evaluating the wit-
> ness's performance, not merely in terms of his embarrassment or
> confusion, or, on the other hand, his successful stubbornness, but
> by reading behind these emotions, to discover his honesty or per-
> fidy. A confused witness may not be a liar at all, and his human fail-
> ing may even elicit sympathy. On the other hand, a [lying] witness
> may succeed in holding his ground, but be exposed as a liar. The
> psychological aspects are intriguing and limitless.

And included in those "intriguing and limitless" possibilities, as
Nizer himself suggests, is the chance in such an atmosphere that,
through a lack of counsel's skill, preparation, or luck, a lying witness may elicit sympathy or a truthful one may be disbelieved.

In the case we have been discussing, many of the doctor's incon-
sistencies, viewed independently, were not devastating, yet when the
damning admissions extracted from the doctor were added to his
shredded credibility, there could be little doubt in Nizer's mind
about what the jury would decide. Deliberation would be a mere formality. The case spoke for itself. The doctor had left the woman to
struggle in vain to deliver a child that could not possibly pass

through her pelvis. For forty-eight hours the poor woman tried to deliver. She tried until it killed her. Nizer wrote:

> How could he have left the patient, wringing wet with perspiration in her heaving efforts, over a forty-five-hour period, to evacuate a child imprisoned in her contracted pelvis? I do not believe it was cruel disregard on his part. Rather it was his ignorance concerning the tragedy that was taking place. Yet was it not such recklessness as was equivalent to negligence? Surely his prior experience in performing a Caesarean section on this woman should have given some intimation that, after forty hours, a crisis was impending. Yet the doctor in this case left the woman whom he saw in prolonged agony, because he thought she would give birth several hours later. Forgetting his wrong medical opinion, where was his humane obligation to be immediately available in her desperate struggle? I knew the jury would understand this, even if it understood nothing else.

When he reached his closing argument, Nizer emphasized that when the woman was having her second child

> . . . it was again in transverse position. Every reasonable indication was that the same physical structure that prevented natural delivery of the first child, would prevent it in the case of the second. Yet he proceeded to permit the woman to labor. Even then, when he had given "the patient time enough to see that she would not deliver herself," to use his description of her first labor experience, he did not perform a Caesarean as he did the first time. Stubbornly he let her press in vain against bones that would not permit the child to pass through—twenty hours—thirty hours—forty hours—forty-five hours—forty-eight hours—until her uterus burst. Was this not gross and inexcusable negligence? Why it was *criminal* negligence! . . .
>
> Only when I had analyzed every one of his shifts, evasions, and contradictions, and read his answers in each instance from the stenographic minutes, did I turn to the heart-rending results from his misconduct. By this time the jurors had been caught up with resentment and anger against the doctor. Now these turned into sympathy for the victims, the dead mother and child, and the live husband and orphan. The emotional impact that had been mounting, finally revealed itself in tears as several of the jurors wept openly as I concluded.

As indicated, Nizer felt very confident as the jury retired to deliberate. But their deliberations went on for hour after hour! After eleven hours, to Nizer's astonished disappointment, the jury returned to announce they were hopelessly deadlocked. The judge thereupon declared a mistrial, after which he summoned the jurors, along with the lawyers, to his chambers to find out what had happened. As Nizer tells it:

Amazement was added to my disappointment when I learned that from the first moment the jurors were unanimous in a verdict for the plaintiff. I was even more astonished when I learned that they were not split because of the amount of the verdict. What then had divided them? Some jurors feared that evidence of the doctor's negligence was so overwhelming that if they decided against him, he would thereafter be criminally indicted and convicted! They did not want him to be thus disgraced and go to jail. They thought this would be too severe a penalty for an outstanding physician. Of course it would be, but where in the world did they get the idea that the civil verdict for damages would lead to criminal proceedings? They reminded me that in summation I, too, had said he was guilty of *criminal* negligence. Indeed I had. In the course of struggling to satisfy the jury that the extreme test of gross negligence had been met, I had characterized his conduct as so reckless and unprofessional as to be criminal negligence. Of course I had not intended this statement to be literal. It was merely a forensic device to pound home the fact that we had met the burden the law placed upon us in a malpractice case. The phrase "criminal negligence" was a reference to the degree of proof, not to pursuit of the doctor in a criminal court. Nevertheless, my first rush of anger and disgust at the jury's lack of comprehension and ignorance gave way to a realization that it had demonstrated sensitivity and wisdom. And . . . if it had erred, it was the lawyer's fault. It was I who had planted or encouraged the fear in its mind by my use of the phrase "criminal negligence." I had failed to explain in summation that all that was involved was money damages, that no criminal proceedings could possibly follow because criminal intent would have to be proved, and, of course, there was none. True enough, it seemed bizarre in retrospect to have worried about calming the jury on the subject of criminal responsibility when we were desperate to prevent our complaint from being dismissed because we might not be able to meet the severe standards of civil liability. Yet it was a lesson I never forgot. Since then, more than ever, I measure the nuance of every word I utter in the presence of a jury. I take nothing for granted. Trials are the wonderland of the unexpected. I never dreamed that we would have a hung jury because we had proved our case.

To the great distress of Nizer and his clients, the case was set for retrial. As it turned out, no retrial was necessary, because the case was then settled.[43]

The second personal injury case Nizer describes illustrates that settlement negotiations can often be as grueling and nerve-racking as a trial.

In discussing the second case, Nizer mentions that early in his career he had learned that insurance companies and others constantly defending personal injury cases, such as for railroads, would bargain very hard, knowing (1) that corporate defendants often investigated the facts surrounding an accident earlier and more thoroughly than did claimants' lawyers; (2) that corporate defendants had more specialized lawyers; (3) that delay in reaching trial often meant agonizing uncertainty for injured victims and their families. Thus almost every offer by Nizer was met with derisive scorn by insurance adjusters.

In the case in question, Nizer represented the family of a young man, John Donelon, who had been killed when the commuter train he was riding home from work was struck from behind by another commuter train. The liability of the railroad was clear enough, but the amount of the damages suffered by the man's family because of his death appeared to be relatively small, for although he was a junior executive at an advertising firm, he had yet to establish himself as a capable and rising "adman." Although several of Donelon's ideas had been very successful, his salary was quite modest, and Nizer would have to prove that Donelon was a bright and talented man whose earnings were bound to rise quite substantially to secure the verdict he wanted.

Mere speculation and insistence by Nizer would not be enough. He had to introduce facts that would show, to the relatively certain degree required by the law, that Donelon's career was on its way up at the time he met his death. The railroad was well aware of the plaintiff's problem, and as a result its settlement offer was a rather paltry $25,000. Nizer knew, though, that if he could prove Donelon's earning potential, the case was worth much more. Despite the fact Nizer lacked the required proof at the time of the $25,000 offer, he rejected it and concentrated on gathering that proof.

After exhaustive investigation, it was discovered that Donelon by sheerest chance had taken a series of intelligence and aptitude tests several years prior to his death. The results of these tests showed that

Donelon scored in the 99th percentile of the population of men in his age group for general intelligence, and in the 70th percentile for practical judgment. In many other categories relevant to high achievement and success in his career, Donelon had also scored well above the 90th percentile. After a bitter legal battle over the admissibility of the test scores, they were accepted into evidence, and Nizer's expert witnesses testified that a man with such high scores was very likely to have a successful and financially rewarding future. However, even though this evidence could, if the jury chose to rely upon it, support a very large verdict, Nizer did not know whether the jury would, in fact, rely upon it. But, such being the nature of a civil liability case, the insurance company was just as unsure about the actions of the jury as Nizer was. As a result, despite the fact that the trial was still in progress, settlement negotiations between Nizer and the insurance company continued. Nizer described this process:

> Following my settlement principles, I threw the burden upon the defendant. What increases was it willing to propose? Step by step the offers went up, sometimes in painful stages—$30,000—$40,000—$42,000—$50,000. I kept Mrs. Donelon [the victim's widow] informed, but advised her firmly to reject these proposals. I was confident that our case had improved greatly and that the risk of submitting to a jury verdict should be accepted.
>
> When the offer reached $75,000, I grew more cautious. Mrs. Donelon continued to state that she would do only as I recommended, and I felt the weight of responsibility more keenly. It was not my money with which I was gambling, it was hers. I discussed the possibilities earnestly with her, applying the most conservative standards. Nevertheless, we decided to hold out for more. The Judge had been advised by both counsel of these developments, and he, too, had misgivings about the risks she might be taking with the jury, the delay of appeals and possible reversal, requiring a new trial. Still we rejected the offer.

As the trial wore on, Nizer dropped another bombshell on the insurance company. Evidence that showed Donelon's capacity for financial growth had been introduced, but the plaintiff also had to introduce evidence of how long Donelon could have expected to live had he not been killed. It was customary to refer to *The American Tables of Mortality* to determine a person's life expectancy. The problem was that these tables were badly out of date; because life expectancy had increased, the tables were inaccurate. Therefore, Nizer consulted his own actuary who, using a current census, calcu-

lated a new life expectancy table. It showed that Donelon could have
expected to live substantially longer than *The American Tables of
Mortality* stated. This meant, of course, that the potential value of
the case was greatly increased. The settlement talks continued:

First, the defendant had been stunned by the scientific proof of
Donelon's capacity for growth. As if he had prepared for his death,
he had taken a battery of tests to establish his potentiality, and we
had gotten it into evidence.

Now the plaintiff had an addition stimulation [the new life expectancy figure] for immediate settlement. The tempo of adjustment talks quickened. Much of the psychological byplay was
dropped. We were no longer given the ultimatum that the final offer
had been made and that it would be withdrawn unless immediately
accepted. We did not have to call the bluff as often, nor engage in
similar counter tactics. I sensed a genuine eagerness, almost anxiety,
to settle the case. The offers rose to $80,000 then in larger leaps to
$90,000. This we were assured with angry sincerity was the last of-
fer. I felt we had reached the end of the settlement rope, and the
choice of acceptance or risk of jury verdict was acute.

Mrs. Donelon continued to express blind faith in my judgment.
We would accept or refuse, as I advised, without any regret or recrimination. This only increased my concern in deciding for her. I
explained that I was confident of a higher verdict from the jury, but
there was no assurance of this. I was deeply troubled in advising her
to reject the offer, only because I knew how precious every dollar
was to her and Bruce [her young son]. A settlement meant immediate and certain cash—no appeals and no delays.

I hoped she would be influenced by my analysis to indicate a
preference, but she wished to be guided, whatever the consequence.
This was touching, but also painful. I had to say that if the responsibility was solely mine, I would advise going to the jury. She had no
delayed reaction of regret. Instead she enthusiastically closed the
discussion with the statement that she had followed me up to this
moment; she was glad to continue do do so. She even tried to comfort me. "Don't worry, Mr. Nizer, if anything goes wrong, I know
you have done your best and I shall be satisfied." I winced at the
mere thought that my guess about the jury might turn out to be
wrong. Yet it was my duty to get her every cent I could. It was a responsibility I could not shirk. I repeated to our adversary that we rejected his offer of $90,000. He turned somewhat surly and said he
would meet us in court for summation.

That night, with more intensity and anxiety than I have labored
in cases involving millions of dollars, I prepared my summation to

the jury. I knew what these dollars we had refused would mean for the rest of Muriel and Bruce Donelon's lives. I was determined to sharpen my skills to their finest edge to sway the jury to a large verdict. It was another one of those nights when I never touched my bed. In the morning I washed and shaved and went to court, prepared to the make the most persuasive argument of which I was capable.

The next morning, however, opposing counsel—a man named Doyle—reopened the negotiations. Lawyers on both sides then conferred with the judge in his chambers. The judge

. . . sensed Doyle's readiness to make sacrifices to settle the case, and also my deep concern about the responsibility I was bearing in holding out. He entered on his mission of compromise with great skill. He warned Doyle that a very large jury verdict might be in the offing and warned me that I had a duty not to pull the string too tight where so substantial an offer was available. He induced me to lower my demand from $150,000 to $125,000, and pushed the defendant up to $95,000. I held out firmly. My summation was ringing in my head. I was not eager to deliver "the oration." Rather, I felt that the hazard of rejecting the offer of $95,000 was not too great because even if a jury were to disappoint us, it would not bring in a verdict much lower. The facts and emotional appeal assured us of that. Furthermore, I sensed that Doyle "had" to settle the case. I could not be sure he had been instructed to do so, but a large jury verdict would jeopardize settlements in all the other pending death actions. Certainly they would not have evidence of a profile graph, or testimony of an actuarial expert increasing life expectancy over the standard tables. If word got out that a jury had brought in a large verdict in a case of a man who earned only $100 a week, what would it cost the insurance company to dispose of its other cases?

These imponderable factors encouraged me to be stubborn, even when Doyle exasperatedly and with a gesture of final exhaustion said that he would recommend to his superiors a settlement of $100,000. I stood fast and insisted on proceeding to summation. The Judge met separately with each counsel, and then advised me that Doyle was ready to recommend to his superiors a settlement of $112,500, but that this was his final proposal. He urged me to bring Mrs. Donelon before him. He would advise her to accept, thus sharing my responsibility and reducing my zeal to get every last dollar for her.

After hearing the Judge's fatherly advice, Mrs. Donelon looked to me, her head poised to bow yes or turn to no, as I would indicate.

Although I was confident that a jury would give her more—else why had the Railroad made this offer—the bird-in-the-hand theory applied especially to a widow and child. Also, the saturation point of justifiable risk had been reached. The Judge had frankly stated to Mrs. Donelon that he had made unusual rulings in which precedent had been broken and that no one could be sure how the upper courts would view them. Even if the jury verdict was higher, how much would it be worth to have money in hand, without the delay of appeal and risk of reversal? I approved, and her head nodded in reflex action.

Note again the key words in Nizer's tale: "gambling," "risks," "bluff," "guess," "anxiety," "imponderable factors," "painful responsibility." More than enough *angst* in the whole process to go around. And this for people already afflicted by the serious injuries or death that led to the litigation in the first place.[44]

4

More on Lawyers' Feats
and Clients' Defeats

As SUGGESTED EARLIER, a personal injury lawyer's work entails a unique combination of substance and illusion. Superficial theatrical appeal must be united with painstaking technical accuracy, which often requires drudgery. A trial judge and, on appeal, the appellate judges will demand that the logic of one's case be valid under the most minute analysis. But in presenting hours, days, and sometimes even weeks or months of highly arcane engineering or medical evidence, the trial lawyer must avoid boring the jury. The amount of technical detail that must be combined with careful calculation of emotional effect can be guessed when one looks at the preparation that goes into a personal injury case.

In a case involving Richard Kooyenga, a husky twenty-one-year-old bricklayer who was paralyzed from the waist down in a scaffolding accident, plaintiff's lawyer, Philip Corboy, spent three weeks on trial. His preparation included 102 exhibits, including many designed to demonstrate the life of indignities the plaintiff faced, such as the catheter, leg bag, and rubber gloves used by Kooyenga to deal with his paralyzed bladder and bowels. Also, according to one observer at the trial, "looming over the jury box was another exhibit, an exact duplicate of the scaffold that tipped over, constantly reminding the jurors of the moment of pain and horror." The result was a jury verdict for $1,578,000.[1]

At a trial about a month later, Corboy represented Daniel Sweeney, thirty-six, a former ironworker who sustained severe back injuries when a crane at a building site in Kankakee, Illinois, buckled, causing him to fall to the ground. As exhibits Corboy used a life-size replica of his client's badly broken back and, placed next to it, a model of a normal back. After six days of trial, the defendant settled for $800,000.

In Jack Star's words, Corboy has "the rare knack of taking extremely complicated legal issues and reducing them to simple, understandable human issues." Star recalls sitting in a Chicago courtroom and watching Corboy win $752,500 for an auto mechanic who had lost an eye from a fragment of an allegedly defective tool while working on a truck transmission. "Corboy," says Star, "had transformed the courtroom into a theater. In the room's center, leaking oil onto the elegant rug, was the truck transmission. On easels, where the jury could see them, were a dozen huge and somewhat mysterious microphotographs of the offending tool—a reminder as to how several metallurgists brought in by Corboy had damagingly testified. ('Juries get bored with the legal talk, and I like to give them something to look at while all the talk is going on,' Corboy says.)"

Corboy's client had previously lost his other eye in a similar accident and now was totally blind. Star's account continues:

> The jury was obviously moved as the courtroom doors opened and a Seeing Eye dog led the blind [plaintiff] to the witness box. Corboy's gentle but probing questioning lasted a long time. The injured man told how he couldn't sleep at night because his eye hurt so much, that he was deprived of such simple pleasures as walking to the corner store or even smoking a cigarette for fear of starting a fire. The mechanic wiped the tears from his sightless eyes as he said most of all he missed seeing the face of his wife—that he had forgotten what she looked like. Leading the blind man to the jury box, Corboy had him raise his smoked glasses so the jury members could see into his sightless, milky eyes. One of the women of the jury shuddered. Another was in tears.[2]

Normally, 95 percent or more of personal injury suits are settled before trial. Corboy's cases, being bigger ones, settle only about 80 percent of the time. "But," says Corboy, "we prepare every case thoroughly, just as though we were going to trial, and this helps us get good settlements."[3]

Preparation by plaintiffs' lawyers often includes the building of complex and costly models. On September 9, 1969, eighty-three persons died in a mid-air collision between an Allegheny Airlines DC-9 and a Piper Cherokee about 12 miles southeast of Indianapolis. Some years later the scene was recreated in a courtroom. The jury hearing the case brought by relatives of the deceased passengers was presented with a scale model of the collision that went so far as to demonstrate how the two airplanes plummeted to the ground. The relative altitudes and speeds of the two aircraft were accurately reproduced by means of a pulley arrangement above a 4-by-8-foot model of the actual terrain. By simply turning a crank, the claimants' attorney could recreate the crash over and over again for the jury. Edward Zagorski, Professor of Industrial Design at the University of Illinois, who constructed the realistic model, recalls, "Everybody sat on the edge of their chairs waiting to see what would happen."

Jesse Stonecipher, Associate Director of the University of Illinois Institute of Aviation, who had investigated the Indianapolis collision and testified for the claimant as an expert witness, comments on how valuable the model was in making very clear to the jury exactly what happened. "I could have sat there all day," said Stonecipher of his testimony at the Indianapolis trial, "and said, 'Now the DC-9 was on a heading of 270 degrees. The PA 28 [was] on a heading of 120 degrees. The DC-9 was traveling at 250 knots. The PA 28 at 100 knots. The PA 28 contacted the DC-9 just ahead of the tail section and ripped the tail off of the airplane, and they both plunged to the ground.' And what do you see after I said that? Practically nothing. But if you've got this model there, it's a visual aid."[4]

Models are increasingly being used in personal injury cases. Zagorski's models ordinarily range in price from $200 to $2,000 but can be much more expensive. Philip Corboy finds that models can be very effective in softening up the opposition either before or during trial, as illustrated by his experience in the case of Daniel Sweeney, the paralyzed ironworker. In another case described by Jack Star, Corboy represented a woman motorist who had suffered brain damage when her car was struck by a train at an unguarded crossing. In order to portray graphically the circumstances of the accident, Corboy hired a model maker from DeKalb, Illinois, to construct a 40-foot-long model of the crossing. Special lighting reconstructed the effect of moonlight at the many points surrounding the crossing. Particularly graphic was a black light source over the entire length of the model showing the reflection from the shadowed snow. "The model maker even used a computer at Northern Illinois University to calculate the proper speed of the time model train approaching the crossing," Star recounts. "Calculations took into consideration the weight of each box car, the type of engine, braking capacity and deceleration."

When the model was finished, Corboy invited the railroad's lawyers and claims managers to see it. They were stunned to see how graphically the model would show how a motorist's vision was obstructed at the crossing. A settlement of $560,000 was promptly reached, vindicating Corboy's $23,000 investment in the model. As a practical matter, Corboy—like most personal injury lawyers—will himself pay for such expenses of trial preparation if he loses the case, but they will come out of the verdict if he wins. Expenses in a typical case, including fees and expert witnesses, investigation, travel, and photocopying, will total around $10,000, but the figure can go as high as $100,000.

With such amounts in effect being risked by Corboy, his young associates who are assigned to prepare cases for him are extremely painstaking. According to Star, each of Corboy's seven young associates (he has no partners) is normally responsible for from 80 to 150 cases at any given time, with years usually elapsing before cases are settled or tried. Corboy's young associates themselves try some two-thirds of the relatively few cases that go all the way to trial, but, Star reports, "Corboy monitors the progress of every case at daily staff meetings, sounding like a tough law professor as he orders his assistants to read precedent-making court decisions and offering street-wise hunches as to what strategies to adopt."[5]

Before a sizable case is ready for trial, preparation by Corboy and his associates will normally fill two large file drawers. For example, in the case of an eighteen-year-old quadraplegic, injured as a result of a railroad crossing accident, the file includes the victim's high school grades; a sworn statement from a neighborhood woman who actually witnessed several prior accidents at the same unguarded crossing; seventeen depositions, including one from the railroad's chief engineer concerning the comparatively modest cost of installing crossing gates; the railroad engineman's personnel record, revealing a prior accident at the same crossing; a financial statement of the railroad's net worth for the purpose of impressing the jury of the capacity of the railroad—probably self-insured—to pay a substantial verdict; a copy of a movie commissioned by the railroad for its presentation, recreating the accident with an actual train; and some newspaper editorials to the effect the crossing was unsafe.

Martin Mayer has written: "All good negligence lawyers are dramatists and actors." Jacob Fuchsberg agrees: "Trying a case is like putting on a biographical play."[6] One problem for the untheatrical lawyer is that jurors, heavily exposed to television, expect a Perry Mason to excite them into a verdict. One solution has been drama lessons for lawyers. Joseph Guastaferro, a director at Chicago's Goodman School of Drama, gives private acting lessons to lawyers. He also works, along with several other actors, at the Court Practice Institute, a Chicago organization that has offered seminars in various trial skills to about 900 lawyers since early 1974. According to Arnie Saks, a film director who coordinates the acting skills portion of the institute's program, lawyers must learn to inject feeling into their presentation. "Say you have a case of a dog biting a mailman, and the mailman sues the owner of the house," says Saks. "The attorney is likely to feel it's no big deal. But he can't show that feeling. We tell him to pretend that this dog bite case is the most important thing, perhaps that the dog bit off the mailman's leg."

Guastaferro teaches his students such things as the use of physical movement. "A nervous lawyer frequently will pace the floor, and the rate and tempo of his own movement will add to the nervousness of the witnesses," he says. "Under cross-examination, if he wants the witness to flounder and flutter, he can pace the room. On the other hand, if it's his own witness, he might remain still, to make his witness look as good as possible to the jury. . . . There are [lawyers] who have rejected my approach as outside the law, as having nothing to do with the pristine, intellectual nature of their work. Fine. I am just trying to help those who want to do a better job."

Generally, Guastaferro finds attorneys to be "pretty pompous." He described one of his former students, a successful Tennessee trial lawyer, as an "urbane, sophisticated fellow who wore three-piece Pierre Cardin suits when he was representing farmers in court. I explained to him that makes him an alien—that there is such a thing as image identification." As a result the attorney altered his style.[7] Philip Corboy, as we have seen, might disagree, but that is one point being made here: The effect of theatrical devices, one way or the other, can be *highly* unpredictable.

In one area there have been vigorous attempts in recent years to make preparation for trial easier for lawyers, but with mixed results. At common law in both England and America, generally speaking, a party to a trial could not require an opponent to disclose the evidence upon which he might be expected to reply. Cases were "tried in the dark," as Irving R. Kaufman of the Federal Court of Appeals in New York put it.[8] One nineteenth-century case stated that "it is a very common thing [at trials] to ask 'if such a witness is here'; the answer given on the other side is, 'You will know in good time, when he is called.' "[9] As a result, many lawyers and their clients have been ambushed at trial with crushing and wholly unanticipated disclosures. An advocate, when confronted with highly damaging evidence for the first time in open court, simply did not have time to examine closely, investigate, and test it.

Dean Wigmore noted in his classic treatise on the law of evidence that "the common law, originating in a community of sports and games, was permeated essentially by the instincts of sportsmanship." He continued:

> This had both its higher aspect and its lower aspect. On the other hand, it has contributed to a sense of fairness, of chivalrous behavior to a worthy adversary, of carrying out a contest on equal and honorable terms. . . . On the other hand, it has contributed to lower the system of administering justice, and in particular of ascertaining truth in litigation, to the level of a mere game of skill or chance. [The English and to a lesser extent eighteenth- and nineteenth-century Americans saw] rules of procedure as expedients for winning the game of litigation irrespective of the ascertainment of truth. The right to use a rule of procedure or evidence precisely as one plays a trump card, or draws to three aces, or holds back a good horse till the home stretch, is a distinctive result of the common-law moral attitude toward parties in litigation.[10]

The same attitude comes through in nineteenth-century commentaries on the English judicial system. Pollock and Maitland, in their history of English law, remark:

> [A]t one end of these [poles or extremes] the model is the conduct of the man of science, who is making researches and will use all appropriate methods for the solution of problems and discovery of truth. At the other stands the umpire of English games, who is there, not in order that he may invent tests for the powers of the two sides, but merely to see that the rules of the game are observed. It is towards the second of these ideals that our English mediaeval procedure is strongly inclined. We are often reminded of the cricket match. The judges sit in court, not in order that they may discover the truth, but in order that they may answer the question, "How's that?" This passive habit seems to grow upon them as time goes on.[11]

It is axiomatic that in a game of skill or chance, as in war, the participants do not reveal their strategy in advance. The football coach does not give his playbook to the other team, and the tennis player does not tell his Wimbledon opponent where he will hit the ball next. Surprise is an all-important factor of the game, whether that game be football, tennis, or a trial at common law in England or America, and to take away the surprise would be to destroy the game. Thus, said Wigmore, "the common law permitted a litigant to reserve his evidential resources (tactics, documents, witnesses) until the final moment, marshalling them at the trial before his surprised and dismayed antagonist."[12]

In modern America, however, our system of justice is supposedly based not so much upon gamesmanship and sport as on accurate and fair adjudication of disputes. Our reliance upon the adversary system as a fact-finding process now assumes that each party to any litigation has all relevant information before him and can put that information to the jury. The essence of every trial is to give the trier of fact (be it a judge or a jury) all of the relevant information and allow it to sift and examine and finally to pronounce the ultimate truth. We no longer want the most sporting or the shrewdest advocate to devastate his lesser opponent. Rather, we want the party with the truth to prevail, regardless of sporting rules or chivalry.

This new approach was codified as early as 1938 by the Federal Rules of Civil Procedure, adopted to apply to the Federal court system and amended periodically thereafter. Most states have adopted similar codes. These rules provide for pretrial discovery of a great deal of the information that one's opponent possesses such as relevant documents, photographs, and other tangible items, as well as the names and expected testimony of witnesses. Secrecy and surprise are not considered appropriate for the modern trial. The theory is that when all sides have the maximum amount of information, they will be able to scrutinize it and if possible find evidence to counter any unfavorable information. To be sure, this results in a less dramatic trial. Despite what the reader may have seen on the old *Perry Mason* television episodes, the star witness is rarely, if ever, produced, to the great surprise of the other side, at the last minute. Nor is one party able to secrete the conclusive piece of evidence—the murder weapon bearing the defendant's fingerprints, or the hotel register showing that a person was at the crucial place at the crucial time—until the last moment. In practice today, virtually all relevant information is available to all parties long before the lawyers reach the courthouse steps.

But such are the frustrations of litigation that the pretrial discovery rule has come in for much abuse, proving, as Assistant U.S. Attorney General Daniel Meador observed, that in litigation one generation's innovations and solutions become the next generation's problems.[13]

In the words of Tom Goldstein, a *New York Times* legal correspondent: "Discovery can last for years, can involve [countless] documents and cost clients dearly. It has been estimated that the cost of pre-trial deposition, including the preparation, the court reporter's time, the taking of the deposition and the reading of the transcript, amounts to $3,000 a day for one lawyer. It costs $2,000 more for a second lawyer."[14] The Wall Street lawyer William B. Lawless, a former Dean of the Notre Dame Law School, in a provocative article entitled "Why Litigants Hate Lawyers," estimates the cost at $5,000 a day, with transcripts alone (which can run to thousands or even hundreds of thousands of pages) costing $3.00 a page. Lawless quotes one disenchanted client as saying, "Attorneys, like nuns, travel in pairs or three at a time with the clock running (they charge by the hour) while the client watches helplessly."[15]

In a way this huge quantity of discovery measures the cruel pressures of its alternative, actual appearance in court. Although lawyers are more accustomed to courtroom combat than others, the trying of cases is a viciously demanding experience even for them. Discovery—either preparing it or conducting it in the privacy of an office or a conference room—is a lot easier and just about as lucrative. No wonder lawyers relish it. Former Attorney General Griffin Bell in speech after speech repeated this anecdote: "When I left private practice in 1961 to go on the bench, the familiar statement of a trial lawyer was that 'I will be on trial.' When I returned to practice in 1976, it had been changed to, 'I will be on discovery.' "

Ironically modern discovery, with all its expense, has brought legal practice around full circle. According to former Federal Judge Simon Rifkind, one of the country's leading trial lawyers, "the practice in many areas of the law has been to make discovery a sporting match and an endurance contest." The new discovery rules were designed to provide information about an opponent's position before trial and to uncover further facts relevant to those already forming the basis of a party's case. But many lawyers will agree with Francis B. Kirkham, a San Francisco lawyer and a leading critic of the discovery process, that discovery procedures are being "perverted into an instrument for attempting to discover a [basis of a claim]." As Assistant Attorney General Meador explained, "In comes the plaintiff, dumps in a vague complaint, and then looks for a [cause for a suit].[16]

George B. Collins, a Chicago lawyer, suggests a response to an opponent's request for documents, whether broad or not: "Give them what they ask for." But, though a lawyer may not be entitled to keep a particular document away from the other side, "You have no duty to make it particularly easy to find." His suggestion is to ship over truckloads of material, forcing the other side to hunt for what it needs. In other words, discovery really becomes "hide-and- seek."

Nor do trial tactics to thwart discovery stop there. New York City lawyers were shocked in January, 1978, by the disclosure that Mahlon F. Perkins, Jr., then a partner in the prestigious Wall Street law firm of Donovan, Leisure, Newton, and Irvine, had admitted to Federal Judge Marvin E. Frankel during trial that as a defense lawyer he had lied in an affidavit about destroying papers requested by the plaintiff. In fact he knew the papers were hidden in suitcases in the law firm's offices. In addition, a key internal memorandum, damaging to the defense, apparently had been improperly withheld not only by Perkins but by the chief defense counsel, John Doar, who had been the Chief Counsel for the House Judiciary Committee during its Watergate-related impeachment hearings. (Court records show that Judge Frankel said to lawyers after hearing Perkins's admission, "I listened sadly and sympathetically as Mr. Perkins went out of his way to take all the blame to himself and to absolve substantially everyone else . . . but I was left with a nagging sense of uneasiness about that.") In his summation to the jury, counsel for the plaintiff, Alvin Stein, spoke of defense expert witness Morton J. Peck, a Yale economist, as a "sordid spectacle of evasion, deception, and concealment." The case exhibits not only human frailties but a fascinating glimpse of the frightful pressures of modern litigation. As Judge Frankel told the lawyers in a court anteroom, "I have heard from the defendant's side notes of a certain relentlessness that seems to me to approach the limits of the normal determination of advocates to win by all permissible means."[18]

Following are further examples of discovery at work in personal injury cases:

On January 3, 1971, the Rudolph Buehlers of downstate Illinois were driving his family home in their 1966 Ford Fairlane. Traveling along a two-lane highway, they slowed to a stop and waited for the oncoming traffic to clear so that they could make a left turn. Four other cars slowed behind the Buehler auto, but a fifth car, driven by

Debra Whalen, moved into the left lane and, at 65 mph, attempted to pass the slowing traffic. Ms. Whalen had nearly completed passing all five of the slowing cars when the Beuhler auto turned across the left lane. Whalen applied her brakes but was able to slow down only to about 35 mph before striking the rear of the Buehlers' Fairlane. Gasoline leaked from the Fairlane's fuel tank upon impact and immediately caught fire. The two Buehler children were very severely burned, and Mrs. Buehler was also seriously injured by the fire.

In addition to suing the driver of the car that struck them, the Buehlers sued the Ford Motor Company, contending that the design and placement of the Fairlane's fuel tank as part of the trunk instead of underneath on straps were unreasonably dangerous in that they allowed fuel to spill under relatively minor provocation, and, if ignited, to allow fire to easily penetrate the passenger compartment, there being no firewall or other safety features to protect the occupants. To win a verdict, however, plaintiffs' counsel had to show that the end result of the crash—the fire—was not simply a freak occurrence but reflected a product defect. It would obviously be beneficial to plaintiffs' case if they could show that Ford knew about the potentially hazardous condition in the Fairlane which could endanger the public but marketed it anyway. (Plaintiffs were represented by Richard Hodson and James Cooksey of Centralia, Illinois and C. E. Heiliginstein of Belleville, Illinois; also pursuing the defective product case against Ford was the lawyer for Debra Whalen, Ray Freeark of Belleville, in that Whalen was contending that Ford was the true cause of plaintiffs' injuries.)

In an attempt to establish that a dangerous condition indeed existed and that Ford knew about it, the plaintiffs' lawyers during May 1972 submitted the following pre-trial interrogatory to Ford:

> Please list all tests performed, of every nature and description whatsoever, and whether performed by the defendant or not, along with results and analyses and interpretations thereof, which were made on the 1966 Ford Fairlane 500 or any Ford preceding it if it was not dissimilar, in which the automobile was subjected to any form of impact collision, upset, fire or other force of any sort whatsoever, or in which the tank or gas was subjected to such force or pressure, and giving the following information:
>
> a. Where and when performed
> b. By whom performed and for whom
> c. Nature of the tests

    d. Results of the tests
    e. Analyses of the tests
    f. Interpretations of the tests[19]

In short, the lawyers wanted to know if Ford had performed any crash tests on 1966 Ford Fairlanes or similar cars. In August 1972 Ford answered that it had performed no such tests.

The domestic auto industry, however, is usually quite thorough in testing its new models. It would be unusual indeed if no crash tests had been performed. During a deposition taken in October of 1972, Ford's opposing counsel discovered from a Ford expert that Ford had indeed conducted crash tests of the type requested the previous May. Confronted with this, Ford turned over a series of reports. Only much later, on the day prior to trial during the first week of July *the following year,* did Ford produce a second series of reports.[20]

So Ford, instead of turning over relevant tests in May 1972, as it was legally obligated to do, at first denied the existence of the reports. Then when confronted with the fact that there were crash tests performed, Ford still produced only a portion of the existing records. It took Ford nearly an entire year from when it first denied the existence of the texts (from August 1972 until July 1973) finally to hand over the second series of reports.

Much to the disappointment of Ford's opponents, however, neither test group contained reports involving rear-end collisions at speeds greater than 22 mph. Some of the tests included in the reports were totally irrelevant to the case against Ford, although two of them had resulted in fuel system failure. But the lawyers were convinced that tests at higher speeds had been performed and continued to press Ford. At a conference in the judge's chambers immediately before trial, they asked Ford's attorney if Ford had completely complied with all of the judicially issued discovery orders. The response by Ford's attorney was: "[Ford has] filed all documents and produced all materials requested [by] the plaintiff."[21] In the course of the trial, however, lawyers opposing Ford were to discover that this statement, like earlier ones on the same topic, was inaccurate.

Through cross-examination of Gilford Gorker, one of Ford's "in-house" engineering experts, it was established that 1965 and 1966 Ford Mustangs had fuel tanks similar to those in the Buehlers' Fairlane. During that same cross-examination, Gorker continued Ford's denial of the existence of any relevant crash tests whatsoever, other than the ones already given to plaintiffs. Ray Freeark, the lawyer for Whalen, the other defendant sued by the Buehlers, confronted Gorker with a series of Ford's own tests, previously unknown to Ford's opponents, which included 30-mph rear-end crashes of *both* a 1966 Fairlane and a 1965 Mustang. Gorker then admitted the authenticity of the documents and the fact that, in both cars, even minor rear-end impacts had caused failures in the fuel system.[22]

It is interesting to note that these crucial tests would never have come to light had it not been for some good luck and the persistence of Whalen's attorney, Freeark. During trial, one of his expert witnesses, Derwyn Severy, arrived from California and reviewed the last collection of tests that Ford had submitted the day before trial. After going through them, Severy said, "I feel certain that there were rear-end tests conducted at speeds in the 30 mph range." Freeark asked him how they could get evidence to prove it, and Severy suggested contacting another lawyer with whom he had dealt in products liability litigation. That call resulted in the lawyer air freighting his computerized list of tests which arrived on the very day Gorker, Ford's expert, went on the stand.[23]

But this was not the full extent of Ford's transgressions. Back in May 1972, when plaintiffs' lawyers had originally requested the crash tests, they had also asked whether Ford or any of its subsidiaries had in their possession any reports recommending against the use of the type of fuel tank design incorporated in the 1966 Fairlane.[24] Ford had denied any knowledge of any such report, but plaintiffs' lawyers had become aware that one might exist. Their investigation led them to the Chicago office of a lawyer who was conducting yet another case against Ford over dangerously designed automobiles.[25] The following statement, prepared by Ian Tampen, a Ford research engineer, was discovered among the Chicago attorney's files:

> A similar case [of a rear-end collision resulting in fire] occurred recently in [the] U.S.A. The Cortina [an English Ford with a fuel tank design similar to the Fairlane's] tank burst and caused an immediate conflagration. No further details are available, however it does indicate that the floor mounted tank is hazardous and should be carefully reviewed and tested in each new model.[26]

Plaintiffs' lawyers summarized the situation in their brief submitted to the Illinois Supreme Court in response to Ford's appeal from a verdict in the total amount of $678,000.[27]

Ford not only failed to reveal or submit its crash tests, which it, under oath, had answered were not made, it up to this day has made no effort to amend its Answers to Interrogatories. Even after Tampen's opinions relative to the hazard of the [type of fuel tank incorporated into the Fairlane] had become known to [plaintiff], Ford's Answers to Interrogatories continued to deny that anyone [had] even made such a statement.[28]

In the words of the Illinois Supreme Court in its opinion in the case: "Ford, notwithstanding that the [plaintiffs'] interrogatories embraced 'its subsidiaries,' when confronted with [Tampen's damaging] document sought to pass off 'this matter as a finding of Ford Motor Corporation Ltd. [its British subsidiary].' "

In its opinion in the case, the Illinois Supreme Court further excoriated Ford's conduct. In speaking about the failure of Ford to produce the 30 mph rear end crash test reports, Justice Dooley stated that the reports were "vital information which had been withheld by defendant Ford Motor Corporation. [That other parties] had obtained this Ford record from some litigation other than the instant one [is] a sad commentary on the effectiveness of the discovery here."[29] Later in the opinion, Justice Dooley, again speaking for the entire court, went on to say that "we cannot condemn too severely the conduct of the Ford Motor Corporation in the discovery procedures here. It gave false answers to interrogatories under oath. It secreted evidence damaging to its case."[30]

And yet, despite Ford's flagrant violations of the rules of discovery, Ford suffered little, if at all, for its conduct. To be sure, the courts were suitably angry, and the plaintiffs were, perhaps, given a little more time to prepare their case, but that was hardly a penalty to Ford. In fact, the longer plaintiffs had to wait for trial, the better it was for Ford. At best, Ford learned from this case that it might as well surrender requested documents promptly in future litigation. At worst, Ford learned that it had little to lose and much to gain by illegally suppressing evidence: If the requested documents remained secret, Ford's case was enhanced; if the documents were ultimately discovered by the plaintiffs, Ford was scarcely in any worse position than if it had given up the records when it was supposed to.

As has already been suggested, suppression of documents is only one way to abuse modern discovery rules. Another tactic involves overwhelming an opponent with thousands, or even tens or hundreds of thousands, of documents in response to his discovery request. There are two variations: First, the party responding to discovery can include the relevant papers—often only several unnumbered and untitled standard-size pages—among file cabinets full of wholly irrelevant documents. The entire lot is dumped on the party requesting discovery. Finding a single typewritten and unindexed page in such a collection would obviously be frustrating and time consuming, if not impossible. The second variation (which you should have guessed by now) involves turning over a truckload of irrelevant documents *without* including the relevant ones.

Perhaps coincidentally, another automobile manufacturer has provided a prime example of this type of abuse. The controversy over the General Motors Corvair is now well known. It was made legendary by consumer advocate Ralph Nader's first book, *Unsafe at Any Speed*. One of the first suits over the dangerous design of that car to reach the courts was brought by Louis G. Davidson, a prominent Chicago personal injury lawyer. On May 11, 1963, his client, Delmar Franklin, then thirty-one years old, was driving his 1961 Corvair down a long, straight, dry grade. His wife was in the front seat alongside him, with his children, ages seven and twelve, in the back seat. A cross wind hit their car, which went out of control and rolled over. Franklin was paralyzed from the chest down; his wife suffered a fractured spine but recovered sufficiently to be able to turn her husband in his bed every two hours. The older child, a girl, broke her arm. It never knitted properly and would be deformed for the rest of her life.[31]

Davidson figured the first thing to do was examine GM proving ground records concerning the stability of the 1961 Corvair. Using proper discovery procedures, he requested those records, but GM refused to produce them. The trial judge, Nicholas J. Bua of the Cook County Circuit Court, repeatedly issued court orders directing GM to produce the material. Not wanting to risk penalties for failure to obey, GM inundated Davidson with 34,000 documents—all unindexed. They contained reports on the windshield wipers, the decorative trim on the car, the heat generated by the engine, and scores of other matters. None, however, involved the stability of the Corvair. GM refused to give Davidson access to several rooms at GM headquarters where other records were kept, even though a court order granted him such access, and GM was allowing attorneys working on a similar case to view the files.[32]

A court order also directed GM to show Davidson certain motion pictures taken of Corvair stability tests. At the appointed time, GM officials carted sixty films into their projection room. Davidson pointed out to them that he was supposed to be supplied with an index to the films. The officials replied that if he had a complaint, he knew where to find the courthouse. He was also informed that the test data that ordinarily accompanied the movies had been destroyed. With his patience slipping away, Davidson turned to the stenographer who was recording the proceedings and started to say for the record that he wished to object to GM's "compliance" with discovery procedures. But before he could finish, the projectionist was ordered by the GM lawyers to start the projector. The sound was turned up to a blare to hinder communication with the stenographer. Davidson angrily settled in to view the films.

He and his associate were there for several days. GM offered no indication of what the filmed tests were intended to prove. The movies showed Corvairs whirring around the proving grounds but gave no clue at all as to the speed of the vehicles or the engineering lessons learned from the tests. The penultimate insult came when promotional films featuring the Chevy II and the Impala were projected. Davidson and his associate could finally take it no longer when an irrelevant movie featuring a comedian appeared on the screen. They angrily left the projection room.

Davidson understandably became fed up with such antics and finally asked Judge Bua to impose sanctions for noncompliance with court orders. Bua, too, was upset. He held GM in default and ordered that judgment be entered against them on the issue of liability, with damages to be determined later. It was the most severe civil penalty that could be imposed.

Bua's order was appealed, and GM won on a technicality. Judge Bua had stated that GM was in "contempt of court," but Illinois procedural laws do not allow an entry of default as a penalty for contempt. Judge Bua, through the state Attorney General's office, told the Illinois Supreme Court that his reference in the order to "contempt" was simply a careless use of language and that the real reason for the default judgment was because of GM's failure to comply with his orders, but he was reversed. Another trial was set, but Davidson settled with GM out of court.[33]

In the words of Tom Goldstein, a reporter on legal matters, "Few topics enrage leading trial lawyers or judges more than what they perceive as abuses in the [discovery] process."[34] Informally and in bar association circles, lawyers are heatedly debating whether and how discovery should be reformed. If discovery is reduced, it is argued, justice will return to the gamesmanship of medieval times;

and yet liberal discovery also seems to reduce justice to a game. The rules may differ to the point of being an entirely new game, but game it remains—and a brutal one at that. While such a circumstance may be acceptable, if regrettable, when the players are corporate giants battling, say, over the rights to a new camera or a new computer, the game is cruel indeed when one player is a desperately injured Delmar Franklin and the other is General Motors.

As a particularly galling example of the frustrations and perversities of trials, consider the problems in trying to prove a drunken driver was in fact drunk. Research has shown that drinking drivers are disproportionately involved in serious accidents. Indeed, about one-half of all traffic fatalities involve drinking drivers, and at least half of those are problem drinkers.

The scene is familiar: A family is headed home, traveling along a dark and nearly deserted highway late some Sunday night. All of a sudden an oncoming car swerves out of its lane. Crash! There is an awful collision and several of the family are badly injured. The other driver, Smith, a man of about sixty, let us say, appears dazed but not seriously injured.

A policeman who arrives at the scene, however, suspects that Smith might have been drinking too much prior to driving. After attending to the injured, the policeman proceeds to investigate. He gives various field sobriety tests to Smith. On the basis of Smith's poor performance during these tests, the officer arrests him for drunken driving and takes him to the police station for a breathalyzer test. Smith "flunks" it, registering a .15 blood alcohol content, more than enough to render him legally drunk.

All of this is crucial to the family. When they sue Smith for the injuries arising out of the accident, they will have to prove that Smith did, in fact, cause the accident by swerving out of his lane, thereby acting negligently. The problem, however, is that there were no witnesses other than the occupants of the vehicles and no conclusive physical evidence to indicate who veered over the center line. Thus, the trial may well end up in a shouting match. The family will contend that Smith was negligent, Smith will deny it, and the outcome will depend upon the proverbial "flip of a coin." But if a jury can be convinced that Smith was drunk at the time of the accident, the plaintiff's case, as a practical matter, will be won.

An open-and-shut case, in light of the police officer's testimony? Not if Smith (or Smith's insurance company) is defended by an experienced lawyer.

One field sobriety test commonly administered to drivers suspected of being intoxicated is the pupillary reaction test. Supposedly,
the less sober a person is, the more slowly his pupils will react to
light. If the arresting officer had administered such a test and offered the opinion that the motorist failed the test, Smith's attorney
might cross-examine this way:

Q. Officer, you say that the defendant's eyes reacted very slowly
   to light when you shined the flashlight in them?
A. Yes, sir.
Q. Did you have any mechanical means of timing the reaction?
A. No, but I afterwards shined the light into the eyes of my part-
   ner, and I could tell that the reaction of his eyes was much
   faster.
Q. By reaction, do you mean the contracting of the pupil of the
   eye?
A. The pupil, yes.
Q. You are not an optometrist, I take it?
A. I am not.
Q. Have you made any special study of the human eye or of the
   defects or diseases of the human eye?
A. No, I haven't.
Q. You realize that not all eyes are alike, that some people may
   have defective vision, or something wrong with their eyes that
   may affect the speed with which they will react to light?
A. I never saw any.
Q. You will admit that some people wear glasses to correct some
   defect in their vision?
A. Yes, some people do.
Q. Not being specially trained in matters relating to the eye, you
   would not know whether or not atrophy of the optic nerve
   would affect the reaction of the pupil to light?
A. No, sir.
Q. Nor would you know whether or not an ocular motor nerve
   weakness would affect the reaction of the pupil to light?
A. No, I would not.
Q. Are you familiar with the Argyle Robertson Syndrome of Lo-
   comotion Ataxia, in which the light reflex is lost?

In the words of Richard Erwin, author of the leading text on the defense of drunk driving cases, "At this point, you are likely to get an

objection from the [other side], but you have made your point, whether or not the objection is sustained.'' The officer's testimony would indeed seem to be undermined. Perhaps more important, doubt is cast upon the credibility of all the rest of the officer's testimony. As to the policeman's testimony that the driver's eyes were bloodshot, again, no serious problem may be presented if the attorney is skillful:

Q. Officer, you have seen people whose eyes were bloodshot and watery who were not under the influence of alcohol, have you not, sir?
[The answer will undoubtedly be ''yes''.]

Q. Then the mere fact that the defendant's eyes were bloodshot and watery would not of itself convince you that he was under the influence of alcohol, would it, sir?
[The answer will be ''no''.]

Q. Likewise, you have seen people who smelled as if they had been consuming alcohol, but who were neither drunk nor intoxicated nor in any way affected by the consumption of alcohol, have you not, sir?

A. Yes.

The officer's testimony that the driver's speech was garbled and incoherent can also be neutralized:

Q. Officer, when you asked the defendant his name, he told you that it was John Smith, didn't he?

A. Yes, sir.

Q. And you wrote it down on the report?

A. Yes.

Q. And you asked him his address, and he told you where he lived, didn't he?

A. Yes.

Q. And when you asked him where he had been, he told you he had just left Little Joe's Bar after having had two beers?

A. Yes.

Q. Now, officer, when he told you his name was John Smith, you were able to understand that, were you?

A. Yes, sir.

Q. And you understood when he told you his address?

A. Yes.

Q. And you understood when he told you that he had had two
   beers? You understood that all right, didn't you, officer?
A. Yes, sir.

In the words, once again, of Richard Erwin:

Proceed down the line, taking everything that the defendant told the
officer, and conclude each question with "you understood the statement of the defendant." Then your final question should take this
form:

Q: Now, officer, will you kindly tell the jury what was incoherent about the defendant's speech that you have testified that you understood?

It makes very little difference what answer the officer gives if he
has committed himself solidly to the proposition that the defendant's speech was incoherent.

Nor is even the fact that the motorist failed a chemical test conclusive as to his sobriety. Erwin explains why:

If the blood alcohol reading is very close—in other words, if it is a
marginal case, such as .11 per cent or .15 per cent—the defense can
sometimes have a better chance with the chemical tests than it would
have without them.

The reason for this is that a strong defense based on the validity
of the chemical tests gets the jury to thinking more about the chemical
tests and less about the original testimony of the arresting officer.
They finally conclude that if the chemical test is valid, the defendant
is guilty; if it is not valid, there is a doubt and he is not guilty,
despite any other evidence that appears in the case.

Finally, according to Erwin:

In addition to the breath-testing and blood-alcohol testing, many
police departments are now using photographs with some degree of
success. The snapshot of the defendant walking the line or putting
his finger to his nose is sometimes deadly evidence against a defendant.

However, it is not always completely fatal. A proper cross-examination of an officer who submits one or two snapshot photographs of the defendant can frequently reduce the effectiveness of
the photographs.

The cross-examination should proceed along these lines:

Q. Officer, I believe you said that the defendant, in walking the
   line stepped off to his left two or three times. Is that correct?

A. Yes, sir.

Q. Now, I show you this photograph that you say was taken when he was walking the line. Does that show when he stepped off the line the second time or when?

A. Yes, that was about when he was halfway down the line and stepped off to his left.

Q. Did he at any time walk the line heel to toe?

A. Oh yes, he walked heel to toe, but he stepped off three times.

Q. You didn't take any pictures of him while he was walking the line heel to toe?

A. No, sir.

Q. You only took the pictures when he stepped off, is that right?

A. Well, I think there were some other pictures. . . .

At this point, defense counsel should demand all the pictures that were taken. Frequently, it will occur that there were pictures that showed the defendant in a perfectly normal position and in which he appears to be perfectly normal. It can then be argued to the jury that it is not difficult to catch a person with a snapshot in an awkward position. Almost all jurors, particularly women, know this and are fearful of it themselves when snapshot-takers are in the vicinity.

Some police departments have been experimenting with motion pictures, and the rumor is that they have a great deal of success. However, the district attorney of one of the largest counties in California has stated:

We found that by taking motion pictures, we could readily get pleas of guilty from a lot of young men who were not used to drinking. The motion pictures amply demonstrated the intoxication of the drivers, and upon being shown the motion pictures, or after having their attorneys look at the motion pictures, it was easy to get them to plead guilty.

However, we ran into a very peculiar situation. We found that the old hardened drunks, who had become acclimated to the use of alcohol over a long period of time, when they found that their picture was to be taken, had the faculty of pulling themselves together and walking about and acting as if they were perfectly sober. Surprisingly, they were able to do this to the degree that the motion picture not only failed to demonstrate that they were intoxicated, but, on the other hand, became the best evidence available to the defense lawyer to prove that they were not intoxicated.

Because of this fact, we found that the worst offenders, offenders with prior records and the habitual drunk, who should
be convicted, were hiring attorneys, subpoenaing the motion
pictures into court, and being found not guilty. Because of that
fact, we abandoned the use of motion pictures as an evidentiary
device in this county.

Accordingly, if you get a case in which a motion picture was
taken, examine the motion picture carefully, having in mind the
type of client that you are representing. If he is an habitual drinker,
it may be that the motion pictures will be his best defense.[35]

Admittedly, these exact questions, answers, and circumstances
will not appear in every case, but they are representative of the ave-
nues open to an alert defense attorney seeking to destroy damning
testimony, in even an obvious drunken driving case against his
client.

At the least, the possibility of the use of such tactics can result in
(1) substantial delay in payment of an accident victim's losses as the
defendant insurance company threatens on this basis to defend what
looks like a clear case against it and (2) a concomitant reduction in
the amount of the settlement, perhaps well below the victim's real
losses, despite what looks like his airtight case, or (3) an outside
chance—or maybe better—that, if the matter is pressed to trial, an
experienced defense lawyer can convince a jury of the defendant's
sobriety, whether or not he was sober.

All this brings to mind the defense strategy outlined by one of
America's most famous trial lawyers, Richard "Racehorse" Haynes,
speaking before a recent American Bar Association seminar in New
York: "Say you sue me because my dog bit you," he said, with his
thumbs hooked in his vest pockets. "Well, now, this is my defense:
My dog doesn't bite. And second is the alternative, my dog was tied
up that night. And third, I don't believe you really got bit. And
fourth," with a sly grin, "I don't have a dog."[36]

Ultimately, there is no way of knowing how many trials are won
by wily tricks. Certainly many lawyers are rather straightforward in
their presentations, depending more for success on painstaking preparation and understandable presentation than anything else. Even
so, the result of a battle between such lawyers on opposite sides is
still a gamble. Keep in mind that whenever a case goes to a jury, the
jury can decide the case *either way* and be right! If that is *not* so, in
legal theory the judge should "direct a verdict" for the only side that
ought to win.[37] What this really means, when you stop and think

about it, is that after months or years of legal battling both before and during trial, the expert lawyers involved (including the judge) throw up their hands, toss the case into the lap of the nonexpert jury, and in effect, say to the laymen, "Here, *you* decide—and any guess you make about which side should win is okay."

Small wonder that the gypsies have a curse: "May you have a lawsuit in which you know you are in the right."

5

The Civil Jury

THE VAST MAJORITY of personal injury cases are settled out of court, not litigated. Studies and jurisdictions vary, but most studies confirm that 95 percent of the cases—perhaps as much as 98 or 99 percent in some jurisdictions—are settled before reaching a verdict.[1] But all settlements are in substantial measure negotiated with an eye to what would happen if the case went to the jury. That explains why the study of the jury and the way it operates is so vital to the area of personal injury law.

At the outset, any litigant must face the prospect of putting his fate in the hands of disgruntled jurors who are paid at a niggardly rate ($15–$30 a day) and are spending most of their time in wearying idleness. Charles Desmond, when he was Chief Judge of New York's highest court, remarked that "the pure waste of time is very great, since many more jurors are called than sit on cases and jurors spend much of their time sitting around waiting."[2] In the words of a *Chicago Tribune* editorial, "Many who are summoned to jury duty . . . are never called [to sit]. Many more twiddle their thumbs for days—time taken away from their jobs and homes—before actually serving on a jury. The result may be not only boredom, but a pool of angry, uncooperative people who feel they have been victimized by the state—hardly an ideal frame of mind for a jury."[3] A study funded by the National Insitute of Law Enforcement and Criminal Justice found that the number of people called for jury duty could be reduced by 20 to 25 percent with no adverse affect on court operations. According to Harvey Solomon, Executive Director of the Institute for Court Management, the solution "basically involves a statistical analysis using some fairly simple techniques but it hasn't been done."[4] So, far from being an exhilarating participation in an important and elevating governmental process, jury duty for many entails long hours of waiting in dingy, dirty quarters, being harassed by surly clerks, occasionally sitting on cases that too often involve the dull reconstruction of humdrum traffic accidents which occurred many years before. A General Accounting Office (GAO) study conducted for the U.S. Senate found that many citizens failed to register to vote because they did not want their names on lists that might be used for jury duty or other nonelection purposes. The GAO survey found that more than one-third of the country's election boards serving municipalities with more than 15,000 residents and fifty-one of the largest city boards believe that the nonelection use of registration lists discourages voter registration. Some boards estimated that as many as 5 percent to 10 percent of potential voters fail to register on these grounds.[5] On the other hand, it is also true that in some big cities at least some people register as Democrats to avoid jury duty. How is this done? If you are known there as a registered Democrat, especially as a party stalwart, you can go to your precinct captain when jury duty comes around and get the call quashed or at least postponed. Thus, at both ends of the spectrum, either never registering to vote or being active in politics, there are people motivated solely by the wish to avoid jury duty.

Once a jury is empaneled, it has enormous power in personal injury cases. As a practical matter, the questions to be decided are turned over to the jury, which receives very little supervisory control from the judge. For example, here is the instruction given to the jury by the judge in personal injury cases in Illinois:

> When I use the word negligence in these instructions, I mean failure to do something which a reasonably careful person would do or the doing of something which a reasonably careful person would not do under circumstances similar to those shown by the evidence. *The law does not say how a reasonably careful person would act under these circumstances; that is for you to decide.* [Emphasis added.]

Referring to this charge, the late Professor Harry Kalven of the University of Chicago Law School, who headed the Chicago Jury Project, the largest study of juries ever done, stated, "It would be impossible to have a clearer statement of the fact that we are delegating law-making power to the jury."[6] What is more, the jury's discretion in estimating the amount of damages is similarly unlimited.

Thus the jury has unique power in personal injury cases. But if the jury is a giant in this area, it is made to be a blindfolded, stumbling giant. The law throws up countless obstacles between the jury and its goal of deciding a case on the basis of thoughtful examination. The schizophrenic pattern of "rational irrationality" in trials—and the gamble it makes of litigation—shows up vividly here: Jurors are manacled in ways unheard of for others who must decide important matters. Jurors are not allowed to take notes. *Imagine* being asked to listen to hours of complicated discussion—sometimes for days, weeks, and even months on end—in order to make a decision on the matter, and yet being denied the right to jot anything down! Jurors are not allowed to ask questions, to suggest what material they might like to see, or to indicate what witnesses they might like to hear. Most of the exclusionary rules of evidence, under which many important matters are withheld, are used *only* in jury cases. If an objection to hearsay evidence, for example, is raised in a bench trial (before a judge sitting without a jury), the judge will normally brush the objection aside and listen to the evidence "for what it's worth." But not in a jury trial. Similarly, many other matters that might seem pertinent are scrupulously hidden from the jury. For example, as has already been noted, the jury is not told whether the accident victim has already been compensated for his losses from accident and health insurance or with sick pay.

The jury also is not told that any award it may give is tax free. Given the fact that the largest portion of the out-of-pocket loss of most substantial verdicts represents the loss of wages, which, of course, are taxable, this is a significant omission indeed. But if such an omission might encourage inadvertent generosity, other rules go the other way. The jury cannot be told, for example, that the victim's legal fees must come out of the award. These fees will often amount to 30 percent or even up to 50 or 60 percent. "Courts shelter juries from such information," according to Professor Joseph Bishop of the Yale Law School, "as sternly as Victorian parents sheltered children from sex."[7]

The biggest item of information that courts go to great lengths to shield from the jury is the matter of insurance. According to one estimate, insured drivers now comprise about 80 percent of all drivers (down from about 86 percent in 1975).[8] As a practical matter, however, any case going to trial will be against an insured defendant. More than 99 percent of all personal injury verdicts and settlements are paid by insurers of one kind or another.[9] But the existence of insurance money is, in the law's eyes, irrelevant; the only thing that matters is whether the individual defendant, insured ot not, was negligent. In other words, theoretically at least, insurance should attach because of liability, not liability because of insurance. To keep the jury honest in deciding the question of liability and to prevent it from considering how nice it would be for the broken plaintiff to be paid from the vast and tempting coffers of insurance companies, any mention of insurance at the trial is treated like a foul expletive at a dinner party and can be grounds for a mistrial. On the other hand, in the jury-selection process, plaintiff's counsel may attempt to circumvent this by asking whether any of the jurors is "in any way affiliated with any company that makes it a practice of investigating or defending cases of the personal injury kind." This is allowed supposedly so that plaintiffs can bar from the jury any insurance company employees or their close relatives. In some jurisdictions, indeed, the plaintiff's lawyer is even permitted in this regard to utter those awful words and ask directly if any of the prospective jurors "works for an insurance company." Sometimes, if the mention of insurance during the trial is only a "slip of the tongue," no mistrial is declared,[10] but a shrewd and aggressive lawyer can make detecting intentional "slips" almost impossible. Anyway, it is assumed that if jurors know there is insurance money involved, they cannot be relied upon to judge fairly the merits of a given case. It seems to be the feeling generally among insurance companies, meanwhile, that most juries know when insurance companies are involved in a case, because jurors can figure out for themselves that financially irresponsible people are not often sued and because they get to recognize insurance company lawyers. As a result, according to Law Professor Leon Green of the University of Texas, "it becomes more and more difficult to mix insurance with negligence law and retain the law's integrity."[11]

In point of fact, insurance companies themselves, as well as plaintiffs, may now *want* juries to know of the existence of insurance. Jurors are most often also carriers of liability insurance and may be conscious of the adverse effect on their insurance bills of verdicts favorable to the plaintiff. Recently several insurance firms conducted an aggressive public relations campaign with respect to "windfall awards," urging jurors to appreciate that they, along with everyone else, must eventually pay for those awards through higher premiums. At least $10 million worth of hard-hitting advertising has appeared in full-page or double-page spreads in publications such as the *New York Times*, the *Wall Street Journal*, *Time*, and *The New Republic*. "Too Bad the Judge Can't Read This to the Jury" is the heading of an Aetna ad showing a judge holding in his hand this instruction to the jury: "When awarding damages in liability cases the jury is cautioned to be fair and to bear in mind that the money does not grow on trees. It must be paid through insurance premiums from uninvolved parties, such as yourselves."[12] Plaintiffs' lawyers from New York to Califonia have complained about such advertising to the Federal Trade Commission, insisting that it mandate corrective ads. Theodore Koskoff, a prominent Connecticut personal injury lawyer, filed a lawsuit on behalf of his plaintiffs, charging the insurance companies, in effect, with jury tampering and asking for an injunction stopping such ads.[13]

At any rate, it seems undeniable that supposedly irrelevant insurance considerations do impinge on jury decisions. Note, too, the contrary distortion: The jury, which cannot be told whether the defendant is insured, may be permitted to assume erroneously that he is—to the detriment or advantage of the occasional uninsured defendant, depending on the jury's prejudice in regard to insurance.

Leaving jurors in the dark about some technical matters may not be inconsistent with the view of the jury as imparting to the law some of the nonlawyer's human instincts and compassion. The law, cold and distant (it is argued), needs the leavening influence of the impulses of those untutored in the technicalities of the law. According to Professors Harry Kalven and Hans Zeisel: "The jury, it is said, is a remarkable device for insuring that we are governed by the spirit of the law and not by its letter; for insuring that the rigidity of any general rule of law can be shaped to do justice in the particular case."[14]

But, as the same authors have said, "What is one man's equity is another man's anarchy."[15] In the first place, there is the problem of the extent to which the law is ignored. Many writers point to the jury's inclination to play Robin Hood with insurance company funds, quite apart from the legal rights of the parties. It has long been thought axiomatic, for example, that jurors refuse to apply the rule of contributory negligence, which bars a negligent claimant from receiving any payment despite negligence on the part of the defendant. Martin Mayer, in his book *The Lawyers*, tells the story of a little old seamstress on a jury who disposed of a plaintiff's fairly obvious contributory negligence with the comment: "He didn't look where he was going—it could happen to anybody—give him his money."[16] But such quixotic ignoring of the law by those charged with applying it can obviously result in chaotic variations. Gabriel Tarde has spoken of the jury's "nonenlightened and unreasoning conscience."[17] Professor Kalven told the following tale:

> The vicissitudes of the functioning jury are well illustrated by an actual case which may be . . . termed "the triple-rape story." The jury-study staff received three sets of reports on this particular case, as it was necessary for it to be tried three times. The first time it was tried, the defendant was found guilty and was given a life sentence; then, for a variety of reasons such as newspaper publicity it was necessary to have the case retried. The second time it was tried the result was a hung jury; so it was tried a third time. This time the defendant was acquitted and the jury actually took up a collection of sixty-four dollars and gave it to him. I offer that to you as an example of the well-known fact that we are dealing with a somewhat flexible institution.[18]

A leading authority on the jury, Professor Maurice Rosenberg of the Columbia Law School, has spoken of his own impatience

> . . . with the jury for its tendency to flout rationality and give rein to what Judge [Jerome] Frank called "juriesprudence." A vivid example of this is attributed to a juror who had just finished serving and explained in these words how the jury had reached its verdict: "We couldn't make head or tail of the case or follow all the messing around the lawyers did. None of us believed the witnesses on either side, anyway, so we made up our minds to disregard the evidence on both sides and decide the case on its merits."[19]

As these instances suggest, the confusion of juries is scarcely their own fault. Judges' instructions to the jury are a perfect illustration of how cumbersome, self-serving, and self-defeating the law and lawyers are, even when their purpose is to help those outside the law to deal with the law. Typically a judge will read the instructions on the law applicable to a given case in a bored or hurried tone, going on for a half-hour or more in a manner that would stupefy any listener into incomprehension. In the words of one of the country's leading authorities on the law of trials, the late Charles McCormick of the University of Texas Law School, jury instructions are typically "given in the most tiresome and unpalatable fashion, so as almost to defy the jury to take an interest in them."[20] Compounding the problem is the fact that the judge will often be reading so-called standard or pattern instructions in the language of appellate court opinions, aiming them at the attorney reader, not the lay listener. Indeed, it is no exaggeration to say that in significant measure the purpose of jury instructions is not so much to instruct the jury but to confuse the judge! A lawyer will often ask the judge to instruct the jury in a certain technical way, with the hope not so much that the jury will be influenced by the language as that the judge may reject the requested instruction and thus create a basis for appeal in the event the lawyer loses at the trial level. Then, armed with "error in the record," the lawyer can continue to bargain for a more favorable settlement, despite the existence of an adverse verdict. His threat to appeal faces his opponents with possible reversal, and failing that the process will consume more of the winning party's time and money.

The anomaly that instructions on the law are aimed at lawyers, not laymen, gains perhaps even firmer support from the fact that, when a point of law is disputed, framing the issue as an instruction to the jury is a handy way to have the law clarified by an appellate court. Counsel for one of the parties to the trial will frame the point of law in summary form in a paragraph or two, supposedly suitable for reading to the jury, and present it to the trial judge. If the trial judge rejects it as an inaccurate statement of the law and the lawyer who offered the instruction appeals, the appellate court has a perfect "laboratory" to clarify the law by approving, disapproving, or modifying the precise language of the proposed charge. Similarly, if the trial judge accepts such an instruction, the opposing lawyer has a basis for appeal. This gives both lawyers an incentive to propose voluminous instructions, and each will comb through the other's in minutest detail. As a result, jury instructions—supposedly a means to clarify the law—are among the richest sources of appeals in American jurisprudence. An Illinois survey covering a twenty-five-year period revealed that reversals occurred in almost 40 percent of the cases appealed on the grounds that the jury had been erroneously instructed.[21]

In response to all the litigation created by jury instructions, attempts have been made by committees of lawyers and judges to standardize jury instructions. By simply copying from the resulting form books, judges are able quickly and competently to assemble a set of jury instructions. But if the use of "pattern" or standard instructions is a boon to judges, it has been a bane for jurors—and indeed for the trial process itself. The instructions are cast in bronze, and the judge reads them like holy writ, never taking his eyes from them. Concerned exclusively with not missing a word, he is oblivious to the degree of comprehension of the jurors. In other words, he is aiming not at the jurors to whom he is supposedly speaking (or rather reading) but at the absent judges of an appellate court.

Because the instructions are drafted for use in a wide variety of cases, they are necessarily very abstract and broad, creating tremendous problems for jurors in applying them to any particular case. And because variations from the broad, abstract terms can create possibilities of error and therefore appeal, judges are loath to supplement them with any concrete examples. As a result, the facts of a given case and illustrative examples are rarely integrated into a standard jury instruction, and the court's instruction is almost never integrated into the trial itself. This occurs despite the recognition by lawyers and judges of the need for such concrete examples.

Therefore "the language used [in jury charges] is in the best tradition of the legal dialect—grammatically complex, lexically abstract and semantically obtuse. Consequently, it is doubtful that jurors can comprehend most of them," according to a perceptive study by Robert and Veda Charrow.[22] Typical of many comments in legal literature is this statement by Judge Swain:

> One of the greatest fictions known to law is that a jury of twelve laymen can hear a judge read a set of instructions once, then understand them, digest them and correctly apply them to the facts of the case. It has taken the judge and lawyers years of study to understand the law as stated in those instructions.[23]

In the words of Jerome Frank, a scholar many consider the most perceptive judge ever to write on trials, "often the judge must state those rules to the jury with such niceties that many lawyers do not comprehend them, and it is impossible that the jury can."[24]

It is important to recognize how insensitive most lawyers and judges are, as a general proposition, to the intelligibility of legalese for nonlawyers. Consider the case of *Garza* v. *Chicago Health Clubs*, a 1972 Federal case. The court was asked to determine whether a notice included in the defendants' loan agreement, in order to comply with the Truth in Lending Law, was understandable to the average person. The agreement called upon the buyer

> . . . to consent to immediate execution upon any such judgment and that any execution that may be issued on such may be immediately

levied upon and satisfied out of any personal property of the undersigned . . . and to waive all right of the undersigned . . . to have personal property last taken and levied upon to satisfy any such execu-
tion.

The court, granting that the clause was written in somewhat legalistic terms, peremptorily ruled the language sufficiently understandable to meet the demands of consumer protection.[25] This judicial attitude carries over to jury instructions as delivered by many judges.
Consider the California instructions on the legal doctrine of *Res Ipsa
Loquitur* (the thing speaks for itself).*
The final sentence of the instruction reads as follows:

> However, you shall not find that a proximate cause of the occur-
> rence was some negligent conduct on the part of the defendant un-
> less you believe, after weighing all the evidence in the case and draw-
> ing such inferences therefrom as you believe warranted, that it is
> more probable than not that the occurrence was caused by some
> negligent conduct on the part of the defendant.[26]

That sentence contains sixty-four words, with approximately
nine clauses. Furthermore, because it states a negative rule, followed
by a negative exception ("unless"), it is very difficult to parse logically. The remainder of the *Res Ipsa Loquitor* instruction is also
filled with unnecessary negatives, adding unnecessary confusion. It
contains many double negatives as well. It goes on, for example, to
say: "However you shall *not* find . . . unless you believe . . ." (note
that "not . . . unless" simply means "if"). The instruction elsewhere
contains these words: "that it is the kind of conduct that does not

---

*Lawyers often "suitably" and inscrutably encase their jargon in Latin, the better
to keep the "unwashed" off balance. Even sophisticated laymen can be brought
up sharp by such legalese. In his book *A Thousand Days*, Arthur Schlesinger, Jr.,
describes a meeting between John F. Kenendy and Philip Graham, the publisher of
the *Washington Post*, at the Democratic Presidential Convention in 1960:

> The two men were driving from the Baltimore to another hotel, where Ken-
> nedy was meeting still another caucus. [Kennedy stated] that he might be
> twenty votes short on the first ballot and asked if there were any chance of
> getting [Lyndon] Johnson votes out of a vice-presidency offer. . . . Graham
> then said that Kennedy could not miss by twenty votes, and, dropping into
> the argot of . . . Law School, observed that his nomination was guaranteed
> by *Res Ipsa Loquitur*. In the midst of the traffic jam and convention hub-
> bub, Kennedy looked up, always ready to learn something new, and said,
> "What does that mean?"

> Arthur M. Schlesinger, Jr., *A Thousand Days* (Boston: Little,
> Brown, 1966), pp. 44–45.

occur ordinarily in the absence of someone's negligence.'' The combination of an implicit negative (''in the absence'') coupled with an explicit negative (''not'') can further confuse the listener. As the Charrow report indicates, the *Res Ipsa Loquitur* instruction is unfortunately not an anomaly but one example of ''the many instructions used by courts which contain linguistic indices of incomprehensibility.''[27]

In one test conducted by the Charrows, only one person out of thirty-five, a Ph.D., understood the California pattern instruction on ''proximate cause.''[28] The concept of ''proximate cause'' is often crucial in personal injury cases. The standard California jury instruction tell us: ''A proximate cause is a cause of an injury which produces the injury in natural and continuous sequence and without which the injury would not have occurred.''[29] In other words, in order to consider the defendant's negligence ''the proximate cause'' of the plaintiff's injury, the injury must be a foreseeable consequence of the defendant's negligence, not highly unpredictable. In the Charrow study about one-quarter of the time the phrase ''proximate cause'' was interpreted as ''approximate cause'' or ''estimated cause'' or some other inaccurate formulation. In addition, the phrase ''natural and continuous sequence,'' produced a variety of misunderstandings. For example, jurors thought that the word ''natural'' referred to a ''natural cause'' rather than a natural chain of effects. Only ten of the thirty-five subjects were able to paraphrase most or all of the instruction without any errors, despite the fact that it was the shortest of the instructions tested—only twenty-seven words. One would think that it would be possible, if nothing else, to memorize such a short instruction, especially after two playings. However, not only did no one memorize it, but four subjects were unable to paraphrase any of it. This is further confirmation of the psycholinguistic finding that one cannot remember what one has not understood. The one subject who paraphrased the entire instruction correctly, the Ph.D., paraphrased by means of an example of cause and effect.[30]

To give another example, California's instruction on ''Contributory Negligence—Forgetfulness of Known Danger'' (dealing with the claimant's own fault) starts out, ''Whether or not it is negligence for one to proceed into a dangerous situation of which he had previous knowledge is a question of fact.'' Keep in mind that the distinction between a question of law and a question of fact is by no means easy to grasp. But apart from that, the subject of the predicate ''is a question of fact" is a sentence consisting of no less than three subordinate clauses. By the time the listener gets to the predicate he or she has probably forgotten the subject,[31] especially if the sentence is read rapidly or droningly amid countless similarly arcane sentences.

Consider, as still another example, the way judges charge jurors on the issue of "Discounting to Present Value." By this device, account is taken of the fact that generally speaking all types of loss the claimant will suffer in the future through injury or death are in effect prepaid by a jury award. The earning power of the money thus paid would produce an overpayment, unless an adjustment is made in the form of a "discount to present value." In other words, the injured party who had expected to earn $10,000 for each of the next ten years, if paid $100,000 now in lump sum, is being overpaid in light of the interest he can earn on the portion of the $100,000 not immediately used for current expenses. In the case of serious disability or death of a relatively young wage-earner, the possibility of overpayment is obviously *very* substantial. The point, though, is a very subtle one to convey quickly to persons unfamiliar with it. But listen to the Illinois Pattern Jury Instruction on the point:

> In computing the damages arising in the future because of injuries, medical expenses, and loss of earnings, you must not simply multiply the damages by the length of time you have found they will continue or the number of years you have found that the plaintiff is likely to live. Instead you must determine that present cash value. "Present cash value" means the sum of money, needed now, which, when added to what that sum may reasonably be expected to earn in the future, will equal the amount of the damages, expenses and earnings at the time in the future when the damages from the injury will be suffered, the expenses must be paid and the earnings would have been received.[32]

Imagine that last sentence being read rapidly at you!

Typical too of the confusing condescension of judges toward jurors in instructing them—leading to a rough sense of justice indeed—is the prominent case of *McWeeney* v. *New York, New Haven and Hartford Railroad*, written by Judge Henry Friendly, for years one of the ablest and most respected lawyers and judges in the United States. In 1956 a railroad brakeman named McWeeney was struck by a moving freight car while he was on the side ladder of another car. He was seriously injured and sued the railroad for the railroad's negligence. He was a bachelor, aged thirty-six at the date of the accident and thirty-nine at the time of the trial. (Note again the typical delay before trial, not to mention the time for appeal.) His pay for the thirteen weeks immediately preceding the accident had been $1,187.61, at an annual rate of approximately $4,800. After a verdict in his favor the defendant railroad moved for a new trial on the grounds that the trial judge erred in refusing ten of the defendant's requests for instructions. (Note how jury instructions served to get error in the record and thus provide a basis for appeal.)

The defendant had requested, among other things, that the jury be instructed in the following terms: "If you verdict is in favor of plaintiff, you must calculate any past or future loss of earnings on the basis of his net income after deduction of income taxes." As we saw earlier, a jury award is not taxable, so the defendant wanted the jury to deduct an equivalent amount of taxes to avoid overpayment. Judge Friendly based his denial of the appeal on two grounds. First, it would mean "imposing on the jury a task the jury cannot readily be expected to perform."[33] Why couldn't they? It is simply too complicated for jurors, Friendly ruled. What would McWeeney's income tax bracket be over the coming years? Supposing he marries? Supposing his wife brings children to the marriage, changing the deductibles.

But the jury is already expected to speculate on, say, the duration of the claimant's injury and the amount of his salary over the coming years. One legal writer asks if the questions of taxation the jurors are asked to speculate about are

> . . . so speculative that we should refuse to let the defendant even try to show them? Indeed, which is more conjectural: the existence of income tax in this country along the pattern we now know it, or the continuation of the plaintiff's salary during exactly the same period? Yet, we have no real difficulty in letting the jury speculate as to the existence of the latter. We will even let the plaintiff try to show that he might have earned *more* salary in the future. If the plaintiff received the advantage of the speculations in his favor, why do we bar the defendant from even trying to show what appears to be a smaller speculation on his favor?[34]

Friendly replied to such criticisms, "Although failure to instruct the jury to reduce a verdict to take account of income taxes on plaintiff's lost earning power, when viewed in isolation, may tend to make verdicts too high there are . . . other factors that countervail this in the ordinary case." Like what? An offsetting factor, says Friendly,

> . . . is that the supposedly overcompensated plaintiff does not retain his entire recovery or anything like it. Whatever the reasons of his-

tory or public policy for the American practice of generally not awarding attorney's fees to the successful party . . . we can hardly shut our eyes to this when asked to require the jury to take another extrinsic factor into account—particularly when we know that even court-prescribed maximum scales of contingent fees, which have been attacked by a counsel as inadequate, provide either a sliding scale ranging from 50% down to 25% or a flat amount of 33½%.

But isn't this an *awfully* rough equation—expecting the rule concerning attorneys fees (about which the jury is not told) to be counterbalanced by the nontaxability of the award (about which the jury is also not told)?

Another offsetting factor, according to Friendly, supposedly justifying the failure to instruct the jury about income taxes, is inflation. Judge Friendly states:

> There is little or no authority in favor of charging the jury to take future inflation into account. Yet there are few who do not regard some degree of continuing inflation as here to stay and who would be willing to translate their own earning power into a fixed annuity. . . . The effect of inflation of [only] 1 percent a year over Mc-Weeney's 29-year [life] expectancy at trial would go a long way towards offsetting any excess in the verdict due to failure to deduct income tax.

Here again is a vivid illustration of courts' cavalier and condescending treatment of juries.

Many judges still will not charge a jury to take inflation into account, despite the still more ferocious raging of inflation since Friendly's 1960 opinion. Indeed, such inflation may well wipe out any advantage the plaintiff would have received from a lump sum *not* discounted to present value: If you assume that money will earn 7 percent annually but that inflation also occurs at a 7 percent rate, the two in effect cancel each other out. In order to compensate the claimant fairly in such circumstances, one should *not* "discount to present value."

Why are jurors kept in the dark about inflation? Because, the courts say, future inflation is too speculative as to whether it will occur and, if so, at what rate. But to ignore inflation is, in effect, to predict that it will not occur. As Judge Godbold said in dissenting from a decision refusing to make allowance for inflation, "the only thing certain about [such a decision] is that it is certain to be wrong."[35] As is typical of the law's sleight-of-hand in dealing with jurors, the rule against charging jurors winks at jurors' "doing their own thing" *sub rosa*, in disregard of the judge's charge. In other words, no court explicitly requires juries to be told *not* to consider future inflation; rather juries may not be explicitly told to take inflation into account.[36] Interestingly enough, the courts that have abandoned the traditional rule against charging juries about inflation often further illustrate *either* deep distrust of juries *or* blind confidence in them. Most courts say jurors may be instructed to take inflation into account only on the basis of "sound and substantial" economic testimony and evidence,[37] while other courts insist that juries be left to their own devices without any expert witnesses on the subject for fear that expert testimony tends to develop "outlandish results."[38] As one judge observed, "economists have fared only slightly better than fortune tellers in foretelling the future."[39]

Such confusion, of course, reconfirms the chaos resulting from the law's demand that damages be awarded only in one lump sum (pp. 19–22). To all the unpredictable variables the jury must thus consider are now added future rates of inflation; some courts insist that juries can only "wing it" on their own in making such predictions, so unreliable are experts, while other courts insist jurors can make such predictions only if they rely on those same experts.[40]

Perhaps it should not surprise us that as a result of all this, jurors come away from the judges' instructions uninstructed. Recall, for example, Louis Nizer's experience where the jury refused to bring in a liability verdict in what seemed to be a simple civil case, because it thought to do so would mean *criminal* punishment of imprisonment for a doctor. Nizer's jury was not alone in its frightful confusion. Another jury, also sitting in a civil case, found for the plaintiff and sentenced the defendant to five years in the penitentiary![41] According to one study, about 40 percent of all jurors believed that they did not clearly understand the instructions of a judge. Many other studies have produced similar results.[42]

On rare occasions a judge will balk at reading an instruction that—though arguably correct—is so incomprehensible as to be useless. In a Washington, D.C., trial, the defendant requested that the following instruction be read to the jury:

DEFENDANT'S INSTRUCTION NO. 4

You are instructed that the Bank as creditor would have reason to believe that certain facts would materially increase the risk beyond which the surety intends to assume if, from consideration of all the

evidence, you find that a reasonable prudent person in the position
of the bank, knowing the specific facts that the bank did know,
would believe that those facts materially increased the risk intended
to be assumed by Allied Equities Corporation.

After the reading of his instructions, the judge caused the jury to be
removed from the courtroom and invited counsel to register any objection either had to the instructions given. The following took place
between the judge and the defendant's lawyer:

> MR. HARPER: We would object to the Court's failure to give De-
> fendant's Requested Instruction No. 4 as to the definition of
> what would have been—would have given the bank reason-
> able cause to believe.
> THE COURT: Well, I had originally intended to give no. 4, but it's
> such gobbledygook that these poor people would have been
> worse off than they are now.
> MR. HARPER: I have no further—
> THE COURT: I'll read this to you, see if somebody in this room
> can understand what it says. [The Court then read defen-
> dant's Instruction No. 4 as quoted above.] That's all one sen-
> tence. Does anybody in this room know what that means? I
> don't. So that's why I didn't give it.

Needless to say, defendant's lawyer appealed on the basis of the trial
judge's failure to read his proffered instruction. He lost, but still he
had gained his chance at winning it and had caused a delay of the
outcome, win or lose.[43]

To cite the words of Curtis Bok, a widely respected lawyer and
judge (father of former Harvard Law School Dean and current Harvard President Derek Bok): "Juries have the disadvantage . . . of being treated like children while the testimony is going on, but then being doused with a kettle full of law during the charge that would
make a third-year law student blanch."[44]

Not surprisingly, in view of its many deficiencies, there have
been many proposals through the years to abolish the jury for civil,
as opposed to criminal, cases. Erwin N. Griswold, when he was
Dean of the Harvard Law School, recommended the abolition of
jury trial in civil cases: "The jury trial is at best the apotheosis of the
amateur. Why should anyone think that 12 persons brought in from
the street, selected in various ways, for their lack of general ability,

should have any special capacity for deciding controversies between persons?''[45] Dean Griswold's statement echoes A. P. Herbert's description of the jury as composed of "twelve people of average ignorance."

Actually, civil jury trial has disappeared almost everywhere else in the world. Hans Zeisel of the University of Chicago, a leading authority on the jury, estimates that 98 percent of all civil jury trials in the world take place in the United States (as well as 90 percent of all criminal jury trials).[46]

But there is little prospect of abolishing civil jury trials here. In the first place, the Seventh Amendment to the U.S. Constitution preserves the right to jury trial for "suits at common law," and similar provisions appear in nearly all the state constitutions. Efforts to amend state constitutions to abolish civil jury trials, at least in personal injury cases, have been uniformly unsuccessful.[47] Why? Because trial lawyers fight so effectively to preserve civil jury trials. Plaintiffs' lawyers like them because of what they perceive to be their pro-plaintiff bias, and in general they are probably right. (See below, p. 104.) One would think that defense lawyers would oppose civil juries for the same reason. But, as we have seen, insurance companies are by no means convinced that juries are necessarily prejudiced against them. According to Professor Maurice Rosenberg, defense lawyers "hold the civil jury in tender esteem . . . because defense lawyers share with the rest of us an instinct for self-preservation. The folklore is that trial counsel can shrug off a $250,000 verdict in a 'maximum' $100,000 case by reminding the vice president of the insurance company client that 'juries will be juries.' '' Insurance companies also support jury trials even when occasional plaintiffs try to avert them, because the longer delay on the civil jury docket (1) affords them an effective bargaining weapon to force the desperately needy plaintiff to settle and (2) allows them to keep its money that much longer, earning interest all the while. The attitude of judges toward juries is a curious mixture. A Columbia University survey of judges produced, in Professor Rosenberg's words, "the paradox that the jury is praised by judges for bringing in community standards to round the sharp edges of the law, but blamed for indulging in irrationality and compromise—even though these may be the very instruments by which the jurors manage to soften the law's metallic sharpness."[48] Finally, a sad reason why almost everyone may wish to preserve the jury is its incorruptability when compared to the judge. It is, after all, much harder to "reach" twelve persons than one. Given the state of the judiciary in the United States—a subject we shall reach shortly—this is by no means an unimportant consideration.

In one part of their varied and monumental study of the jury Professor Kalven and his colleagues attempted to get inside the jury room to see just what makes juries tick. They started out recording actual jury deliberation in a jury room in Wichita, Kansas, with the approval of the trial judge and counsel but without the knowledge of the jurors involved. When this fact became public, a furor arose over so-called jury-tapping. The researchers were censured by the U.S. Attorney General and investigated by a U.S. Senate Subcommittee. So actual taping of the jurors was quickly abandoned.[49] As an alternate device for finding out about the inner working of juries, the Chicago Jury Project then undertook "an experimental jury device to give mock cases to real jurors" and to observe the resultant jury deliberations. Of particular interest was the answer to a question fascinating to all trial lawyers: Who is a good juror for you? In other words, given the enormous variety among people eligible for jury duty, what kind of person makes what kind of juror? Trial lawyers make their living answering this kind of question intuitively and have accumulated a vast lore on jury types.

In the first place, Kalven and his colleagues found that many factors one might think would make a difference in a juror's attitude apparently do not. Age, sex, and marital status, for example, made no difference. Nor did whether one was a Catholic or a Protestant, nor indeed whether one was a Republican or Democrat. As to the factors that do make a difference, occupation and ethnic background seem to be influential. The Chicago study made use of four occupational classifications social scientists commonly use: (1) professional–proprietary class, (2) clerical class, (3) skilled laborers, and (4) unskilled laborers. The results of collating the votes of jurors according to the four occupational categories were as follows: The average award by the professional–proprietary class was $31,000; by the clerical group, $35,000; by the skilled laborers, $38,000; and by the unskilled laborers, $45,000.

As to ethnic factors, Professor Kalven pointed out, the existence of so many second- and third-generation Americans makes ethnicity difficult to work with, but the Chicago study delineated four general categories: (1) blacks; (2) Italians, French, and Swiss; (3) third-generation Americans; and (4) Scandinavian and British. For the same given set of facts, the damage awards were $56,000 by the blacks; $50,000 by the Italians, French, and Swiss; $36,000 by third-generation Americans; and $29,000 by the Scandanivans and British. At one end of the spectrum, then, the black unskilled worker is apparently the best juror for the plaintiff, whereas the Scandinavian proprietor is apparently the worst.[50]

Another factor, long axiomatic to trial lawyers, is the influence of the juror's urban or rural background. This has led to the migratory tort whereby a suit may be instituted a long way from the place of accident because the defendant (such as a railroad) has many places where it can be sued, allowing the plaintiff to pick the area most favorable to his case. Professors Kalven and Zeisel found a pattern of regional variation in damage awards:

> The size of damage awards given by juries for comparable personal injuries was strongly related to the jury's domicile. The larger the community from which the jury came, the larger the award; in addition, juries in the states along the two seacoasts proved to be more generous than juries from the Midwest and the South. City size and region cumulated so that there was a maximum spread between awards from juries from large eastern or western cities and those from small midwestern towns.[51]

Another important factor in addition to bias is how strong the bias survives in the face of jury deliberation. As Professor Kalven said, "It doesn't do you much good to have a '$50,000 man' go into the jury room and have him fall dead the first time someone says $10,000 in counter argument. In other words, you want bias plus stubbornness on your side." Professor Kalven has suggested that one indication of the durability of bias is how intensely the juror participates in the deliberative process. Those who talk the most are the most effective members of the group. Interestingly enough, talk among jurors is divided with remarkable equality, but not surprisingly the proprietary group talks the most, and the unskilled group the least. This would seem to favor the insurance companies: The effectiveness of the jury seems to vary inversely with sympathy for the plaintiff, insofar as the unskilled laborers are the most generous and the propietary class the least generous.[52]

The Chicago Jury Study found that, despite extensive efforts, personality tests and the like apparently could not be adapted to predict biases apart from class or ethnic background. Two questions, however, seemed to be effective in differentiating the more sympathetic juror from the less sympathetic.

The first question was, "Do you ever feel that you have tired yourself out by attempting too much?" The answer to this questions gives a "remarkable index" of the kind of juror the person will turn out to be. A person giving a "yes" answer tends to award an average of $14,000 on the study's award index, whereas the person who answers "no" tends to award an average of $38,000. The test appeared to be much more valid than even the tests of occupation and ethnic background. According to Professor Kalven:

> The success of the question is thought to have some connection with a theory of the Protestant ethic. If one is the kind of person who drives himself by his conscience and therefore is always feeling tired because he is always demanding more of himself than he is capable of doing, that puts him in the lower award category. If he is carefree and has never felt this pressure from conscience, he is in the higher award category.

The second question, which like the first gives a "remarkable index" of what kind of juror a person will be, was: "If you were in trouble yourself would you prefer to be tried by a judge or jury?" Those who answer that they would rather be tried by a judge give lower awards, whereas those who prefer to be tried by a jury give higher awards.[53]

As might be expected, there is both agreement and disagreement among trial lawyers on the Chicago jury findings concerning prejudices prevailing in certain types of jurors.

With the increasing presence of females on juries because of a U.S. Supreme Court opinion outlawing automatic exemption of women, the issue of whether sex makes a difference has advanced to the fore. The Chicago jury study discounts sex as a factor in jury bias, but many lawyers disagree. Andrew McEvoy, a New York lawyer, states: "Generally I prefer women on juries. They're more careful and studied in their analysis of issues." Gerald Lefcourt, a prominent trial lawyer, says, "It's better to have some women [on the jury] if you're going to ask the jury to understand something about [your client's] life. Men are very callous—we're less open about our feelings and so less sensitive to those of others." But, he asserted, "if you have a case in which you have to pick on a woman witness, you have to be careful because women on the jury may sympathize with her." Other lawyers, however, assert that women are harder on other women than men could ever be.

Some lawyers are fearful that a pretty woman on a jury causes friction among fellow jurors. Some women lawyers are aware that their own sex appeal can be influential with a jury. According to Carol Remer-Smith, a youthful female lawyer, "I can tell when the chemistry is working and I don't cut it off. It's one of the things that makes you persuasive."[54]

As the last remark suggests, not only are female jurors increasingly common but so are female trial lawyers. Until a few years ago very few female lawyers ever got to court. The relatively few females who were admitted to law schools (Harvard did not allow any until 1950) were consigned to jobs as law librarians or to back office work entailing probate or title searches, where client contact was severely limited. According to Robert Fiske, the head of the U.S. Attorney's office in Manhattan, who has hired many more female litigators than his predecessors, women "are particularly effective in litigation; they are particularly effective with juries."[55] Others disagree. Either way, the increasing presence of female trial lawyers can induce additional irrational factors in the trial of cases, as witness the remarks of Richard "Racehorse" Haynes, one of the leading trial lawyers in Texas. Female lawyers, says Haynes,

> . . . have had an uphill run at it and still do. For example, we have two female lawyers in our firm, both highly qualified, very intelligent people, very competent and competitive people. When they go to jury trial, if they are much better-looking than the females on the jury, the females on the jury tend to dislike them. If they appear to be too much more intelligent than the male lawyer on the other side, the males on the jury take offense at that. So they really have to tailor their performance in the court to meet the known obstacles.[56]

More generally, the simple factor of how attractive or unattractive a litigant is can have a determinative affect on litigation. According to one study of criminal cases, "the physically attractive defendant has an enormous advantage over the physically unattractive or ugly defendant."[57] The point would seem to apply also to parties to civil litigation.

Admittedly the civil jury has its passionate defenders, especially among—but not limited to—trial lawyers.

Professors Kalven and Zeisel, for example, on the basis of their Chicago Jury Study, asserted: "[C]ontrary to an often voiced suspicion, the jury does by and large understand the facts and get the case straight. [Also] the jury's decision by and large moves with the weight and direction of the evidence."[58] Kalven and Zeisel found, for example, that, based on responses from judges to a survey, about 80 percent of civil jury verdicts agree with what the judges would have found.[59] Kalven and Zeisel also found that the judge disagreed with the jury because he was more pro-plaintiff about as often as the jury disagreed with the judge because it was more pro-plaintiff. In other words, the pro-plaintiff bias of the jury, so widely believed to exist, did not manifest itself on the question of liability. On the question of the amount of damages, however, where the jury found for the plaintiff, its verdict was generally 20 percent higher than the judge's verdict would have been.[60]

Kalven and Zeisel also found that "jury service does not disenchant but actually increases the public's preference for trial by jury."[61] According to Kalven there is "much evidence that most people, once actually serving in a trial, become highly serious and responsible toward their task and toward the joint effort to deliberate through to a verdict." It is true, he said, that jurors object to "housekeeping defects . . . such as the waiting, the loss of income due to serving, and the often miserable quarters in which they are kept." But these are "extrinsic" matters, Kalven argued, which "can and should be corrected."[62]

Other proposals for improvement of the civil jury are being made and implemented but, as we shall see, often themselves engender further problems.[63]

In about twenty states, jurors receive their instructions from the judge in typewritten form.[64] While this may be an improvement, it does not, of course, solve the problem of instructions couched in such technical language as to be unsuitable for the nonlawyer in either oral *or* written form.

To solve that problem, suggestions are often made that instructions be couched in "plain English" that is "clear and understandable" to the layperson. But several problems have plagued such efforts. In the first place, considering the enormous amount of litigation and appeals already engendered by instructions, any fundamental change in their carefully wrought and well-settled terminology (inadequate though it is from many points of view) would probably lead to much more litigation while a generation of lawyers wrestles with, and takes advantage of, the uncertainty of new, untested terminology. Second, conveying technical concepts with absolute accuracy in lucid, easily understood prose is an awesome task, rarely if *ever* achievable. As generations of experts in all fields have discovered, there is often inevitable tension between the precision of technical language and popular, fresh prose.

It can be argued that lawyers are more inclined to use language understandable to nonexperts than any other professional group. Lawyers are almost alone in constantly being forced to translate not only their own but even other technical concepts—medical or engineering, say—into terms meaningful to lay jurors, legislators, zoning board members, and so forth. Perhaps a key reason for all the power lawyers wield in our democratic society is that they are the only powerful learned profession constantly required to communicate with others. Compare, for example, the increasing degree to which the written and oral language of doctors, engineers, scientists, and economists is designed to communicate only with fellow professionals. In an increasingly specialized world—one where ultimate decisions are still made by laymen, such as legislators and jurors—small wonder that power accrues to a profession as learned as any other that almost alone performs the function of translating all kinds of learning for generalist decision-makers.

But that's the point: If lawyers are already better than other professionals (if still often bad) at using technical language in a manner more understandable to nonexperts, how much improvement can we expect of them?[65] Finally, the attempt by the New York legislature to enact a Plain English Law requiring consumer agreements to be in readily understandable language resulted in a fiasco, at least at the outset. Even the sponsors of the law conceded it needed amendment because it was itself insufficiently clear, containing "major ambiguities."[66]

The New Jersey experience has been similar: Edward Frey, director of the Rutgers University Graduate School of Education, states that the "Plain Language" bill before the New Jersey legislature, requiring leases, consumer contracts, and insurance policies to be written at a twelfth-grade reading level, itself is written for college graduates. In addition, Frey states that only about 33 percent of American adults can read at a twelfth-grade level. Furthermore, the bill, which has been rewritten so many times that almost everyone has lost count, contains one 144-word sentence, and another section reading as follows:

> Written agreements covered under this Act shall only permit the following terms:
>   a. Terms whose meaning is generally understandable to persons other than persons with more than a twelfth grade reading level, professionals or specialists in the particular field. These terms shall be excluded when their generally understood meaning is contradictory to the applicable legal or technical meaning.[67]

Attempts to gain more efficiency from jurors by allowing six-person juries and less than unanimous verdicts have generated new problems and uncertainties. (Incidentally, historians believe that the twelve-member jury can be traced to fourteenth-century England and generally disparage the religious explanation that the traditional jury size derives from the number of apostles.) In the last decade thirty-eight states have authorized juries of less than twelve in some civil cases, and thirty-four have sanctioned smaller juries for some types of criminal trials. After a major study, Michael Saks concluded that larger juries "produce longer deliberations, more communication, far better community representation and possibly greater verdict reliability."[67] According to another study of civil cases in New England Federal Courts by the American Judicature Society, six-person juries found for the plaintiff less frequently than did twelve-member juries and generally awarded less damages than did juries of twelve.[68] Still another study indicates that the quality of jury performance drops off when there are fewer members. Smaller juries are less likely to have members who remember each of the important pieces of evidence for use in making decisions. One additional study suggests that the smaller the group, the less likely are its members to be able to overcome their biases.[69]

The paramount point to remember in considering the weaknesses and strengths of the civil jury, and in considering attempts to improve its performance, is that even if it were operating as well as its defenders insist, and even if the steps its detractors advocate to improve it are undertaken and prove to work, litigation will remain a nightmare for those forced to undergo it. This holds true especially for personal injury litigation, with its unique mixture of technology and emotion.

6

The Judge

START WITH THE PREMISE that the great majority of judges are able, conscientious, and hard-working. Indeed, some are superb. Still, a substantial minority remain woefully inadequate—and for that reason vigorous attempts to upgrade the selection, training, and disciplining of the judiciary have taken place in recent years.[1] Apparently things are improving. But, as the following discussion shows, we have perennially had to bear up with a significant number of inadequate judges because of specific factors, and the forces that combine to resist improvement are entrenched and formidable. The net result is that to unreservedly trust even the judiciary—as with so many other facets of the lawsuit lottery—can still be hazardous.

In England, jury trials in almost all civil cases, including those involving accidents, have been abolished. But to depend for trial of cases upon English judges may be different from depending upon American judges. In England, judges are selected from barristers, the small, select group of lawyers who are mainly trial lawyers. Whereas in the United States all lawyers are allowed to appear in major trial and appellate courts, in England only a few are allowed to do so, after going through a careful initial screening and special training. Other lawyers in England do most of the office work, deal directly with clients, engage in commercial counseling, draft wills, and so forth. They are called solicitors, as distinct from barristers.

Appointments to all but minor courts in England are traditionally confined to those who have "taken silk," a special honor of becoming Queen's Counsel, available to only the most distinguished trial lawyers. Because selection is made by the Lord Chancellor on other than a political basis from a small group of people, all specialists and all well known to each other, the quality of selection is generally very high. Also, the comparatively more substantial pay for judges and the lower returns of law practice in England mean English lawyers do not face a financial sacrifice from becoming judges. Added to the enormous prestige of being a judge, all this ensures that the bench is the capstone of a distinguished career and is often eagerly sought by the most qualified and upright of lawyers in England, which is not necessarily the case in the United States.

In the United States, although one hears the expression "elevated to the bench," the best lawyers actually must descend, financially and, at times, in prestige, to become judges. Selection for the judiciary is steeped in politics—sometimes its seamiest side. Even in states where judges are appointed, like Federal judges, by the chief executive, as opposed to being elected, political activity is often a prerequisite to selection. Judge Curtis Bok of Pennsylvania once said, "A judge is a member of the Bar who once knew a governor."[2] But obviously more is involved than just *knowing* a governor. Where political machines exist, as they do in so many of the larger cities, the "only way you get to be a judge," a distinguished New York lawyer with daily experience in the courts said, "is by running errands and kissing asses."[3] According to a recent report of the Illinois Committee on Courts and Justice:

> . . . the path to judicial office in Cook County [Chicago] is not the high-road of education, scholarship, intelligence, character, independence, proven legal ability or standing or reputation in the legal community. . . . What really counts . . . are credits won as precinct captains or in other partisan political service, and political connections, political friendships and relationships with successful political families. . . . [T]he notion that judges are elected by the people is a cruel charade. They are in fact appointed—perhaps the word is anointed—by the ward committeemen and other party slatemakers as a reward for service to the party apparatus and the recognition that they are or will become "good old boys." The real vice of the present system is that it effectively limits opportunity for judicial office to the small segment of the Bar that has gained the price of admis-

sion by demonstrating qualities that have nothing at all to do with essential judicial qualifications.[4]

In their monumental treatise on the government of New York, Wallace S. Sayre and Herbert Kaufman state that "district leaders can extract [from a judge whom they "anoint"] as much as a year's salary plus an additional 'campaign fund' of several thousand dollars."[5] Murray Kempton has written: "The black robe is indeed the prime article of commerce remaining to the party organizations."[6] In *To the Victor: Political Patronage from the Clubhouse to the White House*, Martin and Susan Tolchin point out that wives of judges indulge in wry jokes about how long it will take the family to pay for its seat on the bench.[7] The fortuity of political appointment to the bench is illustrated by Murray Kempton's description of

> . . . the case of [New York] Democratic State Assemblyman Stanley Steingut, whose curious ambition it was to be a leader of his party's delegation in Albany, as his father had been before him. His ascension was blocked by minority leader Anthony Travia, so Steingut got the late Senator [Robert] Kennedy to make Travia a federal judge. But no sooner had Steingut cleared the road than it was barred again, when his delegation, insensitive to hereditary property rights, elected Moses Weinstein as their leader. After a year or so, Steingut finally unseated Weinstein and had his dream; but thanks to the grace toward the fallen which prevails in these matters, Weinstein himself was awarded a state judgeship. Thus two judges owe their seats and we owe an incalculable amount of future legal history to Assemblyman Steingut's urge to re-create himself in his father's image.[8]

The necessity of running the electoral, or at least the backroom political, gantlet repels many of those who might be best qualified for the bench. Other factors also drive off many of the best people. In England barristers are forbidden to form partnerships and must for all practical purposes work alone. Unless there are exceptional circumstances, no more than two lawyers take part in a court proceeding. While remuneration is not strictly on an hourly basis, obviously it bears some relationship to hours spent. In the United States, on the other hand, opportunities for leading lawyers to make huge amounts of money are much greater. Not only, as we have seen, is the contingent fee allowed, but membership in a large law firm means that partners can make considerable sums not only on their own time, but off their juniors'. *Forbes Magazine* noted a few years ago: "Economically speaking, a law firm is a very simple structure. It buys brainpower wholesale—by the year, that is—and sells it retail—by the hour." Much of the time-consuming research work in a big firm is done by the many junior associates, not partners in the firm. Assume a junior is being paid around $20,000 a year. Even a $20,000 salary comes to only $10 to $15 per billable hour. But the junior's time will be billed to the client at from $40 to $70 an hour. So the $20,000 associate may be grossing as much as $80,000 a year for the firm. Even allowing for high overhead costs, about $40,000 of that amount is clear profit.[9] The result is that opportunities to make relatively vast sums of money employing many juniors in the practice of law are far greater in the United States than in England. Hence top-ranking lawyers must often make a real financial sacrifice to go on the bench. Salaries generally fall far short of what a prominent lawyer can earn. Nor does this hold true only for large urban areas. In Spencer, Indiana, (population 2,600) a few years ago, none of the six lawyers in town wanted the vital job of circuit judge because experienced lawyers in Spencer were netting about twice what the judgeship paid.[10]

The dreariness of a trial judge's task arising out of the predominance of auto accident cases may be another factor in driving some able people from the bench in the United States. "It's so boring," says one law professor, "to listen to all those personal injury cases." When I was practicing in the trial department of a large corporate firm in Boston, members of the firm were discussing the decision of a former partner to go on the bench. "How could he stand it," was the consensus, "listening to those auto accident cases day after day?" Just before the 1940 Presidential campaign, President Franklin Roosevelt offered to appoint Dean Acheson to the Federal Court of Appeals for the District of Columbia. Acheson later recalled, "I told the President I just can't sit on my tail and listen to foolishness."[11]

Of course, it is one thing for lawyers to be involved in litigation over matters that might seem humdrum or even "foolish" in the abstract when they are caught up in the excitement and competition of advocacy for their clients; it is quite another for such competitive people to sit, in effect, on the sideline as a linesman. Able lawyers who ascend to the bench sometimes flee after a few years, out of boredom with what strikes them as a "monastic" existence.

Naturally, all of this is sadly reflected in the caliber of some on the bench. According to Samuel I. Rosenman, adviser and speech writer for Presidents Roosevelt and Truman, himself a former trial judge: "Let us face this sad fact: that in many—in far too many—instances, the benches of our courts are occupied by mediocrities—men of small talent, undistinguished in performance, technically deficient and inept."[12]

One finds judges feared because decisions on any given day can turn on their sheerest whim, prejudice—or even sobriety. Some judges are abusive to lawyers and clients alike, with any protest sure to lead to the loss of the case. The luck of the draw, then, can force litigants before lazy or dense judges totally incapable of handling their cases.[13]

Nor do deficiencies stop at mediocrity. Judges are normally installed for life or for long terms with, as we shall see, little or no opportunity for disciplinary action against them. They can become arrogant and overbearing czars in their courtrooms. The judge wears impressive robes; all those present must rise on his entrance; his arrival is heralded by an announcement gravely intoned to a hushed audience; he is addressed as "Your Honor" and sits on a dais in front of large, formal flags and behind an imposing desk, elevated so that, even when seated, his eye level is about three feet above that of anyone else in the austere paneled room. Clerks and bailiffs are models of servility at his beck. Lawyers, both in and out of the courtroom, treat him with elaborate and fearful respect—indeed, "fawning" is the only word that accurately describes it. When out for lunch or an evening, judges become accustomed to being quite literally "paid court to" by sycophantic lawyers, who flatter them, laugh heartily at their jokes, and generally behave like courtiers. One New York lawyer has said (after requesting anonymity),

> After most men have been on the bench a few months, they think they *deserve* praise as one of the trappings of office. The same as having a robe and gavel. If you don't bow and scrape they feel you are putting them down, acting discourteous to them. Sure, it makes me uncomfortable, treating some second-rate political jerk as if he were Learned Hand or Brandeis. But it gets to be a habit. You go through a goddamned ceremony as if you are being received by the Emperor of China. You do everything but kow-tow.
>
> Take my home district, now. Ed Palmieri [in semi-retired status since 1973] is married to a Frenchwoman and as a young man he

lived abroad. Palmieri prides himself on his knowledge of French. Now it happens that I'm fluent in French, and I learned from someone or another than Palmieri loves the opportunity to show off his linguistics. So when I'd go into chambers for a pretrial I'd offer him a pleasantry in French, and he'd beam and respond in kind. This drove the opposing lawyers wild—to hear me and Palmieri chattering away in a foreign language, obviously very much at ease with one another. Now is that flattery or tactics?

Granted the lawyer has no hard proof that his "flattery or tactics" influenced the judge one way or another but, as he put it—illustrating once again the irrational quality of litigation—he felt it gave him "a psychological leg up on the other side. I'm giving you a trade secret, I suppose," he admitted, "but since Palmieri is no longer active, it's of no value to me."[14]

Small wonder that weaknesses manifest themselves in such an atmosphere. Judges who read newspapers during arguments before them are not at all unheard-of.[15] Choleric, ill-tempered, abusive judges plague all court systems. According to Martin Mayer:

> Every jurisdiction has its favorite story—the misogynist who won't allow women to wear lipstick in his courtroom, the conservative who rules that wills signed with a ball-point pen are void, the drunk who leans over the bench and hooks a cigar out of the pocket of the lawyer who has come up for a conference (all these are real incidents).[16]

One can also cite, for example, crusty, conservative Catholic judges who have abused parties before them seeking a divorce. Joseph Goulden names, as a prime example of the mean judge, Charles H. Carr of Los Angeles, who hated such insignia of modernity as long hair. Once, when an especially hirsute lawyer appeared before him, Carr stormed, "I can't tell whether you are a man or a woman." He announced he was recessing court "until I can decide whether to address you as sir or madam." Encouraged by the snickers of his claque of bailiffs, and courtroom hangers-on, Carr went on: "I would have you take down your pants and resolve the question of gender once and for all. But judging from the way you look, I'd have to rule there was not sufficient evidence to render a decision."[17]

Howard James, in his book *Crisis in the Courts*, based on a survey of judges in the Midwest, cites hundreds of judges who work only twenty-five to thirty hours a week despite massive backlogs of cases. In Chicago, traditionally the city with the biggest backlog of civil cases, James, on repeated checks of all 114 courtrooms in the Civic Center, found on a typical day: between 9:30 and 10:00 A.M., judges sitting in only 11 of the 114 courtrooms between 10:00 and 10:30 A.M., 58 of the 114 courtrooms with judges in them; between 10:30 and 11:30 A.M., 45 occupied; between 2:30 and 3:00 P.M., 34 with judges sitting.[18]

During summer months many courts slow down or close, actions reminiscent of the days when courthouses were not air-conditioned. (Many educational institutions enjoying cooled facilities do the same.) One is reminded of Mr. Dooley's comment: "If I had me job to pick out, I'd be a judge. I've looked over all th' others an' that's th' on'y wan that suits. I have th' juducyal timperamint. I hate wurruk."[19] One thoroughly discouraged lawyer said in 1963 (and sadly repeats the general sentiment today):

I have seen a fair amount of this world, from Coney Island to the Riviera, from Harvard to Hiroshima, from . . . messenger [boy] to assistant counsel to an investigation by [an appellate court], from small claims night court to Supreme Court, and the greatest disillusionment of my life was my experience with judges after what I had been taught at . . . law school. I have had a judge tell me to settle a case because the plaintiff and his attorney were good friends; the verdict was in my favor, the judge set it aside, and I had to appeal in order to have it reinstated. . . . There is the judge who refuses to grant a request that opening statements and summation be recorded, who is frequently drunk, and usually works half the day and who, following that record, was approved for [promotion to a higher court by the bar association]. There are many judges who grant adjournments to the first twenty cases on the calendar and then refuse adjournments requested on the later cases, regardless of the reason given, simply because they have lost their patience. There is the judge in [one] county who will keep seventy-five to one hundred attorneys sitting in his courtroom until 5 P.M. although there are only two judges available to try cases and six juries have already been selected, waiting to go into those two [courts]. There are the judges who are consistently an hour or more late for court, but who then order an inquest or dismissal of a case of an attorney who has stepped out of the courtroom to go to the lavatory. And then there are the judges, too few in number, who have been caught and are now in jail.

I see many classes and varieties in my work. I deal with the doctors, mechanics, engineers, court attendants, policemen, lawyers and judges, and my clients, chosen at random, are of every conceivable type. But I have seen more dishonesty in judges than in any other group or class of people.[20]

The corruption of judges shocks us much more than their laziness or arrogance. A Chicago lawyer in his early sixties has described the discouragement that comes when judges are "reached":

A phone call to a judge can change the whole course of a lawsuit— or to the right individual. It's not what you know or what the law is, but who you know—especially in the Municipal Court in Chicago. If you know a politician who has pull there, you can get what you want. It's there, not only in the Municipal Court but in the Superior Court and the Circuit Court. You can go in on a matter, you can have the law with you, and before you know it, you're out in left field. If a client asks you about a particular problem, you read cases and you get the decisions but in the courtroom it's not that way.

In the ordinary neighborhood if something happens, in any matter, the precinct captain or ward politician checks and sees if he knows the judge, or somebody he knows. It all depends on how much influence you can build up. The most damned discouraging thing, one matter . . . was argued for 40 minutes. We had the law with us, cited cases, then the judge gets a phone call—he goes off the bench, and when he gets back, he cuts the argument and, without saying why, rules for the other side. A most disheartening experience in the practice of law. I didn't know what hit me. . . . Then it's not the practice of law but who you know. [The] practice of law is . . . hard . . . and rough, it's really a rough deal.[21]

Most lawyers have confidence in the integrity of jury verdicts. But at least one experienced trial lawyer was very skeptical about a finding of the Chicago Jury Study that judges and juries arrive at the same verdict about 85 percent of the time. The study was done by asking trial judges sitting on jury cases to record what they would have decided had they been sitting alone. "The judge verdicts," said this lawyer, "might have differed widely if they were actually the final verdict and . . . therefore subject to influence."[22]

Part of the problem is certainly that judges, selected and to a significant extent maintained by the political process, remain beholden politically. Said one New York lawyer: "The guys who've made the campaign contributions, who've helped elect the judges, later feel they own 'em."[23] Citing a series of questionable rulings by judges whose qualifications the Illinois Committee on Courts and Justice challenged, the committee notes:

Although the judges' actions may have been proper in each instance, doubts inevitably remain not only among those directly affected by the decision but among the general public. Nothing has contributed more to the lack of public confidence in the local judiciary than the widespread suspicion that some judges put political loyalty ahead of all else.[24]

Martin Mayer has commented, "The words 'courthouse gang' refer to the entire system of county political leadership, which has its office in the courthouse, but judges are normally regarded as part and parcel of what goes on in their courthouses."

The canons of ethics of the American Bar Association call upon judges to "avoid . . . the public endorsement of candidates for political office."[25] But when Howard James of the *Christian Science Monitor* visited Chief Judge John S. Boyle of the Circuit Court of Cook County, Illinois, one day when campaigning for the spring elections was under way, he found a sign on Judge Boyle's desk reading "Daley for Mayor." Court personnel were wearing Daley buttons.[26]

Judge Boyle offers further indications of the politicization of the judiciary in what the columnist Mike Royko in 1968 called Boyle's "new code of ethics for judges." When swearing in new associate judges in Chicago, Boyle (who in 1978 at the age of seventy-eight was defeated for retention on the bench) customarily made a stirring speech about how he expected them to behave on the bench. Boyle's new "New Code of Judicial Ethics—Chicago-Style" was unlike the old dull and lofty code. It had, said Royko, "zing and sock," designed as it was "to discourage . . . judges from doing things that . . . cause big, black headlines, which [could] give Boyle headaches." For example, Boyle used to tell the judges, "Don't let alderman and ward committeemen tell you your job." Granted, there are no such provisions in the traditional canons of ethics. But the old canons were not written by an ex-Chicago alderman like Judge Boyle. Boyle knew, said Royko, that "the sight of an alderman, smiling sweetly at the defendant, is enough to make some [judges] scream 'not guilty' before the case even begins." Boyle would also tell the appointees: "Base your decision on evidence and merits of the case." That may sound like obvious advice to give to experienced lawyers, but Boyle knew, as Royko pointed out, "that other considerations have been known to affect a judge's decision—as well as his standard of living." Royko listed some additional examples of Boyle's choicest canons in order to give some "insight into the way Boyle, who [had] been around politics for 40 years," viewed the administration of justice:

> "I don't want any reports reaching me about [any of you] cursing on the bench."
> "You are not messenger boys for a lot of thieves."
> "If you get off the bench eight or nine times to answer the phone, it appears to people in the courtroom that someone is trying to influence cases."
> "I don't want to hear about you going to police stations in the early mornings to set bonds for a lot of crooks."

Royko summed it up, "they don't teach stuff like that at the Harvard Law School."[27]

All this may help explain the bitter attitude of one able New York criminal defense lawyer, working for the Legal Aid Society, whose "disrespect for judges," according to one report on him, "is so strong and all-inclusive that it amounts at times to class hatred." In a widely publicized interview, Martin Erdmann dismissed most judges as "whores" and appellate judges as "whores who became madames."[28] Ironically, Erdmann's remarks returned to haunt him upon his own recent nomination to the bench.[29]

The obstacles to correcting or removing the arrogant, incompetent, or even corrupt judge are prodigious. Perhaps the biggest is the judges' extraordinary protective instinct toward their own kind, the degree to which they cover for each other and take deep umbrage at criticism of any of their number. A lawyer who complains publicly about judicial inadequacies can invite quick and nasty retaliation. Joseph Goulden notes: "Judges form a mutual protection association as formidable as the Mafia." If, for example, one judge hears that a lawyer in a speech or a law school class has criticized a second judge's ruling, or if a lawyer boasts of getting such a ruling reversed, that lawyer may find himself subjected to not-so-subtle hazing by the first judge the next time he is in court. Such hazing may take the form of forcing the lawyer in his presentation to follow exasperating and technical formalities that normally would be overlooked.[30]

Judges will rarely, then, take action against their peers. Lawyers, feeling that their livelihood depends on the good will of judges, are notoriously reluctant to institute disciplinary proceedings; law schools take no interest in the matter; and the public, without the leadership of specialists who have some competency in the matter, remains ignorant or indifferent. Even the election of judges—itself controversial, as we shall see—tends almost always to rubber-stamp incumbency.

So cumbersome are traditional impeachment proceedings "for cause" against judges that former Attorney General Griffin Bell (a former Federal judge) has said: "Not every judge who perhaps should be impeached can be impeached. Congress does not have that much time."[31] In the state of Illinois, the last two attempts to remove a judge by impeachment, both of which failed, were in 1832 and 1843.[32] In other words, judges are almost never impeached, no matter how grossly improper their conduct is. As to criminal proceedings against judges, of twelve New York State judges indicted by grand jury proceedings in the last five years under a special prosecutor's jurisdiction, every one was cleared, nine of them by their fellow judges before their cases reached trial.[33]

The saddest part of all this is that, as with the jury, (1) the prodigious steps necessary to improve things may create as many problems as they solve and thus may not materially improve things, and (2) even if marked improvement in the quality and performance of the judiciary were possible, we would *still* be left with a horrendously bad method for deciding who is to be paid from insurance after accidents.

As to proposals for improvement, consider the steps implemented or proposed for a better means of disciplining and removing incompetent or corrupt judges. In 1960 California, by constitutional amendment, established a Commission on Judicial Qualifications composed of five judges appointed by the state Supreme Court, two lawyers from the state bar, and two nonlawyer members appointed by the Governor. The commission receives complaints and conducts formal inquiries. As a result, judges may be informally warned, asked to resign or retire, or presented with the option of a hearing before the entire Supreme Court rather than resigning or retiring.

Since 1960, 48 states, in addition to the District of Columbia and Puerto Rico, have instituted commissions to discipline errant judges. At least a few of them have been effective. In New York, for example, since 1975 the commission has censured 65 judges, suspended four, and removed 10, with 73 more resigning.[34] Many people have put an enormous amount of effort into the process of upgrading the judiciary. If the results of all this reform are uneven, the focus on the judiciary—at a time when it is, willingly or unwillingly, assuming more and more power—is inevitable, and probably, in the long run, healthy.

But the frustrations of attempting to invoke even mild sanctions against judges, such as reprimands or short suspensions, under the new machinery are perhaps illustrated by two recent experiences in Illinois.

Chicago Circuit Court Judge Paul Elward was a candidate for re-election to the bench in November 1976. (Incumbent trial judges there do not run against an opponent; the voters decide only whether or not they will be retained.) In September of that year, the Chicago Council of Lawyers, in accordance with its practice, issued a report evaluating all candidates for election to judgeships in Cook County. The report's evaluation of Judge Elward read as follows:

> Judge Elward has been in the Law Division (except for a brief interval in the Criminal Division in 1974-75) since 1971. During that time he has had several assignments, including at one time a highly controversial new call specifically designed to try and move cases along more quickly to trial. He is a *person of substantial intellectual ability who works hard*, but reports from many lawyers also indicate clearly that he has a terrible judicial temperament characterized by extreme rigidity, unreasonable demands and positions, and closed-mindedness. His efforts to achieve worthy objectives—*such as avoiding delays in the court process attributable* to dilatory lawyers—have in several cases been vitiated by the rigidity and excessive zeal with which he has attempted to pursue them. Because of his clear lack of judicial temperament, the Council concludes that he should not be retained as a judge. [Emphasis added.]

An advertisement endorsing Judge Elward's candidacy, exhorting the voters to retain him as a judge, was published in several Cook County suburban newspapers on October 28, 1976, and in the *Chicago Sun-Times* on November 1, the day before the election, under the sponsorship of a "Citizens Committee to Retain Judge Paul Elward." Under the boldface subheading "Ethics and Integrity & Speedy Trials & Equal Justice," sandwiched between two other tributes to Judge Elward, was the following carefully edited extract of the Chicago Council of Lawyers report:

> . . . a person of substantial ability who works hard . . . to achieve worthy objectives . . . such as avoiding delays in the court process.
> *CHICAGO COUNCIL OF LAWYERS*

Immediately below the three endorsements appeared the exhortation *"Vote Yes to Retain Judge Paul Elward."* At the November 2 election, Judge Elward received a favorable vote of 63 percent of the ballots cast and was retained for a new six-year term. The Chicago Council of Lawyers filed a complaint with the Illinois Judicial Inquiry Board, which consists of nine members: three lawyers, four nonlawyers, and two judges. The board investigated the complaint and, in compliance with its authority, filed a complaint with the Illinois Courts Commission, the only body having actual disciplinary power over judges, which, unlike the board, consisted entirely of judges. The complaint alleged that in the form in which the advertisements were published they "were materially misleading as to, and materially misrepresented the evaluation of, [Judge Elward] by [the Chicago Council of Lawyers]" and that by "causing the advertisement to appear retaining only the truncated version of the Council's evaluation [Judge Elward] created the false impression that the Council had recommended [Elward] for retention, when the opposite was true." By that conduct, according to the Judicial Inquiry Board, Elward "also created the false impression that he had significant Bar Association support for retention, when the opposite was true." The complaint finally alleged that Elward's conduct brought his judicial office into disrepute. In accordance with its jurisdiction the Inquiry Board made no specific recommendation as to sanctions, leaving that to the Courts Commission.

But the Inquiry Board might just as well have saved its breath. The Courts Commission *unanimously* vindicated its brother judge and dismissed the complaint. Among the grounds of the commission's decision were (1) that use of the advertisements did not constitute conduct prejudicial to the administration of justice or bring the judicial office into disrepute, and (2) considering the public's exposure to the publication of the Chicago Council of Lawyers Report plus news and editorial comment thereon, "the use of excerpts from the Council's statements did not create the false impressions that the Council had recommended him for retention or that he had significant Bar Association support." In the words of Rubin Cohn, a University of Illinois law professor who is a member of the Inquiry Board, "not a single member of the Commission perceived the ethical issue as sufficiently serious to warrant even the minimum sanctions of reprimand or censure."[36]

But in a celebrated instance when the Illinois Courts Commission did discipline a brother judge, it too might have saved its breath. The Supreme Court of Illinois, made up of still other brother judges, with apparent disregard for the constitutional plan for judicial discipline, overruled the Courts Commission. In 1976 the Illinois Judicial Inquiry Board filed a complaint with the Courts Commission against downstate Circuit Court Judge Samuel Harrod. The commission charged that in the process of sentencing young male defendants, Harrod, in addition to imposing fines in some twenty-six instances, had ordered them to have their hair cut. (Echoes of Los Angeles Judge Carr and his courtroom taunts.) He had also on occasion required defendants sentenced to probation to surrender their driver's licenses to the probation officer, who would then issue a certificate to the defendant to the effect that, although he had a valid driver's license, it had been posted with the probation officer during the period of probation. The obviously intended affect was to identify the defendant as a probationer whenever he was requested to exhibit his driver's license to police officers or to anyone else. The Courts Commission found that Judge Harrod's "haircut orders" and driver's license confiscations presented one of the "clearest cases" of "gross abuse of judicial power" and suspended him without pay for a period of one month. In the words of Frank Greenberg, a former Chicago Bar Association President who is a member of both the Committee on Courts and Justice and the Judicial Inquiry Board, "Judge Harrod's out-of-court reaction to his suspension seems to reflect the same lack of insight into the limitations on judicial power in a democracy that brought him to the attention of the Judicial Inquiry Board in the first place." Harrod had told a Kiwanis Club that his suspension "has intimidated every judge in the state." "Every judge who looks at a defendant is wondering, is he going to turn me in; is his lawyer going to turn me in?" "What it boils down to," Judge Harrod said, "is that they didn't like the haircuts."[37] On Harrod's appeal to the Supreme Court of Illinois, that court overruled the Courts Commission and ordered it to expunge the suspension order from its records. It did so in the face of three facts that even the Supreme Court was forced to admit: (1) the Courts Commission is vested with the sole adjudicative function in the disciplinary system; (2) the commission's decisions are final and nonreviewable; and (3) the Supreme Court may not concern itself with the "correctness of the Commission's determination." The Illinois Supreme Court justified its ruling by drawing a distinction between a review of the "correctness of the Commission's determination," which the court acknowledged to be beyond its purview, and a determination of the scope of the commission's constitutional authority, creating a hole big enough to drive several trucks through.

How had the commission exceeded its constitutional authority? According to the Illinois Supreme Court, the Courts Commission had no power under the constitution to interpret the law but only to apply "determined" law: "Determined" law includes only laws whose meaning has already been determined by a court. Since the commission, in arriving at its decision, had interpreted a statute, it had supposedly committed an unconstitutional act and thereby had no power to punish the judge. But to prohibit judicial disciplinary bodies from interpreting the law is to deny them what every agency created either by constitution or by statute *must* have: the power to interpret the law it administers. Especially in this instance, to limit judicial disciplinary bodies in such a way is to reduce them to vassalage to the very courts they are supposed to discipline (which may have been what the Illinois Supreme Court—subconsciously, at least— had in mind). Very little law of any complexity is so "determined" as not to require interpretation in construing it and resolving intersticial ambiguities. Even the Supreme Court's opinion concerning Judge Harrod will require the Judicial Inquiry Board and Courts Commission to interpret and construe it in determining its breadth and its limitations. To hold that judicial disciplinary bodies have no power to do so is such an extraordinary and wholly untenable legal principle that only judges who are intent—consciously or subconsciously—on hobbling those constitutionally empowered to curb judges would so hold. Furthermore, an Illinois Appellate Court decision invalidating a Harrod haircut order actually was rendered during the commission's proceedings, but the Supreme Court managed to explain it away on the ground that the court's interpretation was somewhat different from the commission's.[38]

The Illinois Supreme Court then went farther by ruling that only conduct which violates specific rules promulgated for judicial conduct by the Supreme Court itself could serve the Courts Commission as grounds for disciplining a judge. A reading of the Illinois Constitution and the Report of its Judiciary Committee, which drafted the pertinent provisions in the constitution, gives little if any support to the proposition that only a violation of the judges' own Supreme Court rules can serve as a cause of judicial discipline. To so hold, says Frank Greenberg, sets the constitution—designed to provide independent discipline of the judiciary—"on its head".[39] Furthermore, the Courts Commission in fact *had* made a finding of violation of a specific Supreme Court rule, but again the Supreme Court strained to hold it inapplicable. The Supreme Court held that Harrod's decision imposing a haircut as a condition of *probation* was not a *sentence*, and therefore did not violate Supreme Court rules on sentencing.[40] An impartial observer might be forgiven for concluding that throughout, the Illinois Supreme Court in straining to reach the self-serving result it sought was resorting to a lot of hair-splitting over hair-cutting.

When it comes to answering "who will judge the judges?" in Illinois, things seem almost back on square one. In the words of the Illinois Judicial Inquiry Board, "by an inexplicable inversion of clear intent [of the constitution] and an analytical approach which strains logic to the breaking point, the Supreme Court . . . has asserted its supremacy in matters of judicial discipline, creating a disciplinary system quite different from that intended by the [new] Constitution."[41] Frank Greenberg commented: "I may perhaps be forgiven if I say the *Harrod* opinion gives me a sense of *déjà vu*. On the Illinois experience with judicial discipline, as in other facets of the political life of the state, the French proverb may apply: *plus ça change, plus c'est la même chose.*"[42]

To top it all off, after the Supreme Court's highly dubious action was cogently criticized by Greenberg and Cohn, both of whom, as pointed out, are members of the Judicial Inquiry Board, the Illinois Bar Association's Judicial Administration Newsletter, published under the informal aegis of the judiciary, (rarely, if ever, will things offensive to judges appear there) called upon (1) the organized bar to discipline lawyers uttering such criticism; (2) the Governor to invoke his power "to remove for incompetence, neglect of duty, or malfeasance in office any" gubernatorially appointed officer, such as a member of the Judicial Inquiry Board, and (3) the legislature to investigate the Judicial Inquiry Board, with an eye toward drastically cutting its budget.[43]

If disciplinary and criminal proceedings are not, as a practical matter, often available against judges, neither are civil actions. Nothing could illustrate the resistance of the imperial judiciary toward sanctions applied to themselves (while ever broadening their own power to sanction others) better than the recent U.S. Supreme Court case of *Stump* v. *Sparkman*. The court ruled 5 to 3 that an injured party had no redress against a judge who approved the sterilization of a fifteen-year-old girl at her mother's request, without letting the girl know or appointing anyone to represent her interests.

The court's ruling said: "A judge will not be deprived of immunity [from suit] because the action he took was in error, was done maliciously or was in excess of his authority." Even "grave procedural errors" admitted of no redress, despite "unfairness to litigants that sometimes results." In effect, dissenting Justice Potter Stewart wrote, the majority opinion means that a judge is free "like a loose cannon, to inflict indiscriminate damage whenever he announces that he is acting in his judicial capacity."[44]

Recognizing how difficult it is to discipline sitting judges, many reformers have focused more and more attention in recent years on the merit selection of judges in the first place. Judges, it is thought, should be appointed rather than elected, and chosen mainly by their professional colleagues rather than political parties. Supposedly this would produce a more efficient, impartial, and generally higher-quality judiciary. Certainly the problems created by electoral selection of judges are real: (1) selection often based on party loyalty and service rather than legal qualifications; (2) continuing political influence on the judiciary; (3) able judges swept from office for simply belonging to the party undergoing a landslide defeat in an election, as happened to some Republican judges on the Goldwater ticket in 1964; (4) the indignity and inappropriateness of judges' courting public favor in the hurly-burly of politics; and (5) the ignorance and indifference of the electorate concerning political candidates. As to the last, consider the sometimes bizarre results. In the words of a *Wall Street Journal* editorial:

> In Texas for instance, [judicial] candidates draw numbers from a hat to determine their place on the ballot. The Houston Chronicle reports that some judgeship races in the recent primary were determined right there. In all five court runoffs in the Houston area, the candidates who survived the first round were either incumbents or number one or number two on the primary ballot. Now it's true that random selection was used in ancient Athens to fill some public offices, but we didn't think that American elections were meant to be that kind of lottery, even for judges.[45]

But here again, the solution—merit selection of judges—poses some problems of its own.

In some respects, given the intensely human qualities and sympathies required, especially of a trial judge, the concerns of public opinion, which, after all, are what politics is all about, *should* be involved. Thus, Edward Costikyan, an excellent lawyer as well as a former head of Tammany Hall, has argued against what he terms the popular myth that judicial selection and politics should be kept separate. Costikyan starts out by questioning whether we can be very confident about knowing who is the "best-qualified" person for the bench. The wisest lawyer may not have appeared in court in years. The best trial lawyer may be not only quick-witted but arrogant when freed from the constraints of advocacy; he may also have little real sympathy for or understanding of the many different kinds of people appearing before the bench. In short, he may have no judicial temperament. The legal scholar may be overly abstract in his thinking or simply inadequate when confronted with what Costikyan calls "the calculated tumult of the adversary system." The person with sympathetic and intuitive understanding of people may simply be an inept lawyer.[46]

Moreover, factors that play a role in political selection figure importantly in the selection of the judiciary, myth to the contrary notwithstanding. Ethnic background, for example, is often rightly a valid factor in considering someone for the bench. Not only must the legislative and executive branches represent various parts of the community, but so must the judicial branch. Otherwise, Costikyan points out, the confidence of all elements in the community in the fairness of the courts can be deeply undermined. If the overwhelming percentage of judges are alumni of Wall Street firms, which traditionally have hired few blacks or Hispanics, what will be the attitude of those minorities of which disproportionate numbers are haled into our courts?[47] (A recent suit by a young Italian-American lawyer named John Anthony Lucido against the awesomely prestigious Wall Street firm of Cravath, Swaine, and Moore alleged that the firm pursues "a continuing pattern and practice of discrimination in favor of white Protestant males generally of Northern European ancestry." Mr. Lucido, who was graduated second in his class from the Notre Dame Law School in 1965, asserted that the firm discriminates by selecting most of its employees from "just four selected law schools," Harvard, Yale, Columbia, and Virginia. Cravath's first ground of defense was that a law firm has a perfect right to exercise such prejudice in hiring and promoting. That defense was struck down, and the case is in further stages of litigation.)[48]

Too often, then, blue-ribbon-panel selection of the judiciary means selection by the bar association, which is dominated by elitist, Ivy League, corporate counsel types, often ill suited to the tasks of either selecting or serving as judges in the lower courts, where, Costikyan comments, "human and not legal problems make up the bulk of the calendar."[49]

Merit selection of judges thus may skew the match between the judge and his actual job. Many in Britain are acutely concerned that members of the highly educated and privileged class decide on the guilt and punishment of people from vastly different socio-economic strata with whom they can have little identification. Britain's rigid merit selection of judges has meant that of thirty-one appointees to the principal trial court (called the High Court) in the five years prior to 1975, twenty-one went to public schools, like Eton and Harrow, and twenty-three to Oxford and Cambridge.[50] The problem carries over to many civil matters. An interesting study in the United States seems to confirm the existence of the problem here as well, now that some thirty states meet at least some of the criteria reformers have established for merit selection of judges. Martin A. Levin, a Brandeis University political scientist, reports on a study he conducted to determine some of the effects of the change. He studied two roughly comparable big-city court systems: Pittsburgh, with judges chosen through partisan elections dominated by a traditionally strong Democratic Party, and Minneapolis, under a "reform" system, with the local bar association playing the dominant role.

After controlling for variations in the cases and defendants in each system, Levin found systematic differences in who became each city's judges and how they performed. "Reform" judges were more likely to come from Northern European, Protestant, and middle-class backgrounds and from private practice; the partisan election system produced more minorities, Catholics, and people from low-income families and party-controlled government jobs.

Reform judges ran highly formal courtrooms. They expressed a rather pronounced contempt for the defendants appearing before them; they often described defendants as "coming from low-intelligence groups" and "crummy people." In the words of the study, such judges "tended to be resigned to the 'criminality' of most defendants and often seem inclined to give up on them." They nonetheless professed to believe prison could rehabilitate such people. As a result they sent more people to jail for longer terms—and discriminated in doing so. A black was more likely to end up in prison than a white who had committed the same crime and had the same prior record. Those who refused to plead guilty, thereby forcing the judges to preside over a full day of trial, and were then convicted were more likely to be sentenced to longer prison terms than they would have received had they initially pleaded guilty.

Political judges, on the other hand, tended to be more lenient than their reform counterparts and more informal in the way they conducted their courtrooms:

> They sought to "help" defendants, especially by "emphasiz[ing] probation and parole." Moreover, they tended to feel that they had a "closeness" and "kinship with the people that come into criminal court," that they are "more human" than the judges of the past and that they have a "greater empathy and awareness of the [defendant's] problems" and "more insight into the different types of people" that came before them. Several judges explained this empathy and "closeness" as part of a general attachment to the "underdog"; others explained it as a product of experience in their previous careers in political parties and government; some said it stemmed from their own minority ethnic and lower-income backgrounds.

In the words of one summary of the Levin piece, political judges "were also without illusions on the question of whether prisons could actually rehabilitate offenders and without a tendency to penalize people who asked for a trial. And they were less prone than reform judges to racial discrimination."[51]

The wisdom of changing over to "reform judges," then, is eminently debatable.

In light of the above, it is not surprising that many blacks perceive racism in the recent move toward merit selection of judges. Just as blacks begin to elect their own to the bench, a system is proposed that—in view of its dominance by the old "white shoe" law firms—will undoubtedly exclude more of them.

Another possible adverse secondary or tertiary effect of removing selection of the judiciary from the political process is the effect on those who take part in politics. Getting bright, able people to take part in the dreary, bone-crushing work of politics has never been easy. One source of attraction for such often thankless labors, as more and more jobs have been removed through the years from patronage rolls, is the possibility of a judgeship. Closing off that attraction might adversely effect the quality of those taking part in electoral politics. That very danger, in fact, has been pointed out to me by some activists vitally concerned with the quality of politics in Chicago and its environs. They see a risk, in other words, that in upgrading the quality of judicial life we may downgrade the quality of political life. The tradeoff may well be worth it, but there is no guarantee that it will.

There is an irony in removing politics from judicial selection at a time when judges are increasingly thrusting themselves (or being thrust by others) into the resolution of highly charged political issues: pollution control, school desegregation, equal employment opportunities, state university admissions, and so forth. (Recall Tocqueville's dictum, being proved true every day, that in the United States sooner or later every unresolved political question becomes a legal question.) Removing politics from the selection of those not only traditionally but increasingly charged with political decisions obviously raises grave questions for a democratic society.

Upgrading the intellectual quality of the bench may pose problems of its own. Brilliance may be a handicap on the bench. A quickminded person can almost die of boredom watching a lawyer of average ability tortuously draw a story from a slow-minded witness, holding the pace of his inquiry down to accommodate the understanding of the dullest-witted juror. A brilliant trial judge can often cause havoc in a courtroom. The juices of judging often do not flow in exceptionally bright people. Judge Charles Wyzanski, formerly of the Federal trial bench in Boston, probably the most brilliant trial judge in the country, was notorious for harassing lawyers and preventing them from trying their own cases as they wanted to. One Boston lawyer said: "If, when I am appearing before Wyzanski, I could just stipulate in advance of the trial that he is smarter than I am, everybody would be saved an awful lot of trouble."[52] Even on the appellate bench, where the whole process is much more cerebral and consists mainly of lawyers presenting arguments usually on esoteric points of law, great brilliance can cause trouble. Felix Frankfurter, a former Harvard Law School professor and manifestly a brilliant jurist on the United States Supreme Court, was notoriously and needlessly waspish and impatient as he snapped questions and comments at even the most able lawyers. Ironically enough, Frankfurter in his memoirs criticizes very pointedly Mr. Justice McReynolds's choleric demeanor on the bench during Frankfurter's arguments as a lawyer before the Supreme Court.[53] I cannot forbear to recall the first argument I ever heard before the United States Supreme Court, when Frankfurter, with extreme querulousness, harassed government counsel. From my vantage point, though admittedly I knew nothing of the case except what I heard during the argument, the government attorney scarcely deserved it, and he certainly upset no other Justice. I later inquired about Frankfurter's reasons of the Justice's clerk, a law school friend, only to learn that the apparently misused counsel was also a former Frankfurter clerk and a close friend. Justice Oliver Wendell Holmes of the United States Supreme Court, surely one of the ablest legal minds the English-speaking world has ever produced, commented on the different qualities needed for lower court service in a letter to Harold Laski: "When I think of [what is] required by a police [court] judge I shudder and turn pale."[54] What a judge may need above all is the right temperament, a sense of fairness and patience, with such ingrained instincts permeating the courtroom. Even in England, with its notable pool of high-grade legal talent to draw from for the bench, when Lord Chancellor Lyndhurst "was asked what method he used in making judicial appointments he replied, 'I look about for a gentleman and if he knows a little law, so much the better.' "[55]

The problem is that no foolproof system of judicial selection exists. Miring the selection of judges in the often seamy politics of America poses all the problems emphasized earlier.

Frustrated by the endless problems of proper selection, some reformers put emphasis on training for judges. Formerly it was nonexistent. A person was a lawyer one day and a full-fledged judge the next. A few years ago, the National College of Trial Judges began a voluntary four-week course for new judges, taught mostly by experienced judges and some law professors. Obviously such training, while better than nothing, is a very modest effort, and many of the judges who need it most may not attend anyway. But even with universal, extended, and expert training of judges, the problems discussed above go much deeper than can be corrected by better schooling of middle-aged people.

Of course, it is important to reemphasize that, as with the jury, there are many things right with the judiciary. The great majority of judges are, as pointed out, able, conscientious, and hard-working.

The problems of intemperate and even corrupt judges may be more acute in impersonal urban settings than in less crowded areas. One lawyer has commented: "I suspect that a judge in a small community is more on the spot and is forced to be more circumspect than is a judge in [a] city of eight million who is easily lost sight of and rarely meets the victims of his act at a church social on the following evening." On the other hand, the same lawyer has observed: "The big cities are the greater part of this country and the trend continues in that direction."[56] Obviously, any attempt to dismiss or diminish a problem in this country on the grounds that it affects only large cities is absurd.

On the question of proper judicial demeanor, Martin Mayer has written:

> In nearly six years of wandering into courtrooms, and in interviews with some dozens of judges, I have found only one judge drunk in chambers and only one boorish in his courtroom. As a group, they have been courteous, serious, levelheaded, conscious of and proud of the honor their community has given them.[57]

Howard James, in his book *Crisis in the Courts*, commenting on the number of lazy judges he found, was careful to balance his account with a description of some conscientious and hard-working members of the judiciary whom he encountered. He was also careful to point out the jurisdictions where judges work a full and demanding day. For example:

> Judges in Los Angeles arrive between 8 and 8:30 A.M., reach the bench promptly at 9, take a 10-minute recess in the morning, lunch from 12 to 1 or 1:30, and quit between 4:15 and 4:30.

> New Jersey judges start at 9:30, lunch from 1 to 2, and adjourn at 4, with 10-minute recesses in the morning and afternoon. Hours are stringently regulated by the New Jersey Supreme Court. Assignment (administrative) judges are the busiest. They start by 8:30 and seldom leave before 5.[58]

We return again to Learned Hand's point: Even given superb judges, with superb juries, litigation—or settlement under threat of litigation—is a dreadful means of "aiding" the injured. (See headnote to Chapter 1.)

7

The Personal Injury Lawyer

PERSONAL INJURY LAWYERS believe passionately in what they do. Even defense lawyers who contest the claims of injured victims see themselves as guarding insurance company coffers from greedy, overreaching claimants, egged on by even greedier, grasping personal injury lawyers looking for what an insurance lawyer regards as their obscene contingent fees. Plaintiffs' lawyers unquestionably do provide invaluable aid to individual claimants. Their defense of the common law negligence system is by no means cynical. They see themselves as representing the underdog, and they tend to be much more politically liberal than their incomes would lead one to expect. But plaintiffs' lawyers often seem to overlook how this system—from which they live so well as individuals helping other individuals—operates. They do not see the way it treats the majority of seriously injured accident victims who don't have a valid tort claim against a generously insured defendant; how harrowing for injury victims is the bitter and often fortuitous struggle the law ordains before compensation can be won; or how terrible are the delays in payment even for those lucky enough to win a settlement or verdict.

One can perhaps better understand the trial lawyer's myopia from a glance at the history and development of common law trials.

The most ancient species of trial in Saxon and old English law was trial by ordeal, or "judgment of God." Ordeal by *hot water* was performed by plunging a defendant's bare arm up to the elbow in boiling water. The *cold water* ordeal was performed by casting the party whose conduct was under suspicion into a river or pond of cold water; if he floated without any action of swimming it was deemed evidence of his guilt; if he sank, he was considered innocent of wrongdoing.[1]

Ordeal by fire similarly required that the person whose conduct was suspect demonstrate supernatural intervention on his behalf. In one version of ordeal by fire, a person was made to carry in his hand a piece of red-hot iron a distance of nine feet. The hand was then wrapped up and sealed. Three days later it was unwrapped, and the guilt or innocence of the accused announced, depending on the hand's condition.[2]

The Normans brought with them to England a variant of trial by ordeal, a mutual ordeal, if you will, or trial by battle, which soon superseded all other ordeals. Like its counterparts, trial by battle was based on a belief in divine intervention: Providence would give victory to the person in the right. Under the custom of challenging witnesses, a party who saw his case going adversely could accuse the inconvenient witness of perjury and demand the right to prove it by force of arms. In the words of historian Homer Lea, this "proceeding . . . adjourned the main case and, likewise decided its result." It is easy therefore to understand the early law's custom, prescribed in some codes, under which witnesses were required to come into court armed and to have their weapons blessed on the altar before giving testimony.[3] Gradually, the custom of challenging witnesses led to the hiring of desperadoes who would testify falsely, which would arouse the anger of the adverse party, whereupon a sword fight would ensue; once again the fight would presumably end the litigation.[4] Gradually, too, a class of professional champions arose.[5]

The interconnection between trial by battle and the substance of the dispute was ingeniously ordained by requirements of some legal codes that the champion adopt the posture of someone who had actually witnessed the incident under dispute. Thus, in England and Normandy, the plaintiff's champion was required to swear that he had heard and seen the matters alleged by the claimant, with the opposing champion automatically swearing the same was false—the whole charade being a total fiction.[6]

With such origins, perhaps it shouldn't surprise us that common law trials are still viewed by advocate-adversaries as battles. Trial tactics manuals and other legal literature are replete with the terminology of weapons and warfare, exhorting the lawyer to "attack," "destroy," "disarm," or "annihilate" an opposing witness.[7] References to "the sword of cross-examination" and to "trial by ambush" are typical.[8] In *The Art of the Trial*, Norbert Savay puts it this way: "A student of the art of advocacy and of the legal contest can profit immensely by a deep and protracted study of war strategy."[9]

Of course, the combat in a trial is verbal and intellectual, but combat it nonetheless is. Charles Curtis, an eminently urbane Boston trial lawyer, has observed: "The justification of the adversary proceeding is in the satisfaction of the parties. . . . The best way to get that done is to encourage them to fight it out, and dissolve their differences in dissension."[10] In Goitein's *Primitive Ordeal and Modern Law*, the author states: "One of the secrets of the success of the legal process in replacing the ordeal is found in the very fact it provided similar satisfactions to that offered by the ordeal."[11]

But lawyers are much more comfortable than laymen with such combat. From their first days in law school, they are encouraged to fight each other with words. By the use of the Socratic method, law professors goad students into intellectual battle with each other and with their teachers. Indeed, the often ferocious and insensitive nature of law school combat has been made legendary in two recent bestsellers, John Osborn's *The Paper Chase* (made into a movie and later a television series) and Scott Turow's *One L*, a diary of a first-year law student. "Nader's Raider" Joel Seligman, in describing the typical teaching methods of Clark Byse, a legendary instructor at the University of Pennsylvania and later at the Harvard Law School, writes that

> . . . for a full forty-eight minutes [Byse's] colloquy concerning a trivial one-and-one-half-page 1891 case goes on, with Byse rapidly shifting hypothetical variations on the case, prodding students to vocalize alternative legal arguments in debate directly with [himself and] each other, and, at one point, chewing out the class for not seeing obvious relationships between his hypothetical questions and earlier cases the class had discussed.[12]

Several law schools, including Harvard and Michigan, have added psychiatrists to their staffs to deal with the inordinate tensions produced by initiation into the combative rites of lawyering. Dr. Alan Stone, the Harvard Law School staff psychiatrist, describes inter-student relations in terms of "enmity, friction, hostility, distaste, contempt and the lack of group cohesiveness and morale."[13] But gradually most lawyers become inured to the combat. Take the word "argument." For most people, arguments are an extreme unpleasantness to be avoided at almost all costs, draining and demeaning when not avoided. To law students and lawyers, the word is a neutral term: "What is your argument for that position?" "Can you really argue that with a straight face?" "I'm on my way to my [moot court] argument."

But if lawyers are relatively comfortable with verbal combat, others are not. And lawyers, perhaps somewhat sensitive about this, proceed to justify all the agony of trial by appeal to an ultimate value: Truth. Columbia Law School's Maurice Rosenberg says, "The underlying hope is that if the law permits the lawyer-gladiators to make the fight, out of the clash and clang of their legal or factual battling, rights of the case will appear and justice be done."[14]

But that assumes that each side will be represented by equally bright and diligent lawyers, scarcely an assured condition.

Thurman Arnold, a brilliant author, Yale law professor, Assistant Attorney General for Antitrust, Federal judge, and leading corporate lawyer, put it this way:

> Mutual exaggeration is supposed to create a lack of exaggeration. Bitter partisanship in opposite directions is supposed to bring out the truth. Of course no rational human being would apply such a theory to his own affairs. . . . Mutual exaggeration of opposing claims violates the whole theory of rational, scientific investigation. Yet in spite of this most obvious fact, the ordinary teacher of law will insist (1) that combat makes for clarity, (2) that heated arguments bring out the truth, and (3) that anyone who doesn't believe this is a loose thinker. The explanation of this attitude lies in the realm of social anthropology.[15]

The result, of course, is that victory—as with trial by battle—still goes not to the party in the right but to the party with the stronger champion.[16] Thus, many lawyers are forced to admit that truth, virtue, and justice are often subordinated to other concerns in common law trials, just as happens in war itself. Consider the subject of cross-examination, the bedrock of the adversary system. Lawyers piously preach that the search for truth has no greater ally than the test of cross-examination. But the contradictory attitude of lawyers toward this basic tool is illustrated by the following juxtaposition from Wellman's classic legal text on cross-examination: Wellman states on page 22 that "no substitute has ever been found for cross-examination as a means of separating truth from falsehood." But later in the book he admits that "the sole object of cross-examination is to break the force of the adverse testimony."[17]

Similarly, Asher Cornelius, in his work *Cross-Examination of Witnesses* wrote:

> [I]f the witness is an honest one and tells a clear straightforward story, do not cross-examine him upon the main story; he will only emphasize it. Cross-examine him for lack of memory, for distances, for marks of identity, for religion, for politics, for anything but his story. . . . In other words, if you are cross-examining a clear-headed honest witness, never give him a chance to repeat his story, but pull the attention of the jury away from it.[18]

In Lake's *How to Cross-Examine Witnesses Successfully*, the author states: "No matter how clear, how logical, how concise, or how honest a witness may be or make his testimony appear, there is always some way, if you are ingenious enough, to cast suspicion on it, to weaken its effect."[20] Suppose, for example, that you are a lawyer and that an opposing witness gives testimony that is highly damaging to your client. Suppose, further, that you know that the testimony is entirely accurate. What do you do? According to a prominent law school dean and trial lawyer, Monroe Freedman, "an attorney is obligated to attack, if he can, the reliability or credibility of an opposing witness whom he knows to be truthful."[21] He should do so, according to Freedman, even though he has "one purpose and one purpose only . . . to impeach the [witness]; to destroy her credibility before the jury and thus to make it appear, contrary to fact, that she is lying."[21]

In the words of Jake Erlich, "I don't have to tell you that a lawsuit is not a disinterested investigation but a bitter adversary duel."[22]

Charles Curtis, the urbane Bostonian mentioned earlier, a leader of the bar and a man very much in love with the practice of law, once remarked that a lawyer's "freedom from the strict bonds of veracity and of the law are the two chief assets of the profession." He also observed, "I don't know any other career that offers ampler opportunity for both the enjoyment of virtue and the exercise of vice, or, if you please, the exercise of virtue and the enjoyment of vice, except for possibly the ancient rituals which were performed in some temples by vestal virgins, and others by sacred prostitutes."[23]

Personal injury lawyers—at least those who represent plaintiffs—are, like criminal and divorce lawyers, often looked down upon by blue-chip law firms doing corporate, commercial, or probate work. In fact, however, personal injury work has become incomparably the richest area of law practice in the United States. When President Carter appointed Cyrus Vance as Secretary of State, he was a member of the prestigious Wall Street firm of Simpson, Thatcher, and Bartlett, and was earning $250,444 a year. As reported in the *New York Times*, "not many did better than he, according to lawyers on Wall Street." According to the same report, however, Wall Street lawyers, although the highest paid corporate lawyers in the country, do worse now than personal injury lawyers:

> "There is no question about it," says Lawrence E. Walsh, a partner in Davis, Polk & Wardwell [another blue-chip Wall Street firm]. "In terms of accumulation of wealth and living style, senior lawyers [on Wall Street] are not matching those of the 1920's. The top of the personal-injury bar does better than [Wall Street] partners."

Confirming this point, James Baccardo, who heads a forty-lawyer personal injury firm in San Jose, California, states, "I've made $1 million for the past 15 years."[24]

The point is that not only a few nationally known personal injury "stars," like Melvin Belli, in big cities like New York and San Francisco, earn *very* high incomes from personal injury work. A recent report on a three-partner firm in Marshall, Texas (population 29,000) indicated that a casual check of the partners' 1975 earnings showed their net (after expenses) to be about $1.6 million on personal injury settlements and verdicts of $4.5 million.[25] And surprising numbers of other lawyers who gain huge fees are strangers to nationwide fame. Here is a 1968 report on a New Jersey lawyer:

> [He] has been in practice for eighteen years [and] isn't at all well known outside Essex County, New Jersey. He isn't an officer of the trade association of personal injury lawyers, the American Trial Lawyers Association; he doesn't get interviewed the way Melvin Belli does; he doesn't have the fame among other lawyers that Jacob Fuchsberg and Harry Gair of New York do in this field. In fact . . . the vast majority of the lawyers in the New York metropolitan area have never heard of this forty-two-year-old attorney. Yet year in and year out he is good for a *net* of nearly $350,000 a year from contingent fees. And even more—if he had not paid out some $280,000 to other lawyers for referring cases to him.[26]

Why such riches for personal injury lawyers? Because, uniquely among lawyers, they are not paid by the hour—"tied to their time sheets," as lawyers put it. Rather, they get a "piece of the action," an equity interest of one-third, and increasingly one-half, of the damages through their contingent fees.

The subject of the contingent fee in personal injury cases engenders bitter controversy. Insurance executives, doctors, and business people often assert that the contingent fee is the primary cause of the evils permeating personal injury liability insurance. By allowing lawyers to buy, in effect, a substantial portion of a victim's claim, the contingent fee allegedly encourages lawyers to seek claims—indeed to excite and exaggerate them. "The contingent fee . . . is a cancer," exclaimed one insurance executive in a typical response of exasperation and frustration at a 1967 conference of lawyers, insurance personnel, government officials, and consumer representatives.[27]

The contingent fee allows a claimant to prosecute a personal injury at little or no financial risk to himself. He need not pay his lawyer a retainer, and he has no worry about paying a fee at the end of the case if he loses. Under the rule in England—at least as formally stated—a lawyer is forbidden to contract for a contingent fee and is entitled to payment for his services, win or lose. (As a practical matter, British lawyers will not in fact press an impecunious client for a fee when a personal injury case is lost. British lawyers also tend to charge for their services according to how successful a result is achieved in such cases, which amounts to something very like a contingent fee.) Another American deviation from the British rules tends to encourage litigation. Not only must the British litigant face at least the theoretical threat of paying his lawyer, win or lose, but if he loses he must pay the winner's lawyers's fee as well. In the United States, a losing party is not obligated to pay the other party's counsel fees, and the result is that little or no financial risk, theoretical or otherwise, deters an injured claimant from suing in the United States. (Here again, though, the contrast with England is not as stark as it seems. A British insurance company is not likely to pursue an unsuccessful claimant, especially an impecunious one, for payment of the insurance company's legal fees.)

Undoubtedly, then, the explicit American rules in regard to lawyers' fees on both sides create a unique atmosphere. A third factor that contributes to the uniquely fertile climate for personal injury cases in the United States, as opposed to England and elsewhere, is the fact that such cases are tried before impressionable juries. None of these circumstances is likely to change. What seems to be happening, in fact, is the Americanization of personal injury law elsewhere rather than the Europeanization of American law. In some measure the rise in personal injury litigation in the United States is a function of a much broader factor than any technical legal rules: the spread of affluence. The plight of the person mutilated by an accident, bereft of any resources for himself or for his family to deal with the aftereffects of the tragedy, arouses general feelings today of compassion, if not outrage. But this is a relatively new phenomenon. John Kenneth Galbraith describes the situation as it existed only a few generations ago:

> In the grim world of Ricardo and Malthus, the ordinary citizen could have no interest in social security in the modern sense. If a man's wage is barely sufficient for existence, he does not worry much about the greater suffering of unemployment. Life is a heavy burden in either case. Men who are engaged in a daily struggle for survival do not think of old age, for they do not expect to see it. When the normal expectation of life is very low, sickness and death are normal hazards. . . . With increasing well-being all people become aware, sooner or later, that they have something to protect.[28]

While earlier accident victims and jurors judging their cases looked upon misfortune as rather a natural concomitant to life, in addition nineteenth-century courts were reluctant to impose liability for personal injury for fear of imposing burdens on infant industries. Such reluctance was apparently a manifestation of the "rugged individualism" that dominated so much of nineteenth-century law, economics, and life. A desperate plight for the mass of mankind is still the same in most parts of the world. The social psychiatrist Robert Coles has recently written:

> Death, Heidegger kept reminding his readers, keeps us more alive, modest and reflective than we may care to know. He was thinking, as philosophers do, of himself and of those who read books such as his. For hundreds of millions of people on this earth life is brief and grim, the next meal a constant uncertainty, disease a daily fact of existence. But for those of us lucky enough to be well-to-do members of advanced industrial societies, the chances are high for a relatively long and healthy if not [necessarily] happy life. The last breath may well come in the person's 70's or 80's; he or she has seen a lot, enjoyed many experiences, known few, if any, hardships— and in an increasing number of instances, been virtually free of major [physical problems] before the final one has been diagnosed.[29]

Thus, first in the United States and increasingly throughout the Western world and Japan, people are no longer serfs, at the mercy of masters or the elements. And when such a person is injured—or is called on, as a juror, to judge the merits of the claim of a fellow creature—a different attitude often prevails, an attitude of rising expectation, of entitlement, as some insurance scholars put it, a demand that reparation be made. This rising expectation has led to much private and social insurance in recent years throughout the industrial world. As a corollary it has also led to expanding tort liability throughout the world. For example, one finds attempts in Europe to adopt more liberal American rules for liability for defective products. But here the uniqueness of the American situation reasserts itself. In the first place, we Americans are surely more litigious than most societies. Why? Partly because we're a nation of strangers, without common origins and traditions or homogeneous traits. With savage rivalries and radical disparities—ethnic, cultural, and geographic—we are far more likely to view each other with distrust and alienation and to sue each other over all kinds of slights and transgressions. Does not our lack of a cohesive sense of national family explain in substantial measure our lack of the degree of social insurance, a way of taking care of one's brothers and sisters, characteristic of such relatively homogeneous nations as Sweden, the United Kingdom, or New Zealand? And our smaller amount of social insurance protection, in turn, probably encourages a unique degree of personal injury litigation, frustrating and ineffectual as it is. Geoffrey Palmer, a brilliant young New Zealand law professor who is a principal drafter of a recent law in New Zealand abolishing all personal injury tort law in favor of a no-fault, government-run social insurance approach to accident compensation, has pointed out that the explosion of personal injury litigation in the United States can be viewed as a reaction to our relative lack of social insurance. In his view it represents a "covert and indirect social engineering" by the courts, which, knowing of the often tragically inadequate social insurance benefits available to accident victims, stretches, distorts, prods, and pushes the common law of tort beyond recognition in a vain attempt to make it serve the ends of social insurance:

> When dealing with traditional rules of tort law, the California Courts [have led the way in stretching] the law. I hesitate to use the word "pervert." The aim appears to be to see that plaintiffs in personal injury cases get paid for serious losses they have sustained where the defendant sued has the money to pay. In some of these cases to assert that the defendant was to blame in the sense that he was at fault or that his conduct caused the harm is not credible to

people of ordinary common sense. Let me mention two recent decisions.

In one 1970 case a [mother and] father and [their] five year old son were staying at a motel in Palm Springs. The motel had a swimming pool. It was the off season and the motel was not crowded. The father and son [neither of whom could swim well, if at all, used the pool and] were both drowned in [precise] circumstances which could not be explained because there were no eye witnesses. A California statute provided that for swimming pools such as the one the motel had, "lifeguard service shall be provided or a sign shall be erected clearly indicating that such service is not provided." The evidence showed that there was no lifeguard service [and] no warning sign. The Supreme Court of California was prepared to hold that the defendant had the burden of showing the absence of the warning [sign] was not a cause of the deaths. A verdict for the defendants given by the jury was overturned since the Court held defendants had not met the burden. How any defendant could ever meet such a burden the Court does not explain. A lawyer from the British Commonwealth would regard that decision as nothing less than remarkable.

In other words, what bothers Palmer is this: There was no requirement that the pool have a lifeguard; with the two swimmers dead, and therefore unable to testify, how could the defendant motel go about proving that a sign saying there was no lifeguard service would have deterred the father and son from swimming when the lack of a lifeguard was obvious with or without a sign? Palmer goes on:

In a 1975 case the Supreme Court of California was dealing with a defendant radio station which had sponsored a contest featuring a disc jockey. The disc jockey, the "real Don Steel" was running a "Super Summer Spectacular," from a fire-engine-red Buick automobile which he drove about the San Fernando Valley. The person who first approached him at each location was given an opportunity to win a small money prize by answering a simple question. Messages would be broadcast "the Real Don Steel is out driving on _____; could be in your neighborhood at any time and he's got bread to spread, so be on the lookout for him." Two teenagers listening to the broadcast had failed to reach Steel at his prior location. When they heard his new location they sped in two cars along the freeway in tandem at over 80 miles per hour forcing the plaintiff's car into a spin where it overturned, killing him. Plaintiff secured verdict from a jury against the Radio Station which the Supreme Court upheld even though the California Court of Appeals had reversed on the ground that the Radio Station had no control or right of control over the drivers of cars on the highway. The Supreme Court was "not persuaded that the imposition of a duty here will lead to unwarranted extensions of liability." It seems to me that theories of recovery against the state of California for allowing such youths to drive at all or against their middle class parents for allowing them to speed about in potent machinery would be just as persuasive. Perhaps my scepticism is unfounded. In the peculiar environment of Southern California it may be that nothing is unforeseeable.

It looks to me as if the courts have begun to try and turn the tort system in the United States into a mutual insurance company against accidents. It is certainly difficult, if not impossible, to defend modern American tort law as a serious attempt to implement a system of recovery based on fault. In California, which in so many ways represents the direction in which the rest of Western civilization will travel, the feeling seems to be that where there is a serious loss someone should be found who will pay for it. So far as losses from accidental injuries are concerned I find the attitude acceptable. As a common lawyer I find the means by which it is implemented distressing. In the end I do not think that the aim can be accomplished through judicial initiatives by the Courts. Certainly it cannot be achieved in a principled and orderly fashion by the sporadic method of common law adjudication. Indeed the only reason it is being attempted through the Courts, I suspect, is that it is politically risky, not to say embarrassing, to pass legislation to pay money to people who are incapacitated by accident. It does not conform to the rhetoric of free enterprise and individual responsibility.[30]

The problem with such sporadic, chaotic, piecemeal attempts at social insurance is that they leave us with the worst of both worlds: skyrocketing insurance premiums as defendant corporations and professionals and their insurers try to prepare for new onslaughts of claims based on novel or perverse theories, and precious little compensation for injury as courts and juries can only fitfully stretch common law tort rules into a genuine system of comprehensive compensation.

A cynic might be prompted to characterize the role of trial lawyers in all this as urging the expansion of tort law—through novel cases and novel theories—so as to make it easier for claimants to be paid, while opposing reforms like no-fault insurance, which would make it so easy to be paid that lawyers would not be necessary.

Unquestionably, the confluence of interest between personal injury lawyers and their clients is often marginal; in fact, outright conflicts of interest are often present.

F. B. Mackinnon, in his monumental study of the contingent fee for the American Bar Association, notes:

> As the fee is payable without regard to time spent on the case, it may be to the lawyer's advantage to settle it quickly, spending as little time as possible on the small claim where the increment in value through rigorous bargaining or trial, while significant to the client, is not significant or perhaps even compensatory to the lawyer. For example, the addition of $100 to the recovery of a claim for which an offer of $300 has been made will add $25 to $50 to the lawyer's fee, but may require more than that amount of his time. However, the additional $50 or $75 may be very important to the client. It is financially more profitable to handle a mass of small claims with a minimum expenditure of time on each than it is to treat each as a unique case and fight for each dollar of the maximum possible recovery for the client.[31]

To counteract this conflict, the contingent fee contract often provides for additional compensation to the lawyer according to the stage at which the case is disposed of. But, according to Mackinnon, "the increase in the rate of fee may lead the lawyer to bring suit or start trial . . . solely to increase his rate from 24% to 33⅓%, and without the likelihood of comparable increment to the client. (Studies show that bringing a case to trial does not, in itself, increase the value of the claim.)" Insurance company lawyers play the same game. They are paid by the hour, with an increased rate for a day or a portion of a day spent in court. As a result, defense lawyers will often drag things out until, say, a jury is picked or later, in order to collect a fee for a "day" or more in court.

The late Lester P. Dodd, a former president of the Michigan Bar Association, writing in *The Detroit Lawyer*, pointedly emphasized the embarrassing questions posed for the bar by many aspects of the contingent fee. Starting from the premise of Canon 13 of the American Bar Association's Canons of Professional Ethics, which asserts that the contingent fee "should always be subject to the supervision of the court, as to its reasonableness," Dodd asked the following questions:

> Is the [contingent fee] contract approved by a court when made? No. Is it automatically brought to the attention of the court when

settlement is made under its terms? No. . . . When his claim is
settled or his judgment paid, a check is issued jointly to the attorney
and client. [T]he client has the option of paying the agreed fee or of
retaining another attorney to ascertain his rights and test the fairness of the fee agreement. A right, perhaps, but a rather naked right
to one who may desperately need his money.[32]

Dodd went on to point out that the contingent fee agreement is
always

. . . drawn by the lawyer. He is a party to it and necessarily represents himself in its negotiation. Can he also represent fairly the
other contracting party? . . . [W]e take in stride and accept as rou-
tine a practice which permits the lawyer to enter into contracts with
his own client under which he acquires a direct personal interest in
[the other's] law suit.

A settlement offer may to one [party to the contract] seem reasonable—to the other unreasonable. One may need money more desperately than the other. . . . Lawyers have been known to refuse to
discuss settlement of a case—"until next year because for tax reasons, I can't afford another large fee this year."[33]

In a 1975 survey of California, attorney Richard J. Kohlman, a
maverick lawyer, who has long fought battles within the bar against
abuses by lawyers of the personal injury liability system, found 50
percent contingent fees commonplace. This, he says, "has special
potential for scandal. . . . [A] 50% fee will always net the client less
than half the total recovery mainly because the lawyer takes his expenses out first." E. Robert Wallach, a former president of the San
Francisco Bar Association and a prominent personal injury attorney, confirms Kohlman's finding: "I agree that there has been an increase in the percentage of contingent fees, and I disapprove." In recent Congressional testimony Murray Teigh Bloom, author of the
bestselling *The Trouble with Lawyers*, cited a 1975 Detroit survey
that found the going rate for contingent fees was 50 percent, regardless of whether the case was settled, tried, or appealed. An ambulance-chasing investigation in Philadelphia recently found that 34
percent of all attorneys there charged 50 percent contingent fees. According to the Philadelphia report, in many cases "the attorneys
managed to get more out of the settlement than the clients."[34] In his
Congressional testimony, Bloom stated that an investigation in Florida "turned up dozens of cases where the lawyer got more money
than the client." He also reported that a 105-count indictment

against lawyers and doctors by a 1976 Miami Federal grand jury found that one of the objects of the conspiracy under investigation was "to reduce payments to accident victims by deducting false and inflated medical bills and costs from the total amount of their settlements."[35]

In his research for his book on lawyers, Bloom unearthed numerous instances of lawyers' overreaching through the size of their contingent fees:

A Gary, Indiana man who, after six years of legal battling, received $25,000 for his serious injuries netted $4,166, leaving his lawyers to fight over the division of the remaining $20,834.

An injured Virginia salesman netted $15,000 from a $33,000 court award.

A ten-year-old Miami boy netted $661 out of a $2,578 auto accident verdict, with his attorney taking $1,260 and the rest going for expenses. (So outraged was the boy's father that he hired a second lawyer—for $190—to rectify the wrong. The court then ordered the first lawyer to pay the boy an additional $666, so that ultimately the boy netted half the award.)

A Los Angeles mother of ten was awarded $90,000 as a result of the "wrongful death" of her husband in an auto accident. Her lawyer, who worked less than two weeks on the case, took 40 percent or $36,000.[36]

Obviously, a personal injury case can often be a lawyer's bonanza. As Bloom put it in his congressional testimony, "No one goes in for ambulance-chasing or personal injury law practice because they like running or the smell of hospitals. They do it because . . . there is an awful lot of easy money in the business."[37] A few phone calls can result in one-third or more of a substantial—or even huge— amount when the insurance company stands ready to pay, and the claimant's lawyer chooses, for one reason or another, valid or otherwise, not to bargain hard for more than the insurer offers.

Another source of quick money for a lawyer occurs when a client suffers a serious accident and the lawyer refers the case to a personal injury expert. Ethically, a lawyer is not supposed to share in the fee when he has simply referred the case and done no legal work himself, but that canon is honored more in the breach than the observance. Apparently such easy money is just too good to pass up, and it is a simple matter to counterfeit the referring attorney's work on the case. How easy all this money is was revealed in an embarrassing case in Miami. Attorney Edward Strickland received a "forwarding fee" of $25,333 from a leading personal injury lawyer, Perry Nichols. Nichols had won a $190,000 verdict for a widow whose husband had been killed in an automobile accident. Nichols took the standard 40 percent, or $76,000, with Strickland getting the customary one-third of Nichols's fee for forwarding the case. The sticking point was that Strickland was a judge and thus was violating the law if he was practicing law on the side. Caught in this bind, Strickland resorted to honesty about how little a forwarding lawyer does. He protested that "the mere referral of the case on the telephone did not take one minute. I played no part in the case, gave no advice, prepared no pleadings." Thus his defense was in effect that referring a case does not rise to the dignity of practicing law! Amen, but it took a strange twist of affairs to get a lawyer to admit it.[38] On the other hand, referring a case does mean giving up two-thirds of the fee. Rather than make such a sacrifice, some lawyers will hold on to a case and, not being experienced in personal injury practice, will litigate where they should not or not litigate where they should. One of the most respected Federal trial judges in the country—formerly a leading trial lawyer as well as scholar—commenting not long ago on Chief Justice Burger's estimate that one-third to one-half of American lawyers are not properly qualified for trial advocacy,[39] said that

> . . . the biggest cause of inept trial lawyering is the non-personal injury lawyer who reads in the Jury Verdict Reporter newsletter that some big name lawyer like Philip Corboy has won a $450,000 verdict for a broken leg. The kid next door then breaks his leg on a skateboard and such a lawyer thinks it's worth $450,000, out of which he's going to net, say, $150,000. (That's a lot of real estate closings!) But his case is not a $450,000 case—it's a $1,500 case at the most. But with stars in his eyes he refuses a reasonable settlement. In fact, professionally and temperamentally he's totally inadequate for trial work. He hates the combat and is completely out of his element. But, not being willing to settle, he comes to court along with his client, and they both take an awful beating. That's where inadequate trial work stems from.[43]

At the other end of the spectrum is the lawyer who knows he is inadequate to appear in court and who is known by insurance companies to be inadequate. And yet out of greed he keeps his own personal injury cases and settles them for a pittance, rather than share a fee with an expert trial lawyer whose efforts could ensure a proper settlement. Furthermore, some lawyers will "wholesale" their cases with insurance companies. That means they will settle all claims of their clients against a given company in a package deal, often for a fraction of their combined value, unconscionably mixing the solid claims with the shaky. After taking his own very substantial cut, such a lawyer then assumes arbitrary power to distribute what is left to individual clients. In view of the wide differences possible even in experts' appraisals of tort cases, the clients have little basis for objecting to what they receive.

Nothing makes personal injury lawyers more apoplectic than an attack on the contingent fee. Basically, when all their bombast is discounted (and bombast is one thing trial lawyers have an abundance of), their defense of the contingent fee rests on three contentions:

1. High fees in some cases are justified by the high risk involved. After all, it is argued, contingent fees are just that—"contingent," with the lawyer getting nothing if the client gets nothing. But, as Professor Maurice Rosenberg of the Columbia University Law School told an American Bar Association Convention in 1976, "plaintiffs recover [something]—whether by suit or settlement—in the vast proportion of cases in which they retain a lawyer." In other words, as the late Bernard Botein, a former New York appellate judge, said "there is very little that is contingent about the contingent fee."[44]

2. The contingent fee allows the impecunious accident victim to retain an able lawyer to match the expertise of the insurance company's adjuster and lawyer, at no initial outlay. It is the "poor man's key to the courtroom." But it is a key that does not in fact unlock many doors for many people. Lawyers are very selective as to the cases they will take. One reason Philip Corboy, the leading Chicago lawyer, wins so often is his *very* careful case selection. Of about 750 cases offered to him in 1976, Corboy rejected all but the strongest 220. About 60 percent of his cases come from referrals from other lawyers.[45] One might ask "What happened to the other 530 accident victims?"

3. Lawyers earn their contingent fees, because clients net more even after paying one-third or more to a lawyer, than without a lawyer. Some studies on this point indicate that lawyers do in fact net their clients more,[46] but others indicate the contrary.[47] Even assuming that hiring a lawyer does increase what a claimant can expect to receive, the necessity of selling a portion of one's claim as a means of paying a lawyer (unheard of, as we have seen, in most other forms of legal service) only goes to illustrate that the contingent fee arrangement is, in the words of the late Professor Albert Ehrenzweig, a lead-

ing torts scholar, no more than a corrective for the "risk involved in the gamble of a negligence suit."[48]

What manner of man is the personal injury lawyer, especially the one who represents plaintiffs? They tend as a group to be flamboyant, flashy, aggressive, gregarious men, brimming with self-confidence, not unlike very successful "hard sell" salesmen. But there is an important extra dimension. Many salesmen tend to be self-conscious about their lack of intellect and refer to themselves ruefully as "peddlers." Trial lawyers suffer from no such self-doubt. The law is an intellectual profession, and trial lawyers above all live by their wits. Trial work may not be as cerebral as, say, tax law, and, as with trial judges, other qualities besides sheer brain power are paramount, but enough brain work is demanded to convince trial lawyers they suffer no lack in this regard. One insurance executive says, "They're great fun to be with. They all work like hell, and they're very able. You know, many of them would be the leaders of the bar in this country—the presidents of the bar associations, the senior partners of the big firms—except that they didn't go to the fancy law schools, they're Jews, the jobs weren't open to them when they started."[49]

Plaintiffs' lawyers do tend to be ethnic types: Jewish, Irish, and Italian names abound. And not only names—they also tend to have an intensely ethnic manner. One is often reminded of politicians when one is with them, which is not surprising since, like politicians, they must maintain their common touch. In their case the electorate is an ever shifting group of twelve jurors. It is this ability to make contact with a cross section of people, to "read" them and play upon their responses, along with enormous confidence that they can do so, that is the trial lawyers' life's blood.

The fact that trial lawyers are aggressive should surprise no one who knows how intensely competitive the courtroom is. Lawyers sometimes refer to it as "the pit." Many lawyers cannot stomach the constant infighting that takes place in court and in preparing to go there. The trial lawyer finds himself in the situation of constantly preparing to do something while someone on the other side is constantly plotting to thwart him. The strain that trial work entails would be akin to that faced by a director who is not only acting in his own play but facing skilled opponents trying to make him and his fellow actors forget their lines. Only a certain temperament can stand the strain, and then only for a certain period and up to a certain point. Trial work, generally speaking, is a younger person's game; the pressures of doing it often lead to heavy drinking. (The trial lawyer who is effective in the morning until he has had several drinks at lunch is by no means uncommon.) Personal injury lawyers, operating in this *enormously* competitive sphere, are usually extremely self-confident, a self-confidence generally enhanced in the case of plaintiff's lawyers by *passionate* belief in their function. As they view it, gigantic and heartless insurance companies will grind down helpless victims unless modern gladiators—they themselves—intervene to protect the injured party, poor and outgunned as he or she is. Many plaintiff's lawyers hate insurance companies. "I'd represent *anybody* in *any* kind of case," says one of the best of them, "but *never* an insurance company for *anything*."[50] They scorn insurance companies' large and posh buildings, erected, as they see it, by bloodless, massive institutions that at the same time would deny the weak and helpless their due. Only trial lawyers, as they see it, stand between the accident victim and harsh destitution.

Something of their passionate emotionalism is suggested by remarks of the one who was generally considered by his peers the best in the business before he went on the bench—Jacob Fuchsberg, a bald and muscular New Yorker who looks like a football coach. "You have to live your case," said Fuchsberg when he was still practicing. "When you say a man is objective, you are not describing a good lawyer. When a case is about to come to trial, I'm hard to settle with, because I've come to know the *people*, not just the file. There may have been an estimate of what the case was worth—which I concurred in superficially—but now I know the *people*."[51] Alfred Julien, another leading personal injury lawyer, will almost always visit his clients' homes, go to dinner with them, and generally become real friends with them. He does this, fellow lawyer Norman Sheresky says, "simply so that he can feel closer to them and . . . more immersed in their causes. The deeper the relationship he develops the easier it seems for him, he believes, to communicate with the jury."[52]

Fuchsberg is in many ways—like so many personal injury lawyers—a bundle of contradictions. At a social occasion, he is a subtle, interesting man, but in court he could be so heavyhanded as to be almost embarrassing. In an American Trial Lawyers film for use in law schools showing a personal injury trial from beginning to end, Fuchsberg starred as the plaintiff's lawyer. Every year I show the film (an excellent one) to my law school classes and every year Fuchsberg's extraordinary unctuousness and studied hesitancies with judge, jurors, clients, and witnesses draw hoots from the law students who are always then shocked when I interrupt their cat calls to say that Fuchsberg was probably the leading plaintiffs' lawyer in the world, earning millions annually. Armed with this knowledge, they begin to see his effectiveness, especially when coupled with his displays of enormous strength as he rasps at opposing counsel in occasional tiffs.

What I think law school students overlook in their newborn but nearsighted sophistication is that most jurors are frightened and a little overwhelmed by the formality and dignity of courtroom proceedings—the robes, the flags, the paneling, the uniformed bailiffs, and so forth. When one is inexperienced and afraid, extraordinary courtesy and deference, even to the point of what might strike someone else as unctuousness, can be very reassuring, especially if accompanied, as it was with Fuchsberg, with displays of strength exerted toward others. Most of us, for example, are often confused and afraid when we go to a doctor's or dentist's office, and the same kind of extraordinary—and even overdone—courtesy shown by nurses and doctors in that situation can be *very* comforting. At any rate, it certainly seems to work and is often adopted by trial lawyers. (One is reminded of Joseph N. Welch, of Army–McCarthy hearings fame, the courtly Boston lawyer with the old-fashioned charm and manner. That was largely a courtroom manner. In his office, where I worked as a younger lawyer, Welch tended to be curt, aloof, and crusty.)

Until fairly recently, defense (or insurance) lawyers tended on the whole to get the best of plaintiffs' lawyers in court. Before, during, and immediately after World War II, a claimant in many communities could not find a lawyer who could compete with insurance lawyers. Since 1946, however, with the founding of The Association of Trial Lawyers of America (ATLA), a revolution in personal injury litigation has come about. Growing to the point where it now has 40,000 members, ATLA has aggressively developed techniques for the effective prosecution of personal injury claims and encouraged their use all over the country by holding seminars on techniques for high verdicts.[53] But still, except in contests between insurance lawyers and plaintiffs' stars or superstars, like Philip Corboy, plaintiffs' counsel is likely to be overmatched. Insurance companies, after all, are institutional litigants whose business it is to know who are the able trial lawyers in every community in the United States and even which ones specialize in cases involving tractors, say, or lower back injuries. But injured claimants usually litigate only once in their lifetimes and drift into the hands of a lawyer by haphazard means. That lawyer may or may not be equal to the case he so eagerly accepts in hopes of the riches promised by a contingent fee.

Mention has already been made of Chief Justice Burger's celebrated criticism that one-half to one-third of American lawyers are not properly qualified for trial advocacy (see p. 144). But trial lawyers at least have to be ready to perform in public, facing an opposing lawyer. Thus trial lawyers may perform better as a group than other lawyers, who can "bury" their mistakes in the privacy of their offices, unscrutinized and untested by judges, juries, or opponents. The biggest cause of trial lawyers' unpreparedness is probably crowded court dockets and inefficient scheduling of cases. Difficulty in scheduling is probably inevitable, as anyone who has ever tried to schedule a meeting of five or six busy people will understand. A trial entails that many and more: judge, lawyers on both sides, parties, witnesses, an available jury, and others. The result is that a young lawyer who starts out by going to the courthouse after thoroughly and even feverishly preparing himself and his witnesses gets used to having his case postponed ("continued," as the lawyers put it) or settled. After a few such experiences, many lawyers stop expecting their cases actually to be reached on any given day and go to the courthouse relatively unprepared, only to find they have to "wing it" when, miracle of miracles, their case is actually called for trial.

At any rate, regardless of the cause of inept trial work and regardless of whether Burger's estimate is high or low, there is certainly a consensus among knowledgeable observers that many American trial lawyers perform ineptly. Even on the defense side, many corporate officials complain that finding able trial lawyers is exceptionally difficult, and if that is true for institutional litigants, it's all the more true for individual claimants. But—as with jurors and judges—even with exemplary lawyers on both sides, a personal injury suit remains a lottery.

In her book *Injustice for All*, Anne Strick passionately condemns the adversary system. Trial-by-battle procedures distort the search for truth and degrade the hapless souls caught up in it, she argues. Lawyer-gladiators inevitably resort to deception, distortion, and manipulation. Legal procedures, whether civil or criminal, inhibit the discovery of what really happened, strangling all subtleties into a rigid choice of "liable or not liable," "guilty or innocent," "either/or." The resulting verdicts, she argues, are unfair, unequal, and long delayed. Harvard Professor James Q. Wilson summarizes her position: The "paradoxical, and unhappy, consequence of a preoccupation with [legal procedures] has been the proliferation of a legal system that, though designed to assert and protect [rights], has come increasingly to distort or mismanage them."[54]

But what is the alternative?

Basically, as one legal scholar has said, "in the intellectual history of mankind, the two principal methods developed for securing and testing data have been scientific research and the adversary trial."[55] The scientific method is largely experimental and inductive; that is, it builds by reasoning from a part to the whole, from the particular to the general, from the individual to the universal. It is often conducted in the laboratory, as it requires control over the variables. Scientific method entails, by definition, the neatness and precision of science. Legal reasoning, on the other hand, is largely deductive, rather than inductive. It reasons from the general to the particular, from the whole to the part, from the universal to the individual; it arrives at conclusions not so much by experimentation as by reasoning, inferring a conclusion from a given premise or rule. In the words of University of Florida law professor Leonard Powers:

> The subject matter of the law restricts the application of the scientific method. The settlement and avoidance of human disputes involve the working of the human mind, not so much in the present as in the past. The physician, by contrast, is dealing with present physical facts with which the instruments of modern science are highly useful. The law's method for making its factual determinations is pitiful by comparison. Further, law making involves value judgments as to human conduct, and the adjudication of human disputes involves the application of this law to factual determinations of past events, including the states of mind of the human beings who are parties to the dispute. Science has only limited utility as to either. This is not grist for its mill. . . .
>
> Law provides rules that are designed either to achieve tolerable solutions of human disputes or to channel human conduct so that human disputes are avoided. Obviously, since persons concerned professionally with the law must know about these rules, the natural approach of the practicing lawyer is likely to be deductive [to reason from those rules to the particular case or problem]. Both his mind and the law books in his library are full of these rules. Where did the rules come from? . . . They did not emanate from the laboratory. . . . Scientific principles are discovered in the laboratory, but the law is made. There can be good law and bad law because it is made by

men; by contrast, to speak of a scientific principle in terms of goodness and badness is to utter nonsense. If it exists, it proves itself. $E = mc^2$, and the highest court in the land cannot overrule it nor can the Congress of the United States repeal it, but the lawyer's rules can be changed. The same lawmakers who made them, or their successors can amend, modify, or repeal them. . . .

Not only does the difference in subject matter result in difference in method but legal method is in many ways the antithesis of the scientific approach. . . .

A practicing physician confronted with a sick patient may call in other physicians, but they do not enter the scene as adversaries. Medical men work together; adverseness is unknown. The physician is trained in the technique of objective inquiry rather than contentious disputation.[56]

The subject matter of the law, then, for the most part does not lend itself to the scientific method. Its subject matter is too sprawling, jumbled, and unmanageable for the calibrations of the laboratory. The use of the adversary method for legal inquiry is perhaps a reflection of the broader area where adversary processes have been brought to bear—with, on the whole, admirable results, namely, the question of *who will govern.* The British taught us that this penultimate question (we shall get to what many consider the ultimate question in a moment) could best be decided by a two-party system, a form of adversary method, if you will. The crudities and tumult of democratic electoral politics are often offensive to many, just as are those of the law, but Churchill's suggestion that we "consider the alternative" makes an unanswerable argument. (And of course, one of the reasons American lawyers so dominate the political process is their familiarity with the adversary process.)

Nor is it without significance that the other question of ultimate significance (at least for some) is turned over to the adversary method: *To whom will we pray?* When the Roman Catholic Church asks who is worthy of sainthood, who may especially invoke God's intervention, it appoints a Devil's Advocate to test the merits of the candidate—a classic use of the adversary method. Distasteful as the law's use of the adversary method may seem, with its relics and suggestions of ordeal and battle, it is by no means without ancient, distinguished, and workable intellectual traditions.

When Anne Strick urges the abandonment of the adversary system in her book, she uses, ironically enough, the bitterly partisan advocacy she so condemns in the adversary system. She proposes as alternatives to the adversary process various forms of dispute settlement by committees of laymen whose task it would be to seek compromise solutions that avoid litigation. Even if adjudication proved necessary, it should be handled by lay judges, assisted by professional jurists and lawyers whose function would be limited to that of neutral fact-seekers rather than adversaries, and who would be paid by the state. Remedies and penalties would be fashioned by "experts" to achieve therapeutic and compensatory ends.[57]

But, as James Q. Wilson points out in reviewing Ms. Strick's book, Americans are very unlikely to abandon the adversary system in either our legal or our political institutions. We Americans are a *very* contentious people with savage rivalries—ethnic, geographic, religious, traditional, economic, and political. To channel those rivalries and their attendant disputes into the *relative* civility of adversary discourse is not without merit. As Wilson puts it, "the adversary system pervades America, not because it is encased by legal traditions and rules, but because of the kind of society we are." Ms. Strick tells us that many societies are much less litigious than we, not only Japan or Korea, but Europe as well. Other countries have far fewer lawyers in proportion to the population than the United States; government and private decisions are appealed to the courts with much less frequency than here. Why? Because, says Wilson, the United States is an adversary culture. It was created, after all, by persons preoccupied with asserting their rights. Not only government but our fellow men were to be checked and limited, above all by a marmoreal law called the Constitution. This creation was followed by more than a century of massive immigration by people distrustful of government and suspicious of power, enduring terrible loneliness and hardships so as to be able to claim their rights and seek their own advantage. If we are now a more interdependent society, Professor Wilson says, than frontier or small-town America, most of us still tend to think in individualistic terms: "We do not accept the decisions of governments, of corporations, or of associations deferentially: We contest them vigorously, sometimes in the street. We have little confidence in 'experts' who might try to plan our lives, resolve our differences, or mastermind our improvement."

Institutional changes away from the adversary system, Wilson says, are unlikely to alter Americans' general disposition to assert their rights more aggressively than any other people in the world. Businesses are going to continue to challenge NLRB or EPA decisions. Taxpayers are going to continue to challenge tax collectors in this almost incredibly sophisticated commercial society where tax laws are unlikely to get much less complex. Labor unions, consumer advocates, neighborhoods, and even other governmental units are going to continue to challenge corporate or governmental decisions of interest to them. And where, Wilson wonders, "would the NAACP have turned in the South to desegregate schools or stop voter harassment if, instead of federal district courts, with all their adversary trappings, there had been neighborhood 'Adjudication Panels' made up of 'lay judges' drawn, as Ms. Strick so disarmingly puts it, from the 'defendant's cultural–linguistic peer groups?' " And where, one might also ask, would the rights of females be without government backing of assertive litigants? Nor is it surprising that the aged, juveniles, prisoners, those in mental institutions, the physically handicapped, and homosexuals are not far behind in aggressively and litigiously asserting their rights.

"The roots of American contentiousness," writes Wilson, "lie far deeper than any set of procedural arrangements and give rise to a set of benefits and burdens far more complex than can be rationalized by any single reform,"[58] such as lessening our reliance on the adversary system.

But Professor Wilson is quick to agree with Ms. Strick about the adverse effects of our warlike system of adversary resolution of disputes. It does entail awful burdens. And thus, if the battles and wars of adversarial resolution are our lot—and, as Wilson suggests, our glory—they must be reserved for those occasions when no alternatives are available. If there is one thing we Americans should have learned in recent years it is that wars undertaken for any but the most essential causes are disastrous. On a much lesser, but still devastating, scale, we have been resorting to warfare, and threats of warfare, as the key element in dealing with millions of claims from injury victims every year. Nothing is worse than unnecessary war. What are the alternatives, then, for accident claims?[59]

Part II
Bypassing the Lawyers

8

No-Fault Auto Insurance as a Solution

DICKIE KRAKOWSKI, SIX YEARS OLD, of Franklin Park, Illinois was seriously injured on July 12, 1972, when he ran into the road and was struck by a passing car. He suffered multiple fractures, internal injuries, and permanent brain damage. Rehabilitation and other medical costs have run to more than $100,000. Dickie's father's health insurance policy paid about 80 percent on most of the medical bills but nothing for rehabilitation expenses. A settlement of $20,000 was gained from the insurance company of the elderly woman who was driving the passing car. After the lawyer's fees and other legal expenses were subtracted, only about $11,000 was left. At last report, the family was $25,000 out of pocket, and its savings were depleted. Bills continued to mount up for speech lessons, physical therapy, and even special dental work, none of which was covered by the family's health insurance.

On October 13, 1973, thirteen days after Michigan's no-fault law went into effect, seventeen-year-old Dale Weber was paralyzed from the waist down when his motorcycle, on which he was apparently violating the speed limit, crashed head-on into an automobile, probably being driven over the center line of the road. As a result of the apparently dual wrongdoing, Dale would probably not have been paid anything from liability insurance if his accident had taken place in Illinois, which has no no-fault law, or if he had been injured two weeks earlier in Michigan, dependent as such payment is on a claimant's being free from fault.

In addition to Dale Weber's being paralyzed, three of his verte-
brae were crushed, his right arm was fractured, and he suffered internal injuries. After some time spent in three different hospitals, he
has been in a rehabilitation program for many months. Under Michigan's no-fault law, the Webers' auto insurance has covered all bills
not covered by the family's health insurance, including his wheel-
chair, crutches, leg braces, and shoes, and even for the labor of at-
taching braces to his shoes. It also paid for hand controls on the two
family cars and driving lessons to instruct Dale on their use, as well
as for rehabilitation therapy twice a week.

According to a *Chicago Tribune* task force studying auto insurance which commented on these two accidents, both families "had
automobile accidents involving severe bodily injuries. But that's
where all similarity ends. . . . [T]he Krakowskis face a never-ending
economic crisis. . . . The Webers have little to worry about financially.[1]

Despite the contrasting operation of no-fault versus fault-finding
auto insurance, passage of no-fault laws—enacted in various forms
in twenty-four states between 1970 and 1975—has been stalled,
largely through the massive opposition of trial lawyers all over the
country. No new no-fault law has been passed in any state since
1975, and an attempt to pass a Federal bill failed in the U.S. House
Commerce Committee in August, 1978, by a 22–19 vote.[2]

Some idea of the widespread political power of trial lawyers is
gained from the experience of a Democratic candidate for governor
in a large Northern industrial state in 1972. Convinced of the merits
of no-fault, he finally was dissuaded from backing it as a campaign
issue through fear of the effect on many of his key campaign workers. "In community after community," a key aide said, "we checked
and found that plaintiffs' lawyers were campaign or finance chairman, etc. They would not have tolerated a pro-no-fault stand. Our
organization might well have fallen apart." The problem is especially acute for ambitious Democrats. With many individual exceptions, able and prominent Democratic lawyers who can be helpful to
a politician at campaign time, especially in smaller cities, tend to represent either plaintiffs in personal injury cases or unions in labor law
matters. Sometimes the two interests overlap in that labor lawyers in
effect provide free or cut-rate legal services to unions in return for
the right to represent injured union members on a contingent fee.

Since 1975 the Association of Trial Lawyers of America (ATLA;
a group composed largely of plaintiffs' personal injury lawyers) has

raised and spent more than a million dollars, with about two-thirds of the funds going to Congressional candidates. Half of these contributions were made in 1978 alone. According to Lynn Sutcliffe, a Washington lawyer who supports no-fault, the ATLA contributions show "a clear pattern of trial lawyers' campaign spending which rewards those who oppose no-fault and punishes those who favor it." Fred Wertheimer, senior vice-president of Common Cause, the public interest lobbying group, remarks that "ATLA did not run a campaign fund, it ran an investment fund."[3] As just one of many examples, the ATLA fund contributed $5,000 to the opponent of Representative Bob Eckhardt (D—Tex.), chief sponsor of the Federal no-fault bill in the House, in a primary election. The ATLA fund was organized in 1975 after no-fault was passed in the U.S. Senate. In 1977 the 40,000-member association moved its headquarters from Boston to Washington, D.C., in order to fight Federal no-fault.[4]

With *many* lawyers throughout the United States having a substantial stake in the present personal injury system, the difficulty of achieving reform by legislation should cause no surprise. Trial lawyers exist in every community of any size. One insurance official explained: "They're affluent, active and articulate. . . . Also, in terms of relative zeal, they have something now that [no-fault reform] would take away, and that gives them a whole different mental set than the rest of us."[5]

Recently, several academic and other studies have rather exhaustively examined the operation of several of the earliest no-fault laws. Before looking at those studies some background information will be helpful.

Under the common law system, as pointed out earlier, after an accident between Smith and Jones, if Smith is an "innocent" party claiming against a "wrongdoer," he is paid not only for his economic loss but for the monetary value of his pain and suffering. But obviously, as we have seen, it is often very difficult to establish who was at fault in an accident, to say nothing of the pecuniary value of pain.[6] Under the no-fault solution, after an accident between Smith and Jones, each is paid, regardless of anyone's fault, by his own insurance company, month by month as his losses accrue, and only for economic losses. As a corollary, each also is required to surrender his claim based on fault against the other.[7] Thus the solution for the ills of auto insurance is seen as relatively simple: Structure the insurance so that it pays (1) for losses regardless of who was at fault, and (2) only for economic losses (essentially medical expenses and wage loss), which are readily reducible to dollars and cents, and not for pain and suffering, which are not. In one simple stroke, then, the two questions that plague auto insurance are eliminated, with payment for additional claims financed by the savings from simplifying the insured event by not having to pay either (1) for determination of fault and the pecuniary value of pain and suffering or (2) for pain and suffering itself. No-fault was designed to make the following improvements in auto accident compensation:

First, it was designed to assure that everyone injured in auto accidents is eligible for auto insurance payment, regardless of his ability to prove fault-based claims. Recall that, according to a massive study by the United States Department of Transportation (DOT), about 55 percent of those seriously injured get absolutely nothing from automobile liability insurance.[8]

Second, it was designed to spend less on smaller, relatively trivial claims and more on serious injury. According to Professor Alfred Conard of the University of Michigan, who conducted an extensive Michigan study, "If there is one thing which [all] the surveys have shown conclusively, it is that the [fault-based] system overpays the small claimants who need it least and underpays the large claimants who need it most."[9]

Third, no-fault was designed to pay claims promptly. According to the DOT study, on the average a period of sixteen months elapses between an accident and any payment based on fault-finding. The larger the loss, the longer the delay. For losses over $2,500, the average delay rose to nineteen months.[10]

Fourth, no-fault was designed to pay more efficiently by using less of the premium dollar on insurance overhead and legal fees. No-fault insurance has been called "no-lawyer insurance" by one consumer advocate.[11] Prior to no-fault in Massachusetts, approximately 80 percent of successful claimants under liability insurance there were represented by attorneys.[12] As a corollary, no-fault was designed to reduce the amount of litigation stemming from auto accidents. Without no-fault laws, typically 50 to 80 percent of civil jury dockets are taken up with auto cases.[13]

Fifth, no-fault insurance was designed to reduce, or at least to stabilize, the costs of auto insurance. Prior to no-fault, the number one complaint about auto insurance was its high cost. It was one of the fastest rising items on the consumer price index.[14]

In response to all these problems, beginning in the mid-1960s, vigorous attempts were begun to initiate no-fault insurance reform.

In fact, studies had been urging such reform since the early 1930s but had been confined mostly to academic journals and were consequently ignored. In 1970 Massachusetts enacted the first no-fault law, followed since by twenty-three other states. The laws come in a bewildering variety—a fact that adds to the pressure for a uniform Federal law—but basically they fall into three categories, with some overlap.

In the first category are *modified no-fault laws*, which provide only modest no-fault benefits and eliminate only relatively few fault-finding claims.[15] States with modified plans are Colorado, Connecticut, Florida, Georgia, Hawaii, Kansas, Kentucky, Massachusetts, Minnesota, New Jersey, New York, North Dakota, Pennsylvania, and Utah.

The second category includes *add-on plans*, which, arguably, are not no-fault plans at all. Although they call for benefits, usually modest ones, to be paid to traffic victims without regard to anyone's fault, they do not eliminate any victim's right to press a fault-finding claim for his pain and suffering against other drivers. Hence the name *add-on*: The laws add on benefits but do not take anything away. States with add-on plans are Arkansas, Delaware, Maryland, Oregon, South Carolina, South Dakota, Texas, and Virginia.

In the third category are *plans approaching pure no-fault*. A pure no-fault plan would eliminate all, or almost all, claims based on fault and substitute relatively unlimited benefits for all medical expenses and wages lost, no matter how extensive. No law goes that far, but Michigan's comes closest. It covers unlimited medical expenses and a maximum of about $53,000 of wage loss, while eliminating fault-based claims unless the victim suffers death, serious disfigurement, or serious impairment of bodily function. Minnesota's law and New York's, as amended, also approach pure no-fault. The Federal no-fault bill too approaches pure no-fault in both benefits and elimination of fault-based claims.[16]

As noted, the drive for no-fault reform has been stalled in the various states, largely over the question of whether laws should be of the add-on variety or otherwise. The trial bar has vigorously asserted, at both state and Federal levels, that no-fault benefits can be paid without eliminating anyone's fault-finding claims for pain and suffering. No-fault backers, on the other hand, oppose add-on laws as a mockery of reform, often labeling them "yes-fault" laws. Trial lawyers reply that under add-on plans auto insurance rates are not only not increased, but reduced. But it is difficult to see how no-fault claims can be added on without eliminating fault-finding claims, and still reduce costs. After all, no one eligible to be paid under fault-finding claims loses anything, and new claimants are added to the rolls. Trial lawyers answer that many fault-based claims are *voluntarily* abandoned, since people who recover their economic losses promptly from their own insurance companies don't bother to press a fault-finding claim against the other driver. Leonard Ring, a former Association of Trial Lawyers of America president, notes that the Delaware add-on experience "has indeed proven that, where the victim has received his medical and wage loss, the incentive to make further claim is extinguished in all but the most serious cases."[17]

Proponents of the purer forms of no-fault that formally ban some fault-based claims argue that statistics for Delaware demonstrate that fault-finding claims are not reduced by add-on plans. (See below, p. 172.) Moreover, even if fewer people than expected bring fault-finding claims when provided with no-fault benefits, despite their right to do so, that situation cannot be expected to persist in the face of the aggressive personal-injury bar and the money that can be made by pressing fault-based claims. Why, such proponents ask, pass a reform that leaves intact the claims that led to the need for reform in the first place, counting on human nature to forgo taking advantage of the right to press claims?[18]

Let us turn to the several extensive statistical studies appraising the operation of no-fault laws to see how the various forms of no-fault have fared in practice.

The principal controversy over no-fault has been whether insurance premiums go up or down upon its enactment. Early actuarial studies seemed to indicate that insurance premiums would be cut. Based on these studies, many states, including Massachusetts, Florida, and New York, mandated a 15 percent cut in auto insurance rates supposedly affected by no-fault. This was a crude gauge when one considers that the same size cuts were required in states where benefit levels and other provisions in the statutes differed widely.

Perhaps nothing is more confusing to the layman than "actuarial science," and actuarial opinions on whether no-fault does in fact increase or decrease costs have fluctuated wildly.[19] In 1976, for example, the New York State Insurance Department announced that the cost of auto insurance had more than doubled during 1975 for many state residents, with some department officials and insurance executives citing abuses in the state's no-fault system as an important factor.[20]

In reply to such findings, proponents of no-fault insurance argue that the "abuses" of the no-fault insurance system are attributable not to any defect in the no-fault principle but to inadequate provisions inserted in no-fault laws largely at the urging of trial lawyers and those insurance companies opposed to true no-fault insurance. In New York, for example, although $50,000 in no-fault benefits are mandated for auto accident victims, prior to December 1, 1977, fault-finding claims could be pressed if medical bills exceeded only $500. Compared to Massachusetts, then, New York provided $50,000 in benefits, instead of $2,000 as in Massachusetts, but kept the same threshold for fault-based claims while mandating the same 15 percent rate decrease! Thus relatively few claims based on fault were eliminated, and insurance companies in far too many instances had to be ready to respond to both no-fault and fault-based claims. Moreover, doctors and lawyers, working together in many cases, arranged to manipulate the no-fault benefits for medical bills to make sure that such bills exceeded the $500 threshold figure. According to one insurance spokesman, "People are learning that all they have to do is have another X-ray or spend another night in the hospital" in order to pass the threshold and file a fault-based claim. Thomas C. Morrill, a vice-president of State Farm Mutual Automobile Insurance Company, the nation's largest, charged that in Florida, where until October 1, 1976, medical bills over $1,000 permitted a fault-based claim, many claims had been built illegitimately to a level that exceeded the threshold established by the law. Once that level was passed, Morrill said, claimants were "free to go for that alluring pot of litigious gold, which our customers [kept] filling for them."[21] In New York, too, according to James March, a former director of research for the state legislature's Select Committee on Insurance, the low threshold acted as "an incentive for doctors to work in cahoots with patients to get their medical fees over that $500 level."[22] In addition, Senator Frank E. Moss (D—Utah), a sponsor of the Federal no-fault bill, charged that New York State trial lawyers attempted to circumvent the no-fault law by circulating a letter that encouraged accident victims to seek larger medical expenses. Furthermore, Senator Moss charged, the lawyers' letter offered an incentive to doctors to go along with such higher charges by offering to collect them from insurance companies without charge to the doctors.[23]

Investigations by the Florida Insurance Department and the Florida Legislature, as well as criminal prosecutions of errant doctors and lawyers, caused Florida to scrap its $1,000 medical bill threshold and phrase the barrier to fault-based claims in less manipulable terms, requiring permanent injury before a fault-based claim can be brought. Another amendment also makes any physician, attorney, insurance adjuster, insurance company, or claimant conspiring to commit claim fraud guilty of a third-degree felony. A hospital administrator or employee who permits the use of hospital facilities by an insured for the purpose of committing claim fraud is likewise guilty of a third-degree felony.[24] The New York State Legislature passed a revised no-fault law, effective December 1, 1977, which substituted a more stringent prerequisite of a "significant limitation of a body function or system" for the previous $500 medical cost threshold. The new law, by adopting the state Workers' Compensation treatment cost schedule, also puts a ceiling on the costs that doctors and hospitals may charge auto accident victims.[25]

In addition to some adverse claims experience under inadequate no-fault laws, the *Wall Street Journal* stated, "no-fault has impaired the financial strength of some insurance firms in another way." It quoted a New York State Insurance Department spokesman as stating that under the old fault-finding system, "a company had a claim reserved for it, went to court, argued and maybe one day had to pay. But in the meantime, that money was earning income. Now, under no-fault, a company has to pay from day one, meaning its investment income is considerably reduced."[26] Surely, though, this is a curious complaint against no-fault. Traffic victims, if not investors, will welcome prompt payment of claims. After all, are insurance companies supposed to be primarily in the business of investing money or paying for accident losses? If readers of the *Wall Street Journal* are confused on this point, the general public should not be.

In addition, there is considerable indication that any price rise in auto insurance has come about not through difficulties under inadequate no-fault laws but from rapidly rising prices, a factor applicable to all auto insurance, fault-based and no-fault alike. Price rises for medical services and auto parts have been especially rapid.[27] According to the Council on Wage and Price Stability, a price index maintained by State Farm showed that in a recent representative year auto crash-part prices increased by 31.7 percent compared to an increase in the wholesale price index for new cars of 12.9 percent during the same year. Crash parts include such items as fenders, hoods, trunk lids, doors, and bumpers.[28] Such disparity in price increases probably reflects the captive market for the seller of replacement parts. Initially when you buy a car, you can choose a Chevrolet, a Ford, or a Plymouth. But once you've bought say, a Chevrolet, you can probably purchase crash parts (the ones most likely to be damaged in a collision) only from GM.[29]

A 1977 U.S. Department of Transportation study points out that only a relatively small part of the average motorist's insurance coverage applies to personal injury. The remaining coverages (such as collision, physical damage, comprehensive, and towing) are not affected by the switch from a fault to a no-fault system. For a typical insurance package covering both personal injury and property damage, the total insurance premium covering personal injury is only about 25 percent.[30] From the perspective of a motorist with this coverage, an increase in the total insurance premium has great psychological and fiscal impact; the relatively minor portion of the premium attributable to personal injury protection, which may have decreased, is almost invisible. A report to the New Jersey Legislature indicates that although premiums generally have increased, the average cost for personal injury coverage actually decreased by 5.5 percent, from $74.29 in 1972 to $70.18 in 1977.[31] A recent study published in the *Rutgers Law Review* evaluates cost–benefit performance of the various types of no-fault laws by measuring the extent to which the laws keep personal injury premiums, as distinguished from property damage premiums, "at or below the level they would have reached had no-fault not been enacted."[32] During the five-year period between 1972 and 1977, total personal injury premiums covering fault-based liability and all supplemental coverages increased 22 percent in fault states; in add-on states such premiums (including no-fault coverages) increased 49.5 percent; in modified no-fault states with low no-fault benefits they increased 18 percent; and in modified no-fault states with high benefits they increased 13 percent.[33]

In Michigan, designated "pure" no-fault, the study found an 11 percent decrease in total personal injury premiums, for both no-fault and fault-finding claims. The Michigan data also showed a 53 percent decrease in premiums covering fault-finding claims for personal injury and an 87 percent decrease in the number of fault-finding claims for personal injury:

> Together, reductions in premiums and [fault-finding] claims are powerful evidence of the efficacy of Michigan's . . . threshold [barring fault-finding claims]. Furthermore, the fact that . . . premium decreases [for fault-finding claims] have more than offset the added cost of [no-fault benefits] suggests that the cost tradeoff envisioned

by no-fault proponents is not only a viable concept, but can be implemented effectively for even the most generous [no-fault benefit] packages.[34]

But, as several of the recent studies have pointed out, simple premium aggregates are only one rather crude way of measuring costs. An arguably better measure is the *value* of the insurance purchased. The improved value per insurance dollar under no-fault is most graphically illustrated by the Michigan experience. Coverage under Michigan's no-fault law pays unlimited medical expenses plus more than $53,000 in wage losses, in addition to coverage of $20,000 for those fault-based claims against a motorist that are preserved under the law. All this insurance is provided at a cost no greater, and apparently less, than the costs, prior to no-fault, of only $20,000 of traditional liability insurance based on fault, under which few seriously injured victims were paid much, if at all. The Michigan Bureau of Insurance estimates that the proportion of premium dollars paid out as benefits has increased by 58 percent under no-fault.[35]

Consider, too, the situation in New Jersey, where no-fault benefits are provided in unlimited amounts for medical costs but only up to $100 a week for a year, or a maximum of $5,200, for wage loss. In addition, fault-finding claims are preserved for anyone whose medical expenses exceed only $100. And yet the annual costs in 1977 of all those no-fault benefits for the average car owner, as reported by a New Jersey Legislative Study Commission, was $40.92, as against $70.18 for $15,000 of coverage for fault-based claims that is preserved under the new law.[36] In other words, fault-finding coverage—with low benefits and many impediments to payments—costs almost twice as much as the huge coverage readily payable under no-fault. One can see how easy it would be further to limit fault-finding claims and to use the money saved to increase no-fault wage loss coverage substantially.

One must also translate these figures into palpable human dimensions. The importance to the tragically injured traffic victim and his family of relatively unlimited medical and other benefits, including comprehensive rehabilitation, has already been indicated by the contrasting experiences of the Krakowski and Weber families (p. 157).

Money magazine has uncovered similar contrasting experiences under no-fault and fault-finding systems:

One day last year, Raymond Wiegers, a Westwood, N.J., equipment salesman, returned home from a business trip to the kind of news every parent dreads. His 17-year-old son Ray Jr. had smashed up the family Buick, injuring himself and three others. In the rainy dusk, the car had skidded around a curve, then flipped over. Ray Jr. had a concussion; two of the others were much more seriously injured. Surveying the episode from the perspective of a year, Wiegers observes: "Everyone's suing everyone else, of course. But in the meantime, thank God all the medical bills have been paid."

Wiegers' thanks should also go to no-fault car insurance, which New Jersey made compulsory in 1973. . . .

To get a victim's-eye view of how no-fault is working, *Money* recently contacted a dozen people hurt seriously last year in crashes in New Jersey and, for comparison, another dozen in Ohio, a state still using the [fault-based] liability insurance system. Most of the New Jersey people had long since been reimbursed for their medical bills, but many of the Ohioans were still embroiled with insurers. "In our experience, this system really works," says Irene Moxley of Ridgewood, N.J. Her son Bruce, 23, lost control of his car in August 1975 and wrapped it around a tree, fracturing several bones. "We're thankful it wasn't worse, of course," Mrs. Moxley says. "But at that, Bruce's medical bills came to $5,400, and the insurance company paid promptly and fairly."

One night two months after Bruce Moxley lost his battle with the tree, Judy Nelson, 16, of Atwater, Ohio, near Akron, was reaching the crest of a hill when she saw horses in the road ahead. She hit one and then another. The crash killed both horses and put Miss Nelson in the hospital for two months. Her bills so far add up to about $12,000, and it looks as though the only hope of getting any of it back is to sue the stable.

A 20-year-old Akron woman would seem to have a simpler case. A few days before last Christmas, another car hit hers and slammed it into the side of a building. Her medical and hospital bills so far total $10,000. But although the other driver was arrested on charges of reckless driving and running a red light, his insurer as of the next October had paid her nothing.[37]

Similarly, the New Jersey Legislative Study Commission examining the state's experience with no-fault commented that unlimited medical benefits under New Jersey's no-fault law

. . . have resulted in insurers paying for an extraordinary range of services in certain catastrophic cases. Some examples may be cited to illustrate the benefits which some New Jersey residents have received as a result of this unlimited coverage. In one case a young man became a quadraplegic as a result of an automobile accident.

As he had no one to care for him, he would normally have been placed in a nursing home, where the kind of care he needed would have been available. The insurer, however, contacted his parents, who lived in England, and they agreed to come to the United States to care for him. The insurer brought them from England, placed a $10,000 down payment on a mobile home for them, and found the father a job. The insurer continued to pay the medical bills for the young man, who has received better and less costly care than if he had been placed in a nursing home or extended care facility.

In another case, a young New Jersey woman attending college in New Mexico was struck by a hit and run automobile. She sustained severe brain damage and partial paralysis, and was sent to a hospital, but the insurer did not feel she was receiving adequate rehabilitative care. The insurer flew her to New Jersey in a specially equipped hospital plane at a cost of $5,000. Her parents wanted her to be cared for at home, but their home, a small Cape Cod–style house, had no bedrooms on the first floor. Consequently, the insurance company built a $15,000 addition, consisting of a bedroom and a bathroom. At the time of the initial injury, the doctors' prognosis was that she would never walk. As a result of both the care she is receiving at home and proper rehabilitative therapy, she is now able to walk to a limited degree.

Aside from the humanitarian aspects involved in providing appropriate rehabilitative care for severely injuryed patients, there are practical reasons as well for encouraging the use of rehabilitation therapy. It is estimated that $60,000 in future medical and nursing home costs are saved for every rehabilitated spinal cord injury case. Such spinal cord injuries, of course, are common to automobile accident victims. Therefore, the extraordinary expenses paid for by the insurers in the examples cited above can be ultimately cost-effective.[38]

A study of "catastrophic" medical claims in Michigan (defined as injuries resulting in medical expenses over $25,000) by the National Association of Independent Insurers, an insurance trade organization of companies generally opposed to no-fault, poignantly illustrates the large amounts available under no-fault to pay for tragic losses most often unpaid under the old fault-finding system. Bear in mind that a U.S. Department of Transportation study showed that those who suffer more than $25,000 of economic losses from auto accidents suffer on the average total losses of $76,341 but receive from fault-finding claims an average of $3,742, or 5 percent of their losses.[39] By way of contrast, between October 1, 1973 (when no-fault went into effect in Michigan), and December 31, 1975, of

260 representative claims for catastrophic medical expenses, 82 (or 32 percent) were for single-car accidents. These, then, were cases where, in all likelihood, no fault-based payment would have been made because, by definition, there was no "other" car or driver to sue. And yet for 82 claimants, almost $9 million had been "reserved" under no-fault insurance (that is, specifically earmarked for payment) for such claims, amounting to an average of about $108,000 per claim.[40] According to the same study, 40 catastrophically injured victims (or 15 percent) were motorcyclists, for whom about $2.5 million was reserved. In view of the typical age and driving habits of motorcyclists, probably few would have been eligible for fault-based payment. In this connection, the NAII data were further broken down by type of injury and average age of accident victims.[41] The Michigan Insurance Department study concludes: "The seriousness of the injuries and the relative young age of the accident victims (32) vividly illustrates the need which is being met by no-fault."[42]

Professor Robert Keeton of Harvard Law School, in testimony before Congress, compared the costs under an early Federal no-fault bill, which provided unlimited medical benefits and wage-loss protection up to a minimum of $15,000, while eliminating fault-based claims unless total disability exceeds ninety days, with the cost for fault-based coverage. Keeton noted that the actuarial estimates submitted to Congress from the three major segments of the insurance industry, which disagree sharply about the desirability of no-fault, ranged from modest savings to modest increases in moving to such no-fault plans from the fault system. Effective no-fault laws, including the one "before this committee now," Keeton testified,

> . . . would not increase the total amount of premiums that the public are putting into automobile insurance. Indeed, it is my own estimate that [they] would decrease it somewhat. But I accept, for the [sake of discussion] the data we are getting from the [insurance] industry studies that show that the total cost would remain at about the same level. But what would we get for our money? What would be the comparison?
>
> Instead of . . . coverage that pays several times the loss in minor injury claims and does not give us guaranteed protection above $10,000 or some such figure as that, with [a] good no-fault law we would get life-time protection for medical expense [stemming from an automobile accident], at least $15,000 of wage protection, something of that order for protection in death benefits, all of that plus

liability protection [for the fault-based claims that are preserved under the Federal no-fault law]. We would get all that for about the same price that we are now paying for this other [fault-based] package.[43]

Keeton's comments raise another goal of no-fault insurance, namely, spending less on small, rather trivial claims and, conversely, more on serious injuries. Professor Joseph Little of the University of Florida Law School found in a study of Florida's no-fault experience that a "shift to greater payments for more serious injuries is clearly seen" under no-fault compared to fault-based payment.[44] The percentage of total personal injury payments to more seriously injured victims almost doubled after two years' experience under no-fault.

A 1978 Michigan Insurance Bureau study similarly found more compensation for genuine losses and for serious victims under no-fault. Under the fault system, it will be recalled, payments for pain and suffering are most often made to the less seriously injured, often really as "bribes" to get rid of the "nuisance" value of smaller claims.[45] But under Michigan's no-fault laws much more of the insurance dollar is being paid for genuine dollar losses of income loss and medical expense, and, because no-fault law eliminates smaller fault-based claims, what is paid for pain and suffering goes to more seriously injured victims (who do, after all, suffer the most pain from accidents).

For the two years prior to no-fault, about 45 percent of payments to victims were for economic loss, and 55 percent were for noneconomic loss. By contrast, for the three years in which no-fault has been operating, 63 percent of payments went to compensate for economic loss, as opposed to 37 percent for noneconomic loss. "This represents an increase of up to 20% in the proportion of loss dollars going to pay for actual economic loss of accident victims rather than for pain and suffering," with more equitable payment even for pain and suffering since, as stated above, only the most seriously injured victims receive payment for pain and suffering under no-fault.[46]

As to the aim of prompt payment under no-fault, a Massachusetts survey by Professor Alan Widiss of the University of Iowa Law School discloses some striking figures regarding timeliness of payment under no-fault as opposed to fault. The figures indicate that the time lapse between receipt by the insurance company of documentation "sufficient for payment of medical expenses" and the first no-fault medical payment received by the victim was between four and seven days in more than 50 percent of the cases; 80 percent received the first payment within a month, and 97.9 percent within 180 days.[47] The time lapse between the date of *accident* and the date of receipt of the first no-fault payment was necessarily longer, being dependent upon the filing of claims and supporting documents by claimants. Even here, 63.3 percent of the claimants received the first no-fault payment within ninety days and 84.8 percent within 180 days.[48] Under the fault system, according to the U.S. Department of Transportation, only 40.5 percent of claims were settled and paid within ninety days of the accident, and only 57.6 percent within 180 days.[49] Reports to the Department of Transportation from the insurance departments of Colorado, Connecticut, Michigan, and New Jersey show comparable statistics, with Michigan's Insurance Bureau reporting that "almost all auto accident claims are settled within 30 days."[50]

As for no-fault's aim of more efficiency by using less of the premium dollar on legal fees and insurance overhead, the Massachusetts study by Professor Widiss suggests a radical reduction in the need for lawyers under no-fault claims. In contrast to the use of attorneys in about 80 percent of the cases prior to the institution of no-fault, attorneys were used for no-fault claims in substantially fewer than 15 percent of the cases. (See above, p. 160.) According to Widiss, "No-fault insurance claims are usually paid without disputes over either the existence of coverage or the amount due the claimant."[51] He states: "A majority of the claimants and defense attorneys surveyed felt that the average [no-fault] claimant did not require legal assistance because the forms were not complicated. Typical of this group was the response of one attorney who observed: 'It's just like Blue Cross or any health or accident claim.' "[52] In Florida, too, overall lawyer involvement per claim diminished.[53] On the other hand, Widiss reports:

> A significant number of claimants' attorneys counseled, as one lawyer put it, that "you always need an attorney when an insurance company is involved." However, this attorney, as well as several others, also pointed out that, even if the attorney is able to do a better job of presenting the client's claim, the amount involved in a [no-fault] claim is usually not sufficient to justify hiring a lawyer. Many lawyers felt this was true even though they also felt that some insurance companies were unjustifiably disputing medical bills, es-

pecially those for hospitalization and X-rays. One attorney, who suggested that some claims departments were paying only a percentage of the amounts claimed, summarized the situation by observing that because "claimants don't stand to gain enough from suing the insurer to make it worthwhile, they are at the mercy of the insurer, and the insurer takes advantage."[54]

Of course, the dilemma of the consumer whose complaint concerns an amount too small to sue for is not confined to insurance companies. One can argue that the dilemma under no-fault is vastly better than the dilemma under fault-finding claims, where insurers often pay little or nothing when the claimant's losses are *heavy*. Far better to have a situation where the claimant is paid so much of his loss—and conversely not paid so little—that the remainder is not really worth bothering about.[55]

As to reduced litigation under no-fault, another Massachusetts study found that the filing of personal injury cases in Massachusetts courts was "precipitously lowered in the wake of no-fault,"[56] including a remarkable reduction of from 42 to 66 percent in courts of unlimited jurisdiction, and an astonishing decline of about 90 percent in courts limited to claims of less than $2,000. The reduction of litigation in Michigan was also significant.[57]

On the other hand, under Delaware's add-on plan, according to a study there, "tort litigation is continuing substantially unabated by the no-fault legislation." Concludes Professor Roger Clark of Rutgers-Camden Law School, who conducted the Delaware study, "It is now clear that, whatever beneficial effects it has had, the Delaware legislation has not discouraged any significant number of potential tort plaintiffs from suing."[58]

In this connection, Professor Widiss reports:

Although the reduction in the retention of attorneys had no overwhelming effects on a majority of the lawyers in Massachusetts, no-fault insurance has had a marked economic impact on the trial bar and on at least a portion of the lawyers in general practice. Many of the attorneys whose practices were substantially affected appear to have offset the economic effects by increasingly engaging in other fields of practice [including real estate, probate, commercial, corporate, tax, and other civil or criminal litigation].[59]

On the other hand, is it true that lawyers deprived of auto suits have caused the recent rise in the number of malpractice or product liability claims? Maybe not. In the first place, the relatively marginal practitioner is apparently the one most affected by no-fault.[60] Whereas many such lawyers are able to handle a simple auto intersection accident,[61] they would be quite out of their depth with the technical, arcane matters involved in medical malpractice or product liability suits. Second, the rise in malpractice and product suits seems at least as great in states such as California, Illinois, and Texas, which do not have auto no-fault, as in no-fault states. And yet it may be that in all states—fault and no-fault alike—personal injury lawyers who were accustomed to the easy fare of auto claims have begun to pursue other types of personal injury cases out of a fear that many auto cases would *eventually* dry up under no-fault laws either already in effect or in the offing.

Over all, Professor Widiss found tremendous satisfaction in Massachusetts with the operation of no-fault as applied to personal injury:

> Seventy-five to 85 percent [of those who had claimed and received no-fault benefits] indicated that they were either "fairly satisfied" or "very satisfied" with the manner in which their claims had been handled and with the amount they had received. . . .
>
> [I]t seems unlikely that many comparable systems exist in which the percentage of "fairly satisfied" and "very satisfied" consumers exceeds 80 percent.[62]

Seventeen to nineteen months after the accidents, insurers had denied liability on only 1.5 percent of the claims, and claims pending or otherwise not paid amounted to some 25 percent of the cases.[63] The 1978 Michigan Insurance Bureau Report contains the results of Michigan public opinion surveys regarding public attitudes to various individual aspects of no-fault and regarding no-fault in general. The results show that the public favors by a 62-to-23 percent margin the idea of providing full medical and rehabilitation benefits to all accident victims. The public also favors, by a vote of 79 percent to 10 percent, the concept of curtailing rights to compensation for pain and suffering in order to provide more adequate medical and wage-loss benefits. Furthermore, by a vote of 53 percent to 18 percent the respondents said they would relinquish their own rights to damages for pain and suffering in exchange for prompt and complete payment of medical bills and lost wages. Finally, a vote of 65 percent to 26 percent favored coordination of no-fault benefits with other insurance benefits in order to prevent double payments for the same economic loss.[64] The report concludes that the "responses . . . show that people do not support the tort system as an effective means of providing accident reparations and that no-fault is clearly preferred."[65]

It is thus surprising to discover that, in response to questions regarding attitudes to no-fault in general, only 17 percent of those polled said that Michigan no-fault is a "good system." Those who said it was a "poor system" comprised 55 percent of those polled.[66] The report states, however, that when these responses were analyzed, it became clear that almost two-thirds of those giving a "poor" rating identified the reasons for that rating as problems that plague the entire automobile insurance system and are not directly related to the no-fault systems as such.[67] An additional 38 percent said that the basis of their dissatisfaction lay in problems related to car damage, not to the aspects of the law pertaining to injury to persons.[68] When the Insurance Bureau evaluated consumer needs in conjunction with the actual performance of Michigan's no-fault law, the stated result was that Michigan's no-fault is successful in "meeting the real needs of the people."[69]

In only three states has no-fault insurance ever been extended to car damage. In Florida the State Supreme Court ruled such an extension unconstitutional; in Massachusetts the no-fault property damage law has been repealed; and in Michigan the Supreme Court in 1978 upheld the constitutionality of no-fault property damage.[70]

Admittedly, as Professor Keeton testified before Congress, the "possibilities for improvement of the [auto insurance] system [applied to car damage] are very modest in comparison with the dramatic improvements effected by a real no-fault system for injuries to people."[71] This is largely because the savings from eliminating payment for pain and suffering and lawyers' fees are not applicable, because cars don't suffer pain, and car-damage cases are often arbitrated inexpensively and expeditiously between insurance companies, without the intervention of lawyers. But savings are still possible under no-fault car-damage coverage, compared to fault-based systems. Note that in the typical two-car accident, four insurance coverages are applicable to the potential damage to the two cars: each driver has insurance covering his liability to the other based on fault, and each driver normally carries collision insurance, a supplementary no-fault coverage applicable to the driver's own car, widely sold even prior to no-fault. Any car bought on time must have collision insurance by order of the lender. Insurance companies, understandably, like a system that calls for four coverages on two losses. But the public should not. By the application of no-fault, each car can be covered at the owner's option by collision-like no-fault coverage, with all fault-based claims abolished. This results in a sensible maximum of two coverages applicable to the two losses.

In fact, however, as the experience in Michigan suggests, most of the public dissatisfaction with no-fault insurance has stemmed from its application to property damage. Why? Well, when someone plows into your car, causing $250 worth of damage, and you either haven't bothered to insure your own car or have insured it with a $100 deductible, you are inclined to become outraged at your own uncompensated losses. People may not be so outraged at suffering the same kind of deductible loss in an accident-caused injury to their person. This may be because they are thankful to have escaped with their lives and/or because they are thankful to be assured payment of all their medical expenses or lost wages. In addition, in states that have applied no-fault to property damage as well as in those that have not, the precipitous rise in auto repair costs has served to cancel out any savings produced by no-fault insurance applicable to injuries to persons.[72]

Even so, Professor Little's Florida no-fault insurance study demonstrates that the application of no-fault to property damage, prior to its being held unconstitutional there, resulted in net advantages to the consumer, albeit less dramatic than those stemming from no-fault for injuries to persons. Little found that, measured by the benefits-to-premium ratio, consumers were getting more for their dollar under property no-fault by a factor of about 10 percent.[73]

Granting all that, the application of no-fault to car damage is still of much less moment that its application to personal injuries, especially because of the likelihood in personal injury cases of much more tragic personal and social losses.

In summary, the U.S. Department of Transportation has concluded:

> State experience with no-fault automobile insurance would appear to confirm the basic soundness of the theory and feasibility of the theory's implementation. No-fault plans of sharply varying objectives and character are widely seen as successes. No problem has arisen in the implementation of no-fault for which there does not appear to be a readily available and feasible solution, given the political will to make the necessary change. No-fault insurance works.[74]

9

What to Do Next?

EVEN IF STATE OR FEDERAL no-fault auto laws were to become effective in all states in the foreseeable future, they will still apply to only some auto accident victims, leaving uncompensated many of the most seriously injured. The latest Federal no-fault auto bill (which did not pass), while relatively generous compared to most states' laws, would still not compensate for medical loss above $100,000 or wage loss above $12,000. Worse still, auto no-fault laws will, by definition, do absolutely nothing for all the victims of nonauto accidents, including those now covered (or, more accurately, *not* covered) by fault-finding liability rules for medical malpractice, defective products, slips and falls, and so forth.

For those who suffer losses in nonautomobile accidents, the prospect for securing adequate compensation is even worse, whether the losses are large or small. Product liability and medical malpractice probably account for the largest losses and the largest number of seriously injured victims outside of automobile accidents. Yet product liability litigation consumes lawyers' time and insurance dollars with even greater profligacy than automobile claims, and with even more dismal results. Most lawyers probably feel competent to handle automobile claims, but in the words of the National Commission on Product Safety, "in the best of circumstances, a products case is still a bruising, frequently heartbreaking, always onerous undertaking for client and lawyer."[1] The issues in a product liability case are far more technical and demanding than those in a typical auto

176

case. Trying to establish whether a driver was going too fast, traveling in the wrong lane, or failing to keep a proper lookout is, if difficult and tedious, still within the ken of almost any adult, particularly a lawyer. But in order to impose liability on a manufacturer for injury caused by a product, an attorney must prove that the product is in some way defective. And proving a product defective almost always involves engineering evidence and testimony of the most technical and arcane kind. In preparation for the trial of a product liability case, an attorney must spend, in the words of one legal text, "hours, if not days or weeks, with his expert [witness] learning about the technology and the minutiae of the product" in question.[2] And while lawyers and engineers are huddling and conferring and appearing in court, a very expensive meter is ticking. An engineer or chemist who studies one side of a case and then testifies will charge anywhere from $1,000 to $3,000 or perhaps higher.[3] The problem is compounded by the inability of engineers and lawyers to understand each other. Most engineers don't understand much law—indeed many of them don't understand much English. On the other hand, most lawyers are verbally, not mechanically, inclined. One can spend the better part of an afternoon explaining to a typical lawyer some complicated engineering item, like a Phillips screwdriver.[4]

The decision to invest all the time and money required by a product liability suit is not lightly undertaken. Manufacturers defend product liability cases with a passion, and they often win. An obstacle facing a victim injured by a manufactured product, one with which a traffic victim rarely has to contend, is the deep umbrage the typical manufacturer takes at a product liability claim. After all, his product is accused of being "defective." Quite apart from the adverse publicity involved, this challenge deeply offends the pride of most manufacturers and denigrates the great effort they believe they expend on such things as careful design and quality control. Thus the manufacturer will commonly defend itself by throwing up an almost endless variety of technical and legal contentions, which can be overcome only after exhaustive trials and appeals.

Rarely can the plaintiff or his lawyer match the resources marshaled by the defending manufacturer. The National Commission on Product Safety describes the predicament of the consumer and his counsel:

> The manufacturer employs a battery of attorneys and technical experts with ample resources at their disposal. The consumer must prove that it was the manufacturer's product, that it did cause the

injury, that the defect existed at the factory, that the suit lies within
the statute of limitations, that the infrequency of the injury does not
absolve the manufacturer from liability and so on.

Meanwhile the defense can muster volumes of evidence against
each statement by the consumer. The defense can also stall: it can
appeal to the next highest court. While the consumer waits and
pays, the defense, if it expects to lose, can offer a modest settlement.[5]

These snags can all lead to prolonged disputes, with that horrendously expensive meter ticking away for both sides as highly paid experts examine all aspects of the accident.

A recent report to the White House from the Federal government's Interagency Task Force on Products Liability confirms what
a disaster this area of the law is for everyone—except lawyers. The
report, along with another submitted to the task force by the Insurance Services Office (ISO), a statistical insurance industry group organized for ratemaking purposes, reveals that the "law of product liability has become filled with uncertainties creating a lottery for
both insurance ratemakers and injured parties."[6] The task force cited
an earlier study by the National Commission of Product Safety,
which found that very few who suffer product injuries are paid from
product liability insurance. Indeed, most injured people, discouraged by the complex litigation process, never even make a claim.[7] So
expensive are product liability claims to prepare and try that many
plaintiffs' lawyers are unwilling to take a case where damages fall
below $15,000 or more.[8] Furthermore, as stated earlier, according to
the ISO study, only 21 percent of the plaintiffs whose claims were
adjudicated to court verdict received awards of damages. Among all
claims, both settled and litigated, some 33 percent of the time no
payment is made.[9] The ISO study also revealed that any payment
made is normally long delayed, with the average personal injury
claim taking seventeen months to close, and larger claims taking
much longer.[10]

The inefficiency of the present system victimizes defendants as
well as plaintiffs. Even when a defendant "wins" a case he still
"loses" substantially through the time, resources, and energy ex-
pended on litigation. The ISO study shows that on the average defendants spend $3,121 to defend cases in which no payment is made.
At the same time, the average payment to an accident victim in the
ISO study (including cases where no payment was made) was
$10,123. For all cases—those resulting in payment and in no pay-

ment—the defendant spent on the average $3,502 defending the claim, or 35 percent of the average payment.[11] If one assumes that on the average one-third of the claimant's payment went for his lawyer and litigation expenses, one can readily appreciate what a substantial portion of dollars is being expended on legal costs.[12]

The task force found that generally product liability insurance accounts for less than 1 percent of the sale price of products, but many smaller manufacturers were especially hard hit. It found instances of premium increases between 100 percent and 500 percent and in some cases 1,000 percent or more in recent years, with premiums approaching 3 percent of the sale price in some branches of the industrial machinery industry.[13] Not only manufacturers of industrial machinery and industrial chemicals but also makers of high-risk consumer goods such as pharmaceuticals, automotive parts, and medical devices have been victimized by escalating premiums.[14]

The scenario for medical malpractice cases follows closely that for product liability. Here too one finds (1) liability turning on very complicated fact situations, almost always calling for expensive expert witnesses, (2) litigation so expensive that only the largest claims are brought, (3) relatively little of the total loss being paid from liability insurance, (4) defendants winning approximately three-quarters of the cases that reach a verdict, (5) rapidly rising claims and premiums, and (6) most of the money going to lawyers and insurance companies rather than to accident victims.[15]

Because the human body is incalculably more complex and less easily understood than any item a consumer could purchase, medical malpractice suits almost necessarily involve factual issues even more esoteric and involved than those found in product liability litigation. The difficulty of proving, for example, that surgical procedures were improperly executed or that their consequences were abnormal has led one malpractice specialist to speak of "the almost Byzantine nature of trying to find fault in malpractice litigation."[16]

As with product liability claims, the last ten years have seen skyrocketing malpractice claims and premiums. In many jurisdictions doctors find themselves paying $20,000 or more a year in liability premiums, with large hospitals facing annual premiums in the millions. But injured victims, here as in all areas of tort law, have benefited little by all this increased litigation. According to my calculations, only 28 cents of the premium dollar goes into victims' pockets, with the remainder claimed in insurance overhead and legal fees payable to insurers' and claimants' lawyers.[17]

The response to these discouraging facts from both sides in the battle, the insurance industry and the plaintiffs' bar, has been especially frustrating. The insurance industry's response has been to insist that the solution is simply to curtail further the rights of injured claimants. The reforms suggested by the American Insurance Association would strip the claimant of rights when he is pursuing claims already overly difficult to win and would offer the claimant nothing in return. The American Insurance Association's Product Liability Legislative Package contains seven fundmental statutory proposals:

1. Reduce the period of the statute of limitations under which a claimant must sue
2. Preclude a manufacturer's liability for modifications and alterations in his products by others[18]
3. Preclude a manufacturer's liability as long as the manufacturer employs a product design "in substantial use in [his] trade or business or in allied or similar trades or businesses[19]
4. Preclude admission in evidence against a manufacturer of his repairs or improvements in his product subsequent to the accident
5. Limit the manufacturer's duty to warn of product defects
6. Limit the occasions on which punitive damages may be assessed against a manufacturer, as well as the amounts of such damages[20]
7. Expand the occasions when the manufacturer may defend based on the victim's own faulty conduct[21]

One need not necessarily disagree with any of these proposals to see that a "solution" to the problems created by current product liability law that merely further restricts compensation for claims is a questionable solution indeed. Every one of these proposals reduces or denies benefits to injured parties; none of them, as a practical matter, is designed to aid the injured. Almost all "solutions" to the medical malpractice crisis being offered by health-care providers and their insurers betray the same bias; many of the proposals are quite similar to those being offered for product liability by businesses and business insurers, often the same companies that insure health-care providers.[22] The irony of such essentially negative and restrictive proposals is that even if enacted they are unlikely to achieve their goals. The American Bar Association's Commission on Medical Professional Liability has concluded that such "tort law changes will not have a significant impact" on the number or size of claims.[23] But even assuming the efficacy of such proposals, should legislatures in an age of rising consumerism leave the solution of the ills of insurance to those who see hope only in lessening and lowering—not bettering or broadening—insurance protection?

The myopia of the insurance industry plays into the hands of its bitter and similarly myopic opponents, the plaintiffs' bar. Robert Begam, a former president of the Association of Trial Lawyers of America, insists that "lawyers, legislators, judges, governmental officials, news media, and citizens [must resist] Big Insurance [moves] to overturn the legal rights of injured Americans."[24] Begam's conclusion is, therefore, that the tort liability system should not be changed in its essentials.

Both sides seem to overlook the simple principle that the experience of no-fault workers' compensation and auto insurance should have taught them long ago: Change the insurance system so that it pays (1) for losses regardless of fault and (2) only for economic losses and not for pain and suffering, which, like fault, is very difficult to determine.

But applying this solution to medical malpractice insurance, for example, is somewhat more complex, because it is more difficult to define the no-fault insured event for medical maloccurrences than for industrial or auto accidents. Under a no-fault system the employer pays an employee–victim injured in an accident "arising out of or in the course of employment"[25] regardless of anyone's fault; the motorist pays any motoring victim injured in an accident "arising out of the ownership, maintenance or use of a motor vehicle"[26] regardless of anyone's fault. But it is not feasible simply to force the health-care provider similarly to pay any patient "injured in the course of medical treatment" regardless of anyone's fault. The problem is how to define whether the patient was injured in the course of medical treatment, as opposed to suffering injury through his own prior condition that sent him to a health-care provider in the first place (his so-called presenting complaint). Assume that a patient goes to a doctor with a thyroid condition. The doctor treats him (perhaps by an operation), and the patient gets worse. A health-care provider could not realistically be asked to pay for *any* worsened condition after treatment; but determining which worsened conditions are due to the doctor's intervention and which to the patient's presenting complaint would be about as intractable a problem as determining the criteria for payment under the present negligence criterion. As indicated in the report of the HEW Secretary's Commission on Medical Malpractice:

> At the outset, the Commission members wrestled with the virtually impossible task of defining the "compensable event" which results from a "medical injury." Every effort to date on this subject has met with the same lack of success. Although we have a reasonable understanding of the terms "work injury" and "automobile accident injury," we have no real mental picture that covers the field of medical injuries. Does a "medical injury" occur when a physician fails to heal his patient or fails to heal him quickly, in the face of the joint hopes by the physician and the patient that an early recovery can be obtained? Illness and accidental injury become inextricably intertwined when fault issues are ignored.[27]

Similar problems attend defining who must pay for what under no-fault product liability. Suppose Jones hires the Smith Construction Company to build a cement patio for Jones's backyard. If White, Jones's neighbor, slips and falls and cracks his skull on the patio, can the Smith Construction Company be expected to pay for all of White's medical expenses and wage loss regardless of anyone's fault or lack of it? If so, can Smith Construction force the subcontractor who poured the cement to pay too? If so, what percentage of White's loss? Can ladder manufacturers really be required to pay for all injuries from falls from ladders regardless of the users' carelessness or the lack of any defect in the ladder; or stove manufacturers for all burns from stoves, and so on?

One apparent solution to compensating accident victims is simply to abandon tort liability of any kind and pay everyone injured by accident on a no-fault basis for his wage loss and medical expenses under Social Security. But it is unlikely that compensation for auto, product, medical, or other injuries will be solved by such a resort to social insurance, at least in the foreseeable future. True, in New Zealand, a sister common law country, liability for personal injury based on fault has been abolished, with compensation for economic losses (and small amounts for pain and suffering) being paid without regard to anyone's fault by a government-run social insurance agency.[28] But New Zealand has long been a relatively socialistic country, with large social insurance programs on which to build such a sweeping no-fault law. New Zealand also has, like Sweden, a small, relatively homogeneous population receptive to redistribution of income among themselves—a population, also like Sweden's, without the often bitter ethnic, geographic, economic, and even class rivalries and the concomitant resistance to social insurance schemes that plague the United States. Even New Zealand's neighbor, Australia, which is sort of halfway between the United States and New Zealand in receptivity to social legislation, has turned a cold shoulder to a New Zealand–like scheme, drawn up by a team that included, at the invitation of the Australian government, drafters of the New Zealand law.[29] Indeed, even in relatively socialistic Great Britain, a Royal Commission, after extensive study, has roundly rejected the New Zealand approach.[30] All the more would the United States resist having Social Security (or some other form of social insurance) automatically cover both wage loss and medical expenses from all accidental injuries. After all, the costs of national health insurance alone in the United States have caused such uncertainty that even that relatively primitive reform, in force everywhere else in the industrialized world, remains to be enacted here.[31]

Even if national health insurance is passed in the near future, it would still cover only a relatively small portion of the total personal injury losses from accidents. No one is suggesting that national health insurance cover wage loss from injury or ill health, for example. And in the case of serious auto and medical malpractice and product liability claims, about 75 percent of injury losses represent wage losses, and only about 25 percent medical costs.[32] With the high costs that any national health insurance will entail, no one expects it to expand to cover middle-class wage losses accompanying medical expenses.[33]

Moreover, if we could cover all or most losses for all injuries under Social Security or some other general insurance scheme, much traditional economic thinking insists that it would be unwise for all injuries, from whatever cause, to be paid from a big, undifferentiated pool of "insurance."

When the law permits dangerous activities, it makes a decision *for* accidents. We know with actuarial certainty that when a skyscraper is built or power tools are used a certain minimum toll in life and limb will be exacted no matter how carefully the work is done. By permitting the activity, society decides, in effect, in favor of exacting this accident toll. This does not, of course, mean that society approves the accidents, but it does mean a willingness to incur them.

If the rules of liability require that an activity pay its way in terms of accident costs (as well as other costs), the market regulates the extent to which that activity will be engaged in, and that extent will in turn be measured by the number of accidents for which society is willing to pay. But if an activity is not required by the liability rules to pay for its accident costs, society is not likely to make intelligent choices about how much of its resources to allocate to this activity and how many accidents it is willing to suffer from the activity. If, for example, the activity of motoring or surgery or the use of lathes does not have to pay its full accident costs, unwittingly more of that activity may occur than people would choose if its full costs were known. In the use of power tools, say, an accident-prone activity, this would mean that we as consumers in buying power tools would vote for more injuries and deaths than we might otherwise be willing to accept if the cost of power tools reflected the full cost of their accident toll.

If our legal system required power tools to pay their own way and consequently increased the cost of power tools (to the extent of liability insurance costs), this would probably result in the sale and use of fewer power tools. And this, in turn, would be likely to reduce the number of accidents from power tools. This is called market deterrence, as distinguished from the deterrence of accidents through, for example, safety regulations for power tools ordained by a government agency such as the Consumer Product Safety Commission.

Liability rules, then, promote proper allocation of resources by assigning the costs incurred by an activity, including the accident losses, to those for which we are willing to pay. In addition, ideally compensation rules should tend to assure compensation for accident victims and to bring about a wide distribution of the costs of accidents. It may well be that, if these last two goals were sought by themselves, the most effective way to attain them would be some broad form of social insurance for all disabling accidents, as is done in New Zealand, or perhaps for disability from any source, including illness, as was proposed in Australia, the cost of which would be distributed over society as a whole by general taxation. The superiority of compensation rules that assign liability to specific enterprises compared to such a broad scheme is probably found in terms of resource allocation. In New Zealand, for example, surgeons or product manufacturers whose services or products cause injury are not forced to pay their victims, who are paid from general taxation. If accident costs are "externalized" in this way—that is, divorced from the activities that generated them—then the activity in question receives a hidden subsidy, which will invite society to vote for more accidents than it should be willing to pay for if it were aware of their costs. In other words, a social insurance scheme, by ignoring the particular causes of loss, may encourage more losses in failing to surcharge those causes. Granted these incentives to safety under present law may work very crudely but they nonetheless deter more than do broad social insurance schemes.[34]

To sum up, in the United States we have always been comparatively content with market solutions, especially when contrasted with massive governmental programs. Thus, for all the reasons just mentioned, we are unlikely to welcome—at least in the foreseeable future—further massive social insurance schemes as the answer to the problems of accident compensation.[35]

What other solutions are available?

10

Harnessing the Lawsuit Lottery: Elective No-Fault Insurance for All Kinds of Accidents

THE CLASSIC VIRTUE of the market system is its flexibility. Let things get bad enough—let a need become obvious enough—and there is a corresponding incentive, primarily but not exclusively financial, for entrepreneurs to devise alternatives to the malfunctioning component. Of course, things by no means always work out smoothly, but, as Adam Smith pointed out two hundred years ago, the almost hydraulic force with which brains, energy, and capital are inclined to flow to those attempting to right the market's wrongs is a healthy influence.

Right now it is hard to imagine anything working much worse than the legal liability system, especially as it applies to personal injury. If things *are* so rotten—and ambitious legislative change seems blocked by a variety of factors and forces—can the market correct the situation the way Adam Smith told us it ought to? It might.

Recall that under the present fault-finding system after an accident a claimant is allowed, in effect, to sell from one-third to one-half or more of his claim to a lawyer in return for the lawyer's services through a contingent fee contract. Why does a claimant do this? Because his claim is such a risky asset he wants to share the risk. In other words, he arranges things so that if he loses his case he at least won't have to pay a lawyer's fee. The claimant unloads even more risk when the contingent fee is combined with the almost universal practice of having the plaintiff's lawyer assume the costs of preparing the case, including the cost of exhibits and so forth, with no recourse against his client if the case is lost.

If a claimant finds his fault-finding claim so distastefully risky that he routinely sells a big chunk of it to his lawyer after an accident, why shouldn't he be willing to trade his *entire* fault-finding claim to an insurance company *before an accident* in return for guaranteed no-fault payment of his economic losses? The no-fault insurance company would then use the proceeds from the fault-finding claims, including amounts for both economic loss and pain and suffering payable to some of its insureds, to pay no-fault benefits for the economic losses of all its insureds. Such a scheme of elective no-fault insurance could be marketed, a la Adam Smith, without the need for any legislation.

Before continuing, some clarification in terminology is in order. First-party insurance is coverage under which the policyholder collects payments for his losses from his own insurance company, rather than from the insurance company of some other person who caused the accident. A classic example of first-party insurance is no-fault auto insurance, whereas the classic example of third-party insurance is liability insurance based on fault-finding, or tort liability insurance, as lawyers call it.[1]

A scheme of elective first-party no-fault insurance could work like this: An insurance company could offer to its insureds no-fault coverages in increments of, say, $10,000 up to any amount, including a million dollars or more.[2] The coverage would be for economic loss, consisting mainly of medical expenses (including rehabilitation, rarely covered under health insurance today) and wage loss, resulting from personal injury in any kind of accident. Nothing would be paid for noneconomic loss, such as pain and suffering, nor would payment be made for losses already recompensed from another source, such as sick pay or health insurance. In return for such a guarantee of no-fault benefits payable regardless of how the accident happened, the insured would transfer to his no-fault insurance company his entire fault-based claim against any third parties who caused the accident. In accordance with the concept of no-fault insurance, *any* person buying the coverage would be paid in the event of suffering loss from an accident, not just those with valid fault-finding claims. The no-fault benefits would be paid periodically as loss accrues.[3] Furthermore, the insurance company would also agree to pay the insured for his economic losses in excess of his no-fault coverage out of whatever amount the company could recover in a fault-finding claim against any third party, without subtracting any legal expenses incurred in gaining such payment. The no-fault insurance company is in a position to offer such free legal services to its insured because it must pay its lawyers to pursue its own claim anyway, just as today it defends an insured against a fault-finding claim under liability insurance at no additional cost to the insured beyond his premiums. By this device the insured will be guaranteed whatever level of no-fault benefits he wishes to purchase, plus whatever amounts of economic loss in excess of that limit he is eligible for under a fault-finding claim.[4] The transfer of the fault-finding claim to the no-fault insurance company would have to be made at the time the agreement for potential payment of no-fault benefits is instituted, before any accident to the insured. Otherwise, if after an accident a victim could choose whether to press a fault-finding *or* a no-fault claim, those with valid fault-finding claims would opt for litigation and others would collect no-fault benefits, which would leave the insurance company without enough winnable fault-finding claims to provide income for paying no-fault benefits.

Note that anyone wanting sure protection for losses due to injury to himself will want to buy first-party no-fault insurance which will be funded—at least in substantial measure—from claims against all those, including commercial parties, who will want to continue to protect themselves and their assets from tort liability by buying third-party liability insurance.

True, the complex questions of fault and the value of pain and suffering would still have to be settled between the no-fault insurance company and the insurance company of the third party who injured the no-fault insured. But those issues would now arise between two insurance companies, which would be more likely to settle the matter expeditiously by informal means and without expensive litigation, as happens now with many intercompany claims.[5] And even if the matter could not be settled quickly, at least the protracted, expensive litigation would take place between large, impersonal corporations, without forcing its agonies of expense, delay, trickery, and uncertainty on lonely, frightened, wounded accident victims.

Note that this plan for no-fault benefits will not be compulsory.[6] Rather it will be elective—allowing but not compelling any insurance company to offer it, and similarly allowing any potential accident victim to refuse it. In view of the apparent public preference, evidenced by many polls, for certainty of insurance payment as against the gamble of a lawsuit, widespread adoption of no-fault can be expected. Recall that in Michigan, after experience with the most sweeping no-fault auto insurance law in the nation, the public favors by a 79-to-10-percent margin the curtailing of rights to payment for pain and suffering in order to have more medical and wage loss benefits. Furthermore, by a 53-to-18-percent margin, members of the public said they would relinquish their own rights to sue for payment for pain and suffering "in return for prompt and complete payment of medical bills and . . . lost wages." (See Chapter 8, p. 173.) These Michigan results corroborate many earlier studies showing a strong public preference for certainty of payment for out-of-pocket loss caused by an accident over a gamble for payment of out-of-pocket loss plus pain and suffering.[7]

Consider, then, the advantages to an insured under elective no-fault insurance. He is assured of automatic payment of economic loss at whatever level he has chosen in the event of any kind of accidental personal injury; he is also assured of payment of whatever economic losses he would have recovered under a fault-finding claim, without the necessity of incurring attorneys' fees or other litigation expenses for either no-fault or fault-based payment.[8] In practical terms his net payment will often be almost as great as, and sometimes greater than, whatever payment he would have received from a fault-finding claim, and he will suffer much less uncertainty and anxiety.

To take a hypothetical case: If after an accident between Smith and Jones, Smith had a valid fault-based claim against Jones and recovered $55,000 ($30,000 in economic loss and $25,000 in noneconomic loss), he would normally pay at least one-third of that or $18,333, to a lawyer, leaving him with a net of $36,667. If Smith had bought $30,000 or more of elective no-fault insurance, he would be paid for all his economic losses automatically without the uncertainty and stress of a fault-finding lawsuit and without paying anything to a lawyer. If he had instead elected to buy only $10,000 of no-fault insurance, he would still receive a net of $30,000, with $10,000 (the amount he chose) payable automatically without the uncertainty and stress of fault-finding litigation, and the rest recovered from Jones by his no-fault company pressing the fault-based claim. If litigation expenses amount to 50 percent (not at all unusual, as we have seen; see Chapter 7, pp. 142–43), Smith would have received net payment of $27,500 (one half of $55,000) from liability insurance, as against $30,000 under elective no-fault insurance.

It is true that legal rules now in existence might at first blush seem to inhibit the implementation of elective no-fault insurance: rules prohibiting the sale of personal injury claims and rules against "maintenance" and "champerty," which supposedly prohibit lawyers from sharing in the proceeds of a suit.[9] But such rules were instituted long ago (1) to prevent speculators from taking advantage of desperately injured accident victims, forcing them to sell their claims for a pittance in order to get something to live on, and (2) to prevent "officious intermeddling" in others' affairs by such speculators. Neither situation will result when an insurance company promises to pay promptly for economic losses of accident victims in return for the right to press their claims against third parties causing injury.[10] After all, as we have seen, the law already allows the accident victim to sell, in effect, a third or more of his claim to his lawyer in the form of a contingent fee in order to pay his lawyer, thereby creating an exception to rules against maintenance and champerty.

In this connection, ask yourself why plaintiffs' lawyers are so much better able than plaintiffs to bear the risks of personal injury suits. Because, in the words of Melvin Reder, a University of Chicago economist, lawyers have much better "portfolio diversification." Lawyers handle many different claims, whereas normally a claimant has only one in a lifetime. So lawyers are in a far better position to undertake the risks of pursuing a claim.

Logically, Reder argues, we should allow a plaintiff to transfer his *entire* claim. Not relishing risks, the typical injury victim would be willing to sell all or at least most of his "risky asset," and the logical buyer would be his lawyer, who has already bought a portion through the contingent fee. On the other hand, as Reder admits, prohibitions of maintenance and champerty would seem to make it unethical for a lawyer to purchase outright for cash his client's *entire* claim. But even if plaintiffs' lawyers were allowed to buy claims, they would want to split the risk further. A given case, after all, might require an attorney to invest a significant portion of his annual income in preparation for trial. So, Reder says, even if lawyers were allowed to buy injury victims' entire fault-finding claims, they would probably want to resell them or exchange shares in large claims among themselves. Indeed, that goes on now: By hiring other lawyers to try their cases in court, by retaining referring lawyers or others as co-counsel, or even by practicing in partnerships, lawyers already pool their risks.[11]

But if personal injury lawyers have considerable means of spreading their risks compared to their clients, they cannot match the risk-spreading abilities of the insurance companies. An insurance company is by definition a classic means of diversifying risks with mathematical (actuarial) certainty among the company's insureds. Moreover, if the risks are of too great a magnitude even for all the company's insureds combined, a company can easily reinsure its larger risks with still other insurance companies. But on the plaintiff's side, apart from selling one-third or more of his claim to his lawyer, the plaintiff often is locked into much more risk than he can comfortably bear, a far less diversified portfolio of risk, if you will, than is wise for him.

Why should not insurance companies, once again a la Adam Smith, step in to fill this desperate need and allow potential personal injury victims to pool their risks with the best risk-bearers of all? After all, an insurance company, as we have seen, is a much better risk-bearer than a lawyer or even a group of lawyers. In addition to its actuarial safety, an insurance company has all the stability and fairness that the law imposes on such enterprises through extensive governmental regulation of insurance. Admittedly, regulation is often weak (p. 209–10), but it is still more rigorous than for most enterprises, and far greater than for law firms. In other words, why not go a step farther than Reder and allow anyone who so wishes to sell his *entire* fault-finding claim to a highly regulated financial entity like an insurance company, thereby removing the risk of an accident victim's uncompensated loss? Why should plaintiffs' lawyers be the only ones allowed to buy fault-finding claims, and then only in return for legal services?[12]

To put things in historical perspective, shortly after the turn of the century enlightened forces in business, labor, and government banded together to pass no-fault workers' compensation acts throughout the United States. Convinced of the waste and tragedy of requiring injured employees to sue their employers in cumbersome litigation to establish who was at fault in an accident, these forces overcame the bitter opposition of trial lawyers, among others, and passed laws requiring employers to pay any employee injured in the course of employment for his medical expenses and wage loss without regard to anyone's fault. In return the employee gave up his right to sue his employer based on fault for pain and suffering.[13]

A half-century later a similar scenario is being played out for no-fault auto insurance. The principle underlying both workers' compensation and no-fault auto insurance laws is to use amounts that would otherwise be spent on fault-finding claims to pay everyone's economic losses on a no-fault basis; to redistribute the money, if you will, so that all those injured would be paid promptly rather than a few paid relatively large amounts, arrived at fortuitously and after long delay. In essence, then, the two key difficulties of the common law fault-finding system that no-fault workmen's compensation and auto laws were designed to correct were (1) the gaps in coverage resulting in great numbers who were paid little or nothing and (2) the delay in payment of claims. Both flaws arise from the deliberately complex and demanding fault-finding standards for paying claims under the common law. No-fault's twin objectives of eliminating gaps and delays in payment are interrelated. Improvement in the timing of payment depends on extension of payment to everyone. Acceleration of payment rests on simplifying the criteria for payment, and this, in turn, rests on extending the coverage so as to hold to a minimum the job of distinguishing between eligible and ineligible claims. Extending coverage, then, is the key to all workable no-fault proposals. But where is the money for the newly covered victims to come from? The answer is from money saved from not paying (1) for pain and suffering, (2) for finding fault and determining the pecuniary value of pain and suffering,[14] and (3) to the extent that people have already been paid from other sources, such as health insurance or sick pay.

Admittedly, the first-party no-fault insurance being proposed here applied these principles with a slightly different twist, but the principles are very much the same.

In the case of workers' compensation, the potential injurer in effect buys the potential fault-finding claims of his employees by agreeing to use the savings from not defending or paying fault-finding claims to help pay *every* injured employee less extensive no-fault benefits. No-fault auto laws accomplish much the same result. Motorists are compelled by statute to cover themselves for no-fault benefits and, by paying into the same system as all their potential victims, to buy off all fault-finding against themselves. As with workmen's compensation, each motorist pays for no-fault benefits with the money he formerly spent on insuring against his fault-based liability to others.[15]

Under the first-party no-fault plan that I now propose, it is not the potential injurer who buys fault-finding claims by agreeing to pay no-fault benefits, but someone else. Yet, as I indicate, the principle is the same. The main difference is that the fault-finding claim remains alive, precisely because it is not the potential injurer who is buying it. But nonetheless, money now used to pay (1) for some victims' pain and suffering, (2) for losses already paid from other sources such as health insurance, and (3) for litigation expenses will be spread out more evenly to pay benefits to everyone regardless of fault. Admittedly, the savings from not having to litigate the issues of fault and the value of pain and suffering are not as great under this first-party no-fault scheme, because fault-finding claims must still be asserted. But, as indicated, dealing with such claims should prove less expensive than at present because of the expeditious settlement that can be expected for claims pending between large commercial establishments such as insurance companies. (See above, p. 188.)

A major objection plaintiffs' lawyers can be expected to mount against elective no-fault insurance is the victim's loss of payment for his pain and suffering. In this regard, Philip Corboy, the prominent personal injury lawyer, has adduced the testimony of a nurse in a case involving severe burns suffered by a certain Jake Crouch when a transformer on which he was working exploded, spewing burning oil on him. Corboy's purpose is to illustrate the reality of pain and to justify the law's attention to compensating a victim for it. The nurse describes in detail the extensive (and, one gathers, hugely expensive) treatment of the patient, including the careful professional application of Sulfamylon cream and professionally supervised whirlpool treatments. She then testifies:

> [Jake] very soon after he was admitted became aware of the fact that the treatment would be a long one. . . . He would look to the future and getting out of the hospital and the possibility of getting back to work. . . . [H]e liked to be out on his job and he felt this wasn't going to be possible and this was a factor in his depression, that his life style would have to change. He often discussed with me what would happen to his family. He worried about how they were making out . . . as far as financial arrangements . . . and I would say a great deal of time he was severely depressed.[16]

The patient in this case was awarded $650,000 after a lengthy trial, as Corboy indicates (he does not tell the length of time between injury and trial). But Jake Crouch was one of the lucky ones in being paid at all from the fault-finding liability system. Moreover, as the nurse's testimony poignantly indicates, what he most needed was treatment—both physical and psychiatric (for his depression)—and assurances that his family would be cared for. In short, as with most of us if seriously injured, he was primarily concerned with payment for his economic losses, not for his pain and suffering. Indeed, there is an implication that, had he been quickly compensated for his economic losses, his pain and suffering would have been considerably reduced.

Reference has already been made several times to the overwhelming preference in Michigan and elsewhere for prompt, assured payment of economic losses stemming from accidents over the gamble of possibly being paid through a fault-finding suit for economic loss plus pain and suffering (p. 173). Indeed, an Illinois survey of even those who were successful in pursuing a fault-finding claim against a third party showed how few of them knew about, learned about, or cared about being paid for pain and suffering.[17] Almost three-quarters of the accident victims surveyed did not know about or expect to receive payment for pain and suffering at the time of the accident; nor did most of them ever learn about it, even if they were represented by a lawyer! It may be because lawyers take their fees out of payment for pain and suffering that they fail to inform their clients about such payment. Indeed, this raises an answer to lawyers' protest against taking away a victim's payment for pain and suffering: It isn't so much victims who miss such payment as their lawyers.

The Illinois study also found that accident victims didn't learn whether they had been paid for pain and suffering. Among those who had been paid more than four times their economic loss (and thus had been compensated relatively generously for their pain and suffering), only 34 percent *thought* that they had been paid for their pain.[18] Nor was there any correlation between the amount of pain suffered and the amounts paid for it.

Also significant was how little difference payment for pain and suffering made to accident victims emotionally. Very few victims ended up with any feeling of resentment against those who had negligently injured them.[19] Whether they were paid for pain, or how much, had no significant bearing on any feelings of resentment about the accident. Nor indeed did payment for pain and suffering significantly affect other attitudes toward the accident, such as how satisfied the victim was about his treatment by the other party's insurance company. In addition, whether victims *thought* they were paid for pain and suffering had no effect on their attitudes about the accident, about the party negligently causing it, or about the other party's insurance company. Nor did the belief that payment for pain had been received assuage any pain experienced.[20] In short, most accident victims are ignorant of, and indifferent to, payment for pain and suffering through a fault-finding claim against the negligent party injuring them.

True, the above study concerned auto accidents. But because they take place in public, where the victim can *see* and easily comprehend the faulty behavior of the party injuring him, auto accidents might be expected to generate even more personal feelings than accidents stemming from the relatively remote and impersonal behavior of other parties leading to medical malpractice, product liability, or slip and fall injuries.[21] Of course, some observers find the reason for the rise in recent years of malpractice claims in patients' anger at the medical profession.[22] But fault-based claims have risen spectacularly against many other defendants besides health-care providers, casting some doubt on any peculiar animus against doctors. Furthermore, patients *very* rarely press criminal charges against malpracticing doctors, which would seem to cast doubt on how outraged patients are at erring doctors (p. 25). So maybe it is compensation patients want from all those suits, not revenge. If so, first-party no-fault provides it much better than insurance covering fault-finding. Finally, even if recrimination is a primary motive, the plan of elective no-fault insurance proposed here *preserves* fault-finding claims, in which the outraged patient or other accident victim gets to take part, often to his economic advantage.

In addition, no-fault insurance, by paying promptly for losses, including for medical treatment to relieve pain, probably does a lot more toward alleviating pain and suffering than the fault-finding system. The years since World War II have seen dramatic innovations in the development of treatment to relieve pain, not only analgesics but other more innovative devices, such as the application of electric signals to the nervous system to kill pain and the therapies administered to Jake Crouch.[23] With such medical innovation, an insurance system paying, as does no-fault, for medical treatment that alleviates pain should be most welcome. An insurance scheme assuring prompt and sympathetic treatment, including medication and psychiatric and rehabilitation services, would seem far more helpful than an insurance system that haphazardly dumps large amounts of money on occasional victims after years of fighting and frustration. One cannot, after all, overlook the very real pain inflicted by the fault system on accident victims through the uncertainty and delay attendant on a fault-finding claim. Injury victims who cannot know *when* they will be paid, *what* they will be paid, or *if* they will be paid suffer racking anguish, as do their loved ones. Professor Conard

and his colleagues, in a Michigan study of accident victims subjected
to fault-finding claims, emphasized victims' "reactions of disappointment and even bitterness" and their "dislike of uncertainty."
Conard and his colleagues said their findings "painted an emphatic
picture of anxiety, frustration, disappointment and resentment felt
by injury victims in the course of the adjustment and litigation processes."[24]

On the other hand, research done by Dr. Lester Keiser, Chief of
Neuropsychiatry at Memorial Hospital in Hollywood, Florida, has
found that "no-fault insurance has the benign affect of reducing the
psychic shock, strain and subsequent 'traumatic neurosis' encountered by accident victims." According to a report on Dr. Keiser's
research, "Under the old automobile insurance system, with its frequent and lengthy law suits, the nervous strain experienced by an accident victim is often intensified in the ensuing wrangles with claims
adjusters and lawyers." The victims' rage, aggravated by protracted
litigation, according to the same report, can often lead to their being
"so absorbed in nursing their symptons and pressing their claims
that they completely alter their lives. Dr. Keiser notes that no-fault
insurance [enacted in his home state of Florida] obviously does not
eliminate the inevitable emotional distress that follows an accident.
But what it does do, he says, is eliminate many of the conditions that
make such a trauma worse."[25]

Keep in mind that all this proposal would do is allow contracts
for no-fault insurance, not require them. Why *not* allow such alternatives to fault-finding insurance? After all, perhaps the most distressing aspect of the common law's system of personal injury insurance is that it compounds its problem by requiring everyone, in
effect, to buy fault-finding insurance, which, from the individual's
point of view, is largely worthless and horrendously expensive, even
though some people hit the jackpot.

Suppose, instead, that a customer were given this choice when
buying a power tool or undergoing an operation:

"Do you wish to buy tort liability insurance?"

"What's that?"

Any effective truth-in-insurance law would then require that the
buyer be told:

Your chances of being paid any benefits under the insurance are extremely small. Most people who are injured by this procedure or
product are not paid from this insurance. In fact, about two-thirds
to three-quarters of the premium is used up by insurance overhead

and legal expenses on both sides. And even if you are one of the rare ones who ever collects under this insurance, you would only be paid when about two years or more has elapsed after you put in your claim. Also there is a real chance that before you are paid you would have to go to court. In addition, even if you go to trial and win, it is very likely that there will be an appeal—or several appeals—which can take an additional year or two or more before you would be paid, assuming you win the appeal(s).

In fact, lawyers have seen to it that no one is forced to explain the dubious value of insurance covering fault-finding. There is little point in telling the consumer or patient about the relative worthlessness of such insurance anyway, because he is not allowed to reject it even if he does not want it. On the contrary, because liability based on fault is imposed by common law, such liability insurance must be indirectly bought by everyone who buys a product or undergoes medical treatment; almost any reputable manufacturer, retailer, or health-care provider will buy such insurance and add the cost of it to the price of the product or service. Court cases abound with pronouncements from judges to the effect that any manufacturer, retailer, or health-care provider who tries to dispense with his liability coverage for fault in the sale of a product or service will not be allowed to do so, even if he offers a correspondingly lower price.[26] Courts have been concerned that such disclaimers of liability for fault would leave consumers without any remedy for serious injury in return for, at best, a comparatively niggling price advantage. But this is not to say that such courts would prevent anyone from selling his rights to be paid based on fault-finding to someone who is in a position to assert those rights—in return for a guaranteed prompt payment of the seller's real losses. I predict courts would welcome, not strike down, contracts for elective no-fault benefits.[27] By such devices the market can attempt to correct many of the evils and abuses of the present liability insurance system.

Would the fact that the fault-finding claim is being pursued primarily or solely in the interests of an insurance company deflate jury verdicts for pain and suffering and consequently reduce the funds available to pay no-fault claims? Several factors militate against such a likelihood: In the first place the jury need not be informed that the plaintiff is an insurance company, just as it not now told in personal injury cases that the *defendant* is an insurance company.[28] Moreover, since at the outset such lawsuits by insurance companies will be relatively rare, juries probably will not suspect on whose behalf the claim is being pressed. To the extent also that the accident victim retains an interest in the claim (as when his economic losses exceed the level of no-fault benefits he selected), the problem is lessened. But even assuming assertion of the entire fault-finding claim by an insurance company and a widespread practice among no-fault insurance companies of pressing such claims, a shrinkage of pain and suffering verdicts, while perhaps more likely, need not be substantial. The University of Chicago jury study found how conscientious jurors are in following the law rather than their subjective prejudices, including those against insurance companies.[29] Just as jurors apparently do not mistreat insurance companies when they are defendants, so they probably won't mistreat such companies when they are claimants. Finally, if and when no-fault insurance companies press their insureds' fault-finding claims to the point where the size of jury verdicts in such cases is affected, at least insurance companies (along with their insureds), who are after all often defendants in such suits, will benefit from the new climate, along with everyone else who is paying, directly or indirectly, liability insurance premiums. And it would certainly seem unlikely that the proceeds from fault-finding claims will be so reduced as to cause abandonment of a no-fault coverage that has become popular enough to be widespread.

A converse worry about elective no-fault insurance is that placing fault-finding claims completely in the hands of insurance companies could bring about an increase in personal injury litigation, with its attendant costs to society. Under this new system a no-fault insurance company would assert a fault-finding claim against the liability insurance company of the party whose fault supposedly caused the injury: Would not two insurance companies—relatively impervious to the risks of losing a fault-finding claim (being "risk neutral" or even "risk preferrers," in the economist's terms)—be more inclined to initiate and litigate claims than would many individual accident victims? The latter, after all, often fear lawsuits and fear still worse losing one that is started. As a result, individuals probably start fewer and settle more claims than insurance companies. Also, a lawyer for an individual accident victim, being paid by contingent fee only if he wins, may be more inclined to drop or settle a claim than an insurance company lawyer, who is paid by the hour, win or lose. As a result, elective no-fault might lead to more claims and litigation than the present fault-finding system.[30]

In answer to these objections, first, the lack of expertise on the part of most individual claimants and even their lawyers in appraising the value of personal injury claims may lead to *more* litigation than would result if experienced insurance company lawyers on both sides are negotiating over the same cases.[31] Second, unlike plaintiffs' lawyers, who on the whole deal with clients who are at their mercy, insurance company lawyers and claimsmen are subject to the discipline of their employer, a commercially astute organization inclined to eliminate needless litigation. Third, even if the total amount of litigation increases, that is not necessarily a bad thing. The greatest evil of the present system is the existence of a vast pool of insurance dollars that is paid to needy claimants inadequately, not at all, or in a dilatory, haphazard manner, while other claimants, usually less needy, are being overpaid. So it is by no means necessarily a condemnation of elective no-fault insurance to say that such insurance will result in more claims and litigation. That could be beneficial, if litigation is between sophisticated commercial parties shrewdly asserting arguably valid claims against each other. It would offer the concomitant benefit of imposing (or "internalizing") costs on the activities causing them (p. 184), while at the same time the litigation generates funds for prompt payment of the real losses to needy accident victims.

Elective no-fault insurance permits the insurance industry to harness the fault-finding system to its own and the public's advantage. Insurers seem almost panicked over current trends in liability insurance and their inability to control them through legislation or court decisions. An article in *Business Week* reveals the depth of the insurance industry's frustrations with current personal injury law:

> Almost to a man, insurance executives think that the tort system is running amok, not only in product liability but in . . . auto liability, and personal liability as well. . . .
>
> It is one thing to blame the tort system, however, and something entirely different to change it. . . .
>
> The fragmented [insurance] industry must deal with the courts and legislatures of the 50 states and the federal government. The problem of getting any [governmental] action on a program for changing the liability laws is so great that no one hopes for a quick change.[32]

But, far from requiring vast and revolutionary changes of the type enacted in New Zealand, writing no-fault insurance contracts with a simultaneous purchase of the insureds' fault-finding claims need not await statutory authorization. Elective first-party no-fault can be implemented by mutual agreement of the parties victimized by the legal system, bypassing the lawyers who really are the only beneficiaries of the legal system they have devised. Elective no-fault, being implemented by private parties of their own volition, can be applied where it looks likely to work and ignored when it won't; an accurate check on costs and benefits can be kept every step of the way.[33]

Elective no-fault insurance could be offered in a variety of ways. An auto insurance company could offer no-fault insurance benefits for auto accidents to its insureds in states without (or with inadequate) no-fault auto laws.[38] Workers' compensation insurance companies could offer employees, pursuant to collective bargaining, benefits supplementing inadequate no-fault workers' compensation benefits for injuries in the course of employment; workers' compensation insurance companies could also offer no-fault benefits to employees and their families for off-the-job accidents.[34] Health and disability insurance companies, either writing individual policies or through group coverage, or casualty companies writing homeowner's coverage, could offer to their policyholders no-fault coverage for all kinds of accidents. Credit unions, professional or trade associations, and others could also offer such coverage to their members. If a unionized employer were to opt to offer improved no-fault coverage through workers' compensation or through some other coverage such as his group health and disability coverage, the employees' rights would be further protected, because the matter probably would be bargained over with the union.[35] Also note that, regardless of whether no-fault coverage, along with a concomitant "purchase" of fault-finding claims, is instituted pursuant to collective bargaining, a significant advantage arises because the victim's or his employer's own insurance company provides the coverage. A claimant will deal, therefore, with an insurance company with whom he or his employer has a continuing relationship, as opposed to claiming against a stranger's insurance company, which owes no loyalty to him, as is the case under traditional fault liability insurance.[36]

Two mounting complaints in our society are against (1) more and more government spending and bureaucracy as a solution to social problems, and (2) more and more legalisms, as litigation, legislation, and other legalistic devices proliferate, and lawyers with them. In fact, complaints about more and more government bureaucracy and more and more lawyering are interrelated beyond the fact that lawyers draft the laws creating the bureaucracy and then often staff it. Laurence Silberman, a former U.S. Deputy Attorney General, has pointed out in a thoughtful article entitled "Will Lawyering Strangle Democratic Capitalism?": "Capitalism, of course, is based on private market-orientated decision-making, whereas the legal process, although it normally takes the form of an adversary proceeding in which private interests play their part, is in reality a way in which the government asserts power." In Silberman's view, "Lawyers today are more and more simply a structural continuation of the bureaucracy."[37]

Complaints about governmental bureaucracy and lawyering are, of course, nothing new. From our first President, who specified in his will that no lawyer was to probate his estate, to the current occupant of the White House, who not long ago attacked the legal profession on the grounds "that we are over-lawyered and under-represented," there has been a long tradition of hostility to lawyers in the United States.[38]

But, as suggested earlier (pp. 152–53), in an increasingly complex and sophisticated society we are not likely to diminish substantially our need for governmental solutions to many problems beyond the capacities of private enterprise and individuals to solve, or to diminish our need for lawyers to represent those in our society with understandably opposing views and interests. Anyone who wants to return to some halcyon day of unfettered private enterprise has probably forgotten about the Depression or the days of uncontrolled license to market unsafe food and drugs and watered stock. Anyone who wants to crack down on everyone from executives accused of bribing to drivers accused of drinking can hardly expect them not to defend themselves. It is common today for those frustrated by our overlawyered society to quote Shakespeare's lines from *Henry VI, Part II*: "The first things we do, let's kill all the lawyers."[39] It should be pointed out that those words were spoken by a character named Dick the Butcher (which incidentally makes them embarrassing lines for doctors to use), a member of a gang of rabble led by a demagogue planning to take over the country and destroy all title to property. As a prelude to *that* enterprise, a necessary first step was to dispatch all lawyers, to destroy law itself. Knowing the full context, almost anyone might be embarrassed to use Shakespeare's words in condemnation of lawyers.

So our need for governmental bureaucracy and lawyers makes it all the more necessary to reserve our legislation, bureaucracy, litiga-

tion, and lawyering for matters where they are essential. As Silberman has put it: "Today, there is an increasing awareness in the industrial democracies that a certain degree—a tipping point if you
will—of government intervention into the workings of the economy
begins to erode the natural vigor of capitalism. Reliance on the legal
process contributes to the sum total of governmental intervention
and thereby endangers our economy."[40] Later Silberman says:

> Unless our political institutions mount a virtual counter-revolution
> against the legal process, our only hope of preserving the vigor of
> democratic capitalism may be for the legal process to become so un-
> wieldy that private . . . decision-making gain[s] a comparative ad-
> vantage. But then the legal process would be less available for those
> matters for which it is truly needed.

What is needed, then, is to identify specific instances where the legal
process is being applied unnecessarily. In this connection, Silberman
asserts, "That . . . automobile accident claims, for instance, are disposed of through elaborate adversary legal procedures is a costly national scandal."[41] "Is it too much," he asks, "to ask of American
lawyers that they accept major responsibility for finding ways out of
this dilemma? I do not think so. After all American democracy was
founded and set on its course by lawyers—albeit lawyers who were
also simultaneously farmers, businessmen, architects, and philos-
ophers."[42]

First-party no-fault insurance would be an instance where lawyers and others could attempt to allow private decision making to
replace unwieldy legal processes. Perhaps the most significant advantage of elective no-fault insurance is that it attacks the cruel social problem of providing adequate compensation for accident victims without requiring any legislation or any new governmental
bureaucracy to administer it. And it does so by a scheme designed to
by-pass lawyers and their often incredibly self-serving complexity
and cumbersomeness. True, litigation remains a possibility between
insurance companies, but insurance companies have at least the
leverage, sophistication, and power to control *all* their expert employees—lawyers and nonlawyers alike—better than do individuals.
Indeed, corporate counterattacks to diminish legal expenses and litigation are on the rise. At a recent American Bar Association
meeting, Lester Pollack, Chairman of the Finance Committee of
CNA Financial Corporation of Chicago, a major insuring institu-

tion, castigated lawyers as "Roman gladiators," more interested in scoring against opposing counsel than in getting quick settlements. At the same meeting, J. A. Pritzker, Chairman of Chicago's Cerro-Marmon Corporation, accused lawyers of engaging in courtroom "overkill" instead of expressing "the spirit of the transaction" that businessmen cherish. As a result of such reactions, according to the *Wall Street Journal*, "corporate clients are no longer watching helplessly. In many board rooms the motto is 'Think Settlement.'" Even the much maligned "gladiators"—at least of the corporate variety— echo these sentiments. Jerome S. Weiss, former president of the Chicago Bar Association, calls litigation "the most expensive luxury you can think of. As a corporate attorney, I avoid courts like the plague."[43] Finally, to the extent large institutions choose not to avoid litigation, at least under elective no-fault insurance, as suggested earlier, that is a commercial decision, and the agonies and delay of litigation do not fall primarily on pathetically injured accident victims and their families.

In one sense reformers are becoming more cautious about the unpredictable side effects of their reforms. Who would have predicted, to take one example, that the only lasting effect of Prohibition would be the rise of organized crime? No-fault auto insurance in its various forms will probably have an adverse effect on the plaintiffs' personal injury bar in our country. And *perhaps* this should give us pause, because personal injury attorneys *are* a unique breed. Despite their enormous wealth, they remain cut off, by choice and design, from the establishment. There are not many groups in our society, except perhaps the top luminaries in entertainment and the arts, who achieve great monetary success and yet are not drawn into the network of the corporate establishment. Even theatrical or artistic types must sell their talents to or through large corporate enterprises, and at any rate they are often childish people, notoriously ineffective in the practical world of affairs. But not so plaintiffs' lawyers. They are *very* effective people in the day-to-day world, and yet stridently independent. They and their families do not belong to the best country clubs or the Junior League. In contrast, the insurance company lawyers tend to welcome the corporate, Ivy League or Big Ten law school patina. Plaintiffs' lawyers remind one, once again, of politicians and labor leaders, who also, while moving at high levels of power, must cultivate the common touch. Unlike plaintiffs' lawyers, though, both politicians and labor leaders must hew carefully to their constituents' lines. Plaintiffs' lawyers, then, are unique as a rare breed who truly are independent. Their ability to wring large verdicts from juries for individual claimants, along with huge fees for themselves, makes them immune from pressures that require conformity in most of their economic peers. No buttering up of big clients is required of them, no wooing of corporate executives or bankers.[44] (True, they have to be nice to judges, but even there they can appeal.) Most of them are free spirits. And, unlike most very wealthy people, they tend to be ethnics and political liberals. It is no coincidence that Hugo Black represented injured claimants, and made huge sums doing it, before he ran for the Senate in Alabama, from which he went to the Supreme Court.

As a result, mourning the passing of plaintiffs' lawyers, unlike mourning the passing of, say, the cowboy, is more than just an exercise in nostalgia. Personal injury lawyers represent a rare resource, *very* talented, highly trained, energetic, dramatic, colorful individuals, taking on the establishment with little if any fear of retaliation or of stepping on peers' toes. Indeed, they make their living by taking on the establishment. Admittedly, they do so in the narrow area of personal injury, but, through accident causes that affect many, their efforts can exert enormous leverage against concentrations of economic, social, and political power. No other country has such the unique "crucial mass" of hardened, tough, disciplined, independent but basically responsible gladiators ready to strike anywhere their services can pay off, because no other country has the contingent fee. No-fault can be viewed as choking off this rare breed's source of income and influence. Insurance companies pursuing fault-finding claims will probably retain their own corporate-type lawyers. Even if they turn to present-day plaintiffs' lawyers, to that extent the latter will cease to be as independent as when they were being hired by individuals. Perhaps, to repeat, all this should give us pause.

But probably not for long. In the first place, elective no-fault of the type being proposed here *is* elective; for the indefinite future the legal system applicable to personal injuries as we know it will continue to function for those who, for one reason or another, are not covered by no-fault. Second, we can hardly expect the seriously and even tragically injured in our society to continue to subsidize an anti-establishment cadre that depends on the cruel and capricious fault-finding system. Third, as stated above, plaintiffs' lawyers, for all their talents and individualism, have on the whole litigated only very narrow issues of personal injury on an isolated and episodic basis. More general public issues of pollution, corporate or union corruption, and so forth have on the whole escaped their attention. Perhaps a choking off of personal injury litigation will excite their interest in broader issues more in the public interest than winning an isolated if gargantuan—but long-delayed—verdict for an occasional accident victim.

11

Some More Doubts—and Hopes

IT WOULD BE A MISTAKE to think that elective no-fault insurance at a stroke is going to serve as a panacea for the ills of personal injury compensation, even if widely adopted. The frustrations of insurance, whether operating under no-fault or fault-finding, are very real and worthy of emphasis. Consider the following exchange:

> As a principal spokesman for the country's property and liability insurance business, we wish to register our objection to several inaccuracies, misleading statements and the over-all tone of Russell Baker's Sunday Observer column [in *The New York Times Magazine*, "Fine Print"] of November 11.
>
> While we don't question the facts involving Mr. Baker's slow seepage claims under his homeowner's policy, we would like to explain the situation.
>
> The homeowners policy was never intended to cover slow seepage such as that which occurred to Mr. Baker's home. The policy does cover accidental damage caused by a burst or broken pipe and it would be unrealistic to cover conditions like slow seepage which fall into the category of maintenance. . . .
>
> > Alfred G. Haggerty
> > Assistant Vice President
> > Insurance Information Institute
> > New York City[1]

206

MORE FINE PRINT
by Russell Baker

. . . Alfred G. Haggerty [has denounced me] on the ground that a column published here was unfair to the American insurance industry for which Mr. Haggerty seems to be the official writer of angry letters.

Mr. Haggerty's letter was right. The column to which he objected was indeed unfair to the American insurance industry. I planned it that way. Any industry that takes so much money and gives nothing in return when the plumbing leaks through the ceiling, I reasoned, can certainly put up with a little unfairness. If it can't, it can always set aside some of this month's premium collections to buy itself three Martinis and enjoy a good bout of self-pity.[2]

That exchange of remarks is but a small part of an ongoing dialogue that, if anything, may grow more acrimonious as the years go by.

It is no coincidence that Kafka was a clerk in an insurance office, nor that the prototypical bureaucratic nightmare of a large barn of an office, glaringly fluorescent-lighted, with endless lines of metal desks, manned by equally endless and faceless functionaries, is usually seen as an insurance office.

The insurance industry is indeed capable of Kafkaesque operations. Regardless of whether you buy Mr. Baker's particular complaint, consider the following examples:

After a businessman had applied to an agent for auto insurance, an investigator visited the businessman's home to speak with him. In writing up his report, the investigator mentioned that he noticed several paintings of nudes on the wall. The businessman was turned down for the insurance as a moral hazard.[3]

A female Princeton University faculty member had her auto insurance canceled by State Farm, the nation's largest auto insurer, because of a report that she was living with a man "without benefit of wedlock." That's the way insurance people still talk about such things in their reports.[4]

A roofer named Michael Egan injured his back in 1971 in a fall from a roof. Under a disability policy with Mutual of Omaha he was entitled to lifetime benefits of $200 a month for disability from an accident but only three months of benefits for disability stemming from sickness. In 1972, Mutual of Omaha reclassified his disability as a sickness, thereby ending his benefits, without asking for any medical determination. After a twelve-day trial of Egan's suit

against Mutual of Omaha, California Superior Court Judge Howard
McClain stated in a five-page opinion that the "evidence is clearly
sufficient" that Mutual of Omaha adjusters "violated good faith
and fair dealing" in reclassifying Mr. Egan's disability. In particular he noted that the failure of Mutual of Omaha to order a medical
examination of Egan or to consult his doctors showed "a total disregard of the rights of the insured." Even the defense testimony, according to Judge McClain, demonstrated that the company acted
without sufficient information to make its reclassification.[5]

The New York State Insurance Department cited Blue Shield of
Greater New York for various derelictions. Taking an average of
five minutes to answer a telephone call was one such complaint.[6]

Unfortunately, getting an answer from an insurance company to
a telephone call may not help much. Karl Herrmann, Insurance
Commissioner of the State of Washington, testified as follows before a U.S. Senate committee investigating auto insurance:

> A graduate student in economics at the University of Washington,
> in Seattle, had his auto insurance suddenly cancelled. The letter,
> which lacked specific reasons for the cancellation, was signed by a
> Mr. "T. Case." The student tried to reach Mr. Case repeatedly by
> telephone, but could never locate the signer of the letter. He was al-
> ways told by the insurance company's telephone operators that
> "Mr. Case is out to lunch," or "He's in conference," or "He's sick
> today."
>
> One day the student was discussing his problem with an official
> of the university. A secretary whose husband worked as an adjuster
> for the company involved overheard the conversation and explained
> why it was that "Mr. Case" was always out. "That stands for
> 'Tough Case,' " she said. "There is no such person. It's the way the
> company has of avoiding further discussion with cancelled policy-
> holders."[7]

Nor is the problem limited to treatment of individual complaints
and insureds. For years widespread complaints have been heard
against insurance companies' "redlining" of ghetto and other areas
where coverage is uniformly refused. Daniel Patrick Moynihan,
while a professor at Harvard, observed:

> A sociological phenomenon of sorts appears to be at work. Insur-
> ance agents are for the most part careful middle-class persons who
> are suspicious equally of working-class (not to mention lower-class)
> types who might tend to get into trouble, and educated types who
> might cause it. Occasionally the categories overlap. A University of
> California professor on his way back from a world tour stopped in

Cambridge last spring to give a series of lectures. He and his wife took a small furnished apartment and bought a car, thinking to drive back to Berkeley. He applied for insurance at a nearby Sears, Roebuck branch, but unaccountably was turned down. Several days later, a stranger mailed the professor the rejected application form. It had apparently been thrown away by the insurance agent who had written across it in ball point pen, "Lives on Wrong Side of Massachusetts Avenue."[8]

Why should so much insurance be so inadequate in so many ways for so many parties in the United States?

Some people blame inadequate government regulation. To be sure, such regulation is often woefully weak, as are the laws under which regulation operates. Insufficient and poorly paid staff is the norm. Commissioners on leave from the insurance industry or on their way there at the end of their tenure are commonplace. At the other extreme, appointment as an insurance commissioner often goes as a plum to a governor's political supporter or contributor who has little or no qualification for the job. Former Governor Michael Dukakis of Massachusetts, an early and influential legislative supporter of no-fault insurance, has written:

> Like other regulatory agencies at the state level, insurance departments have tended to become constituent agencies. Contact with the insurance industry is close and continuous. Moreover, the ability of the state agency to match the assembled accounting and actuarial knowledge of the industry may be limited. . . . [T]he size and expertise of the agency's staff . . . is rarely endowed with the kind or number of personnel required for the job of confronting the vast resources of the industry. For example, in Massachusetts only one or two key people are doing the critical job of evaluating rates and coverages filed with the commissioner each year.[9]

But even if regulation and the laws under which it functions were tighter, would the results be any different? Some observers argue that the industry's problems stem from overregulation already. The industry is plagued, they say, with "inept and stodgy management"—what one Wall Street investment banker described as "dinosaur clubs disguised as top management, who do not have the constitution to change."[10] But what is the cause of that? *Too* much regulation through the years, they say. "Let's face it," a member of the New York Insurance Commissioner's staff says, "this is a hothouse industry, just like the railroads. Nearly every time it wants to make a move it has got to get approval from us. This is not the sort of atmosphere which bright young men thrive in.''[11] Take the case of those ringing Blue Shield phones. George Goodlett, a Blue Shield spokesman, attributes the problem at least in part to workers' performance. "We have a 15 percent ceiling on administrative expenses," he says. "As a result, our pay scale is very low and this is reflected in the quality of our help.''[12] The problem, however, does not stop with clerks. H. J. Maidenberg, a consumer columnist for the *New York Times*, has written, "Secondary management salaries in the traditionally low-paying insurance field are set either to repel aggressive, bright executives or to force many in the industry to leave.''[13]

Assuming, for the sake of argument, better regulation *is* the answer, could Federal regulation do any better? Not in the view of consumer advocate Herbert Denenberg, Pennsylvania's former Insurance Commissioner. "The history of Federal regulatory agencies is anything but encouraging," he says. "Medicare and Medicaid, for example, are a mess. We've got problems with our present system, but at least we don't have to contend with a giant bureaucracy.''[14] Nor would governmental *ownership* of insurance promise much, if any, improvement. Take state-run systems of workers' compensation, as an example. There are a number of them in the United States, both operating alone (seven states) and in competition with commercial companies (twelve states). Under neither system have they noticeably outperformed private enterprise. Although they cost a little less, they operate, according to their critics, with less efficient and slower handling of claims and without performing many of the services that private insurers offer their policyholders.[15]

One problem with Federal intervention is that although insurance matters may loom large in Albany or Springfield, they tend to pale to insignificance in Washington. To an official trying to decide how much of America's military resources should be committed to peacekeeping in the Middle East or how to deal with inflation, casualty insurance matters can seem relatively unimportant. One factor in the defeat of no-fault in Congress in recent years has been the Federal government's preoccupation with inflation, the energy crisis, and the like, preventing key Federal officials from focusing on such a mundane matter as auto insurance.

The problems of insurance, then, surely transcend the question of what segment of government will regulate it and in what way. The problems, as Moynihan suggests, are to some extent cultural. In the first place, most of us are quite uncertain as to precisely what we want from insurance. Indeed, most of us are wildly inconsistent in our demands: We want swift and complete payment of our claims, but we want very cheap insurance. Insurance companies are castigated for haggling over health insurance claims on the one hand, and on the other for shoveling out money indiscriminately in payment of those same health insurance claims, thereby supposedly adding unnecessarily to health insurance costs.

The abuses of insurance companies in resisting claims must be seen against the widespread abuses of claimants in pressing them. Insurance companies are classic examples of large, impersonal, bureaucratic institutions that many people, who otherwise would not dream of stealing, have few qualms about "ripping off." Insurance company personnel relish telling of their victimization through such chicanery. A few years ago one insurer found itself paying a disproportionate number of claims for hospitalized children from a given area. Stranger still, the hospitalizations were occurring over weekends. On investigation, it turned out that the device of using hospitalization insurance to get expert and "cheap" babysitters had spread through the community. The writer Morton Hunt cites a case in Boston where "240 persons filed claims for a collision between a streetcar and a truck—but the streetcar had a top capacity of 68."[16] In Chapter 2, I cited numerous similar examples of fraudulent claims.

Such tawdry tales point up another cultural aspect of the inherent problems of American insurance. Insurance companies are, as Moynihan suggested, prototypical bureaucracies, employing orderly, conventional middle-class folk. But these very orderly, conventional folk are paid (more accurately, underpaid) to deal with very unconventional disorders: fires, riots, thefts, deaths, injuries, and catastrophes of all kinds. A study by the sociologist H. Laurence Ross of a large casualty insurance company in New York City documents the type of person employed by the typical insurance company and his attitude toward the events and people he must deal with. In his book *Settled Out of Court: The Social Process of Insurance Claims Adjustment*, Professor Ross offers some insights into insurance processes and personnel:

> From the standpoint of prestige and income, the occupational position of the adjuster can be described as lower white-collar, comparable to such positions as bank teller, bookkeeper, retail salesman

and many other jobs in the insurance field. These occupations . . .
pay modestly . . . and require modest but not extraordinary levels of
intelligence and judgment.

Entry into claims work was virtually always casual and unplanned.
Rarely did a claims man have claims or insurance in mind as a career, even as recently as his college days.

Another theme often noted in the interviews [with adjusters] appears . . . to represent a liking of and appreciation for power. Facing the claimant, the adjuster has the ability to "help" or deny the
need for help, and his discretion does in fact give him a degree of
power not often met in jobs of a comparable status level. ("Like
I'm some sort of a God in my job, deciding who is right and who is
wrong, and helping the poor slob.")

In many ways . . . observations about the claims man's job parallel
those made in several studies of the police patrolman. Both occupations present work situations with a great deal of intrinsic satisfaction such as variety, challenge, and power over others, and a great
deal of necessary but non-legitimized discretion. Both are fields
with great visibility and open recruitment and great security, yet
members of both occupations experience problems in the area of
relative pay and status. Low levels of ambition, appearing as reluctance to leave field work, are again common to both. . . . [T]here
are parallels in social and political attitudes among the incumbents
as well.

The adjuster's job requires him to take suspicious view of claims
and of claimants. Many of the men . . . had developed a skeptical
attitude toward the motives of the claimant public which is in keeping with a philosophically conservative outlook. For instance, while
driving by a boatyard, one man mentioned the fact that claims for
boat damage tend to coincide with the end of the boating season,
when bills for storage have to be met. In a business district, he
stated that the better the times for business, the fewer the claims,
and conversely, when business is bad, fire claims mount. Another
man noted that when home losses are reported, he always looks for
additions to the house, such as refinishing the basement or adding a
porch, which might produce a need to assert the claim for theft or
other type of loss. A third adjuster who does much hospital liability
work sees the patient's need to pay hospital and doctor bills as the
source of many claims of malpractice and hospital liability.[17]

On a broader level as it pertains to the cultural aspects of insurance, we live in an age of more and more "sophisticated" people,

insisting on their "rights," and insisting on treatment as *individuals*—people not about to be pushed around by cops or anyone else. But as young Winston Churchill, helping Lloyd George to push through social insurance in the great Liberal government of the early twentieth century, said, "Insurance brings the miracle of averages to the rescue of the masses."[18] *Any* process of "averaging," however, let alone dealing with us all as "the masses," is by definition a bureaucratic, impersonal business. Macaulay said: "In proportion as men know more and think more, they look less at individuals and more at classes. They therefore make better theories and worse poetry." Naomi Bliven has written: "Any long demographic retrospect suggests that nearly all the people now alive in the Western world are descended from serfs. We are the children of pawns; industrialism promised to make us all knights."[19] Our serf ancestors, in the face of misfortune or disaster, dumbly accepted their fate. Insurance, an outgrowth of industrialism, assures us of at least some rather mechanical, impersonal help. But, like knights—and Russell Baker—we all become very annoyed when we feel we are misserved. Like knights, we want poetic perfection.

Of course, no one is really a knight any more, nor does poetry accompany every service. Does this mean we just grin and bear it, with a bit of growling and kicking on occasion? Not at all. There are many ways that insurance can be vastly improved. There are at least partial solutions to some of the worst problems plaguing insurance. (Note: only *partial* solutions to *some* problems. Daniel Patrick Moynihan has pointed out a fact that we, with all our competence, have overlooked: that the existence of a problem does not necessarily mean the existence of a solution.)[20] But effective solutions are not likely to be sweepingly dramatic—"poetic," if you will. No panacea is available to build "Jerusalem in our green and pleasant land." "After a period of chiliastic vision," writes Moynihan, "we have entered a time that requires a more sober assessment of our chances, a more modest approach to events."[21]

It is precisely in that spirit that my proposal for elective no-fault insurance is offered. It will still leave us at the often not-so-tender mercies of insurance companies, but, as experience under no-fault auto insurance indicates (pp. 157–75), an insurance mechanism is infinitely superior to the lawyers' fault-finding system. Given all the inevitable problems that will always plague insurance, it clearly makes sense to enable the consumer to eliminate, if he wants, its most glaring and intractable difficulties by having claims (1) based on the simple occurrence of an accident instead of a finding of fault; (2) payable for clear, identifiable losses as opposed to amorphous, litigable items like pain and suffering; and (3) payable by one's own insurance company, as opposed to a stranger's. (According to a survey of New York insurance agents, 85 percent of them believed that an insured fared better in terms of efficient settlement of claims under first-party contracts, whereby an insured claims against his own company, than under third-party contracts, with claims made against someone else's company. Only 10 percent disagreed with this conclusion, with 5 percent undecided.)[22]

In short, elective no-fault is not, to repeat, any kind of panacea, but most of us will end up much better treated after an accident by insurance rules from insurance companies than by legal rules from lawyers.

Admittedly, though, in depending on initiatives by the insurance industry, first-party no-fault insurance may not get off the ground. Workers' compensation came into being through innovations not by the insurance industry but largely by progressive business forces and public interest groups, such as the National Civic Federation, which claimed to represent business and the public as well as some labor interests. (See Chapter 10, p. 191.) Similarly, no-fault auto insurance at the outset had no backing from the insurance industry.

It was to tap initiatives of private entities other than the generally timid insurance industry that I proposed in 1975 *third-party* elective no-fault insurance. (Recall that third-party insurance entails claims against someone else's insurance company, p. 187). This proposal, as with first-party no-fault, would be implemented by private enterprise without the necessity of authorizing legislation. Businesses and professionals—health-care providers, manufacturers, retailers, and so forth—would be encouraged to identify hundreds of maloccurrences stemming from their products and services that can be readily isolated and for which it will be feasible to apply the no-fault bargain: prompt payment for economic losses in return for waiver of the right to sue based on fault for possible, but uncertain, payment of economic loss *plus* pain and suffering. For such identifiable injuries, the savings realized from eliminating payment for (1) insurance overhead and legal fees, (2) pain and suffering, and (3) losses already covered by other sources could be used to finance prompt and expeditious payment regardless of fault. The advantages to health-care providers and businesses, as well as their insurance companies, would be (1) potentially lower premiums; (2) greater certainty of the extent of potential liability, in that liability would no longer turn on the vicissitudes of unpredictable fault-finding litigation but rather on defined, predictable compensable events; (3) avoidance of being stigmatized and paying a windfall gain solely because of fortuitous injury to a customer or patient; (4) use of insurance dollars to pay genuine losses as opposed to devoting large amounts to payment of legal fees and insurance overhead; and (5) the good will arising from prompt payment to customers or patients, instead of the ill will stemming from resistance to claims for injuries attributable to the use of one's products or services. At the same time, providers of goods and services would not be required to cover *all* risks connected with their output, the prospect of which is so forbidding. Rather they are allowed—not required—to select risks for which no-fault insurance *is* feasible.[23]

As examples of the way third-party no-fault would work, a manufacturer of a power tool could elect to take out a no-fault policy to pay for economic losses—medical expense and wage loss—payable whenever an amputation results from the use of the power tool. Payment would be made without regard to the victim's possible carelessness or the lack of any defect in the tool. Similarly, a doctor who knows the inevitable risks of, say, cardiac arrest in even normal patients in the course of a given surgical procedure could agree to pay for economic losses stemming from such an adverse result of an operation, regardless of anyone's fault. In both cases, the prior agreement to make no-fault payments would wipe out any claim based on fault, just as happens under no-fault auto insurance and workers' compensation.

If a business or health-care provider had agreed to provide third-party no-fault benefits to a person already covered under a first-party contract, under normal insurance rules the victim could claim against his own insurance company, which could then get automatic contribution from the third party's insurance company.[24]

Admittedly, however, most producers of goods and services have been reluctant to consider electing third-party no-fault insurance to cover their risks. There have been a few exceptions. At the behest of the Toro Company of Minnesota, a leading manufacturer of power lawnmowers, a bill authorizing manufacturers to elect no-fault insurance was introduced in the Minnesota legislature and has been the subject of hearings.[25] (Although such legislation is arguably not necessary, Toro wanted it before proceeding to initiate no-fault.) Efforts are currently under way, sponsored by the American Bar Association's Commission on Medical Professional Liability, to have doctors and lawyers define compensable events for medical treatment for which no-fault benefits might be paid under a scheme of third-party no-fault insurance. On the whole, though, there is probably more hope with experimentation in the near future under first-party no-fault. Despite the overall timidity of the insurance industry, several large insurance institutions are exploring experimental first-party no-fault programs.

In the meantime, there is one legislative possibility for further application of no-fault that is very promising, and that concerns industrial accidents covered both by workers' compensation *and* by product liability insurance. Recall that under workers' compensation acts, employers guarantee on a no-fault basis all medical expenses and at least subsistence wage loss to employees injured on the job in return for the employee's surrender of his fault-finding claim against his employer.

Through the years plaintiffs' lawyers have realized that although the employer is thus exempt from fault-finding liability, third-party suppliers of industrial equipment to the place of employment, suppliers of such things as punch-press machines, are not. The result has been a rising number of so-called third-party product liability suits. According to one study, almost one-half of the total of product liability payments for personal injury (42 percent) went to employees injured on the job and therefore presumably already covered by workers' compensation.[26]

Plaintiffs' lawyers are quick to point out that the reason so many injured employees sue third parties, in addition to collecting workers' compensation benefits, is the inadequacy of workers' compensation benefits. Until 1974, for example, the maximum weekly benefit for disabled workers in twenty-three of the fifty states was below the official poverty level for a family of four—then $82.69 a week.[27] But if one wishes to augment workers' compensation benefits, which are at least assured, if often inadequate, doing so by the dilatory, wasteful, haphazard lottery of fault-finding claims is about as bad a way as one could find. In addition, despite attempts by the states to upgrade their workers' compensation benefits since 1974, a bill in Congress would mandate even higher benefits by Federal standards.[28] Herein lies the rub: Despite strong labor backing, higher workers' compensation benefits are being stoutly resisted by business, especially if mandated by the Federal government. On the other hand, business wants relief from the growing threats of product liability suits, and such relief can be gained, as a practical matter, only by Federal action, inasmuch as most product sales and claims extend across state borders. Labor, however, understandably opposes eliminating product liability claims for workers, at least without some *quid pro quo*. The makings of a healthy compromise are thereby suggested: The Federal bill for Federal standards should increase workers' compensation benefits and at the same time make receipt of such benefits the sole source of payment for industrial accident victims, at least as against third parties who themselves cover their employees by workers' compensation. In other words, business will be obligated to pay higher workers' compensation benefits but, at the same time, will gain relief from product liability claims. With such obvious advantages for both management and labor, both powerful lobbying forces, the chances of legislative success in overriding trial lawyer opposition are markedly better than for other no-fault proposals, which have some general consumer support but no backing by such vested interests.

One additional feature should be added: If the bill simply abolishes product liability claims against third-party suppliers, it would allow manufacturers of industrial equipment to escape the costs of injuries caused by their defective products. In other words, at a stroke, manufacturers of industrial equipment would shed almost all financial responsibility for any injuries caused to other than their own employees by their defective products, with the costs falling solely on their purchasers' workers' compensation insurance. As a way of overcoming this objection, I propose that workers' compensation be made the sole source of payment for any industrial accident victim, but an employer paying workers' compensation benefits should be allowed to claim against any third party causing injury to an employee to defray the costs of the workers' compensation benefits. In other words, the injured employee retains his absolute right to workers' compensation benefits regardless of his own fault or the lack of any fault on his employer's part; but such an employee loses his common law claim not only against his employer but against any third-party supplier to his employer. On the other hand, his employer is entitled to claim against any such third party injuring an employee up to the amount of the workers' compensation benefits that are payable.[29]

Here, too, although the cumbersome issue of fault must still be litigated as between the employer and the third party, such litigation—which would normally take place only between commercial establishments—would be more likely to be handled expeditiously. If settlement is not reached, arbitration could be readily used (neither party being in a position to exploit sympathy from a jury), and even more ambitious contractual arrangements to dispose of matters *en masse* might well be resorted to. For example, the parties might agree, either at the time of sale of the product or on an annual basis, on a rough calculation of employers' compensation premiums allocable to a third party's machinery rather than litigating cases one by one. In this way, the highly wasteful fault-finding tort system with its need to litigate case by case the issues of both fault and pain and suffering would be by-passed.

The type of statute proposed here would result in benefits to all parties concerned: employees, employers, third-party suppliers of industrial equipment, and insurance companies. Although individual employees would lose their fault-finding claims, as a group they would lose very little, because in any given case there is little likelihood of payment, and because of the delay and waste accompanying any payment. And for the little that employees lose, they will be recompensed by an increase in more certain and therefore more valuable workers' compensation benefits.

The employer, under this "sole source" system, gains too in that he no longer has to bear indirectly the costs of product liability while bearing directly the cost of workers' compensation, as he now must do in a manner that runs contrary to the bargain promised to employers when workers' compensation acts were passed early in the century. After all, under the present system, manufacturers of industrial equipment naturally try to include in the price of their equipment the cost of product liability insurance necessary to cover claims made by persons already paid from workers' compensation. As a result, employers end up paying for both workers' compensation and fault-finding liability claims. This proposal also operates greatly to the advantage of manufacturers of industrial equipment. Under the proposed sole source provision, such manufacturers escape exposure to common law product liability. They are not, however, permitted to evade all losses attributable to their products, as they would be if an employer had to bear all costs of injuries to his employees caused by defective products. Finally, the insurance industry, plagued by the uncertainties of the product liability market to such an extent that many insurance companies are shying away from that market, should welcome a change that will restore more stable conditions to product liability coverage.

It is not clear by what means the fault-finding system of personal injury compensation will ultimately be displaced by no-fault insurance, whether by first-party or third-party elective no-fault; by a combination of the two; by sweeping reforms of the New Zealand variety (p. 182); or by some other compromise system. What ought to be clear, however, is that the present system of lawyers' fault-finding gives us the worst of both worlds—soaring premiums and scanty benefits—and is doomed to fall. Indeed, the only surprising thing is that this outmoded way of dealing with accidents should have lasted so long into the twentieth century.

Daniel Patrick Moynihan, in urging favorable consideration of elective no-fault insurance, calls no-fault auto insurance "the one incontestably successful reform [proposed in] the 1960's." Moynihan also attempts to place elective no-fault liability in a broad sociopolitical and economic context. He cites the rise in distrust of business and professionals, as well as government, exemplified in the increasing aggressiveness and futility of the consumer movement:

> There is an element . . . in the new consumerism which is not reassuring at all. . . . I fear that American education is increasingly turning out persons of socially active dispositions who do not understand or accept how the American economic system works and that this is going to have the most baleful consequences for that system. It is going to become overregulated and oversued, undercapitalized and underproductive.

"It is here," Moynihan asserts, "that [elective no-fault liability insurance] assumes an almost unique importance for, while modest seeming, it addresses the largest of questions." Since elective no-fault insurance for products and services is self-executing, without the need for a cumbersome new bureaucracy, such as those ordained by the Occupational Safety and Health Administration (OSHA) and other such regulatory bodies, it is, for Moynihan, a prototype of the kind of innovative, pragmatic, cooperative, and mutually beneficial reform that is essential to our society. It is, he writes,

> . . . conservative . . . in the sense that Justice Frankfurter was conservative [It] values highly those things the legal system can do, and . . . is concerned that [the legal system] not seek to overdo. An overextended system, dealing with ever more peripheral issues, eventually becomes incapable of dealing with those vital and central issues for which it was created. The image of empires collapsing on their marches comes to mind. [The proponents of elective no-fault liabil-

ity do] not want us litigating ourselves into a stalemated and para-
noid society. We could do so. We could take all the fun out of it, all
the pride out of it, and that would be such a waste, such a loss. . . .
[C]onfrontational, adversary relations are developing seemingly
everywhere. They can't succeed. When everyone sues, no one gets
satisfied. (Our experience with the automobile brought us after the
fact to that realization.) . . . The legal system becomes ever more en-
cumbered. . . . Justice . . . is not done. . . . Free systems come more
and more to be seen as threatening; regulation ever more normal
and necessary. . . . This is the way systems die.[30]

Earlier Moynihan, in discussing the advantages of no-fault auto
insurance, had stated that the proponents of no-fault insurance "are
right in the all-important perception as to what it is Americans are
good at. We are good at maintaining business relationships once a
basis of mutual self-interest is established. [No-fault insurance]
would establish one."[31] Elective no-fault insurance allows insurance
companies and their insureds to by-pass lawyers with all their self-
serving cumbersomeness in dealing with all kinds of accidental injuries. It too, then, is an excellent example of establishing a relationship based on mutual self-interest. As such, Moynihan writes, it is
not merely "concerned with aspects of tort liability [but is concerned
with] those particulars whereby a free society remains free."[32]

Professor Luke Cooperrider of the University of Michigan Law
School has pointed out that the common law fault-finding system is
roundly condemned not only because it treats accident victims very
badly, but because in the course of doing so it wastes resources that
could otherwise provide more adequately for victims' needs. Personal injury lawyers often counter with the argument that the common law fault-finding system is being blamed for not doing what it
was never designed to do. It is, after all, a way of resolving conflicts—by its very nature contentious. How could a fault-finding system be otherwise, or how could it even come to be thought of as a
likely mechanism for the efficient treatment of the massive social
problem of compensating accident victims? But that argument, says
Cooperrider, begs the question. Assuming it makes sense, for either
compassionate or economic reasons, for society to undertake to replace the economic losses of the many who are fortuitously victimized by injury from our technological environment—and indeed this
is clearly the trend even in fault-finding litigation (pp. 138–40)—then
surely it makes sense to find a more efficient way of doing it than a
system of fault-finding provides. It makes sense, Cooperrider says,

to try to put compensation on an insurance basis rather than a litigation basis. If a comprehensive social insurance system providing not only for medical care but for maintenance of income as well seems destined not to be in the foreseeable future, then we must look to the private sector. There, admittedly, a significant part of the problem is already treated on a first-party basis through medical and disability insurance, through various employment-related fringe benefits, and even through significant public social insurance programs. But the crying need is to provide supplements to replace the very large economic losses *not* absorbed by the insurance sources already in place, and also to bring as many as possible of the less well-connected members of our society under the umbrella of protection. The most immediate source of funds to divert in order to help with this part of the problem seems to lie in the fault-finding liability system. There is no other way, Cooperrider argues, "of bringing in from the cold those who do not presently enjoy sufficient benefits provided by our conglomeration of private sector medical expense and income protection devices." This is what automobile no-fault statutes, in their limited way, have accomplished for auto injuries, and workmen's compensation for industrial accidents. If a scheme of elective no-fault insurance is by no means as neat and as comprehensive as that which was possible with respect to industrial and automobile accidents, Cooperrider contends, it is nonetheless clearly the most feasible way of beginning to attack the problem of compensating for injuries not now covered by auto no-fault, workers' compensation, or other insurance sources.[33]

In sum, elective no-fault insurance provides the only practicable means of immediately "bringing in from the cold" many of those whose losses from accidents outstrip their present sources of help. Only personal injury lawyers will be hurt by such a step.

Appendix

Making It Work

UNDER FIRST-PARTY ELECTIVE NO-FAULT, the first-party insurance company guarantees to its insured not only the level of no-fault benefits chosen by the insured but whatever amount of economic loss above that level the insured is eligible for from any third party whose conduct or product is faulty.

This provision concerning distribution of the tort recovery could cause problems of conflict of interest betweeen the insurer and its no-fault insured, unless corrective devices are employed. Consider a hypothetical case: Alton buys $10,000 worth of no-fault benefits from Allied Insurance Company. Alton is injured in an accident with Baker and suffers $30,000 in economic loss. Allied, of course, must pay Alton up to $10,000 in no-fault benefits as losses accrue, pursuant to the no-fault contract. When Allied proceeds to settle Alton's tort claims with Baker (or Beneficial Insurance Company, which insures Bakers' tort liability), Allied may wish to settle the case expeditiously for, say, $15,000 rather than litigate extensively for possibly more. Allied may be convinced, for example, that in the event of actual litigation a jury could find against Alton. Or Allied may, at year's end, have five claims against Beneficial, which has six against Allied, which the two companies want to settle all together. After all, the possibility of such expeditious settlement of claims between insurers and self-insurers is one of the virtues of first-party no-fault insurance. But even if the case is settled individually be-

tween Allied and Beneficial for $15,000, Allied might find it difficult
to satisfy Alton as to the allocation of the $15,000 between economic
and noneconomic damages, especially if the lump sum had been discounted for reasons of doubtful liability. How much of the $15,000
was precisely attributable to economic loss, and how much to pain
and suffering (and therefore belonging to Allied)? The problem is
that when a settlement amount is agreed on between Allied and Beneficial it is not normally broken down into component parts—rather
a lump sum figure is, for the most part, intuitively arrived at. Obviously, then, the manner in which Allied efficiently disposes of
Alton's tort claim and purports to distribute the proceeds could lead
to conflicts of interest, disputes, or, at least, disappointment and
misunderstanding. But unless Allied has the power to dispose absolutely of Alton's claim, without the intervention of Alton, some of
the effectiveness of first-party no-fault insurance is lost.

The solution I propose is this: Allied will retain the power to dispose absolutely of Alton's tort claim, but will also undertake an obligation to pay Alton, besides the level of no-fault benefits Alton has
purchased, the equivalent of whatever amount of economic loss in
excess of that limit Alton is eligible for under tort liability. The
amount, if any, of Allied's obligation to pay Alton's tort recovery
for economic loss will be determinable ultimately by giving Alton a
right to require arbitration, in a procedure solely between Allied and
Alton, on the issues of the fact and amount of Baker's tort liability
to Alton for economic loss. In other words, Allied, quite apart from
any settlement it makes with Baker or Beneficial, must allow Alton
to submit the amount of Baker's tort liability to Alton for economic
loss to arbitration. Thus, Allied gets unfettered control over Alton's
tort claim, but, as I said, Alton is assured of not only whatever level
of no-fault benefits he has purchased, but whatever economic loss in
excess of that limit he is eligible for under tort liability.[1]

Assume again that Alton elected $10,000 of no-fault benefits, but
now he suffers $8,000 of economic loss and $12,000 of noneconomic
loss. Alton receives $8,000 in no-fault benefits from Allied, which,
in turn, succeeds to Alton's entire tort claim against Baker of
$20,000 ($8,000 in economic and $12,000 in noneconomic loss).[2]
Allied will be using the $12,000 recovered for Alton's noneconomic
loss (pain and suffering) to fund payment of the economic loss of its
insureds without tort claims. Note that, where Alton has insured
himself for as much or more in no-fault benefits as he suffers in economic loss, no problem of distributing tort proceeds due to Alton

arises. This would be true in the great majority of cases. But the exceptional cases must be considered.

In our first hypothetical instance, Alton elected $10,000 of no-fault benefits and suffered $30,000 of economic loss plus, let us further assume, $25,000 of noneconomic loss. Allied pays Alton $10,000 in no-fault benefits as loss accrues. Allied also proceeds to claim against Baker (or Beneficial, Baker's liability insurer). Allied and Beneficial may negotiate at the end of the year a bulk settlement of all mutual claims against each other, or Allied may settle the claim individually with Beneficial, as suggested earlier.

Various possibilities can occur, then, as Allied deals with Baker or Beneficial.

1. Allied may be unable to extract any settlement from Baker (because of doubtful liability, for example), or Allied may settle with Baker for $15,000, which includes $7,000, say, allocable to Alton's economic loss, less than Alton's no-fault limit of $10,000. In either event, Allied would make no offer to Alton of any amount in excess of no-fault benefits. But Alton would have the right to arbitrate with Allied as to whether he is entitled to more from Allied, as representing his economic loss above the no-fault limits due in a tort claim from Baker. Alton would have to pay his own lawyer if he wishes to retain one for such a proceeding. (More on such arbitration proceedings below.)

2. Allied may settle with Baker for an amount in excess of Allied's no-fault obligation to Alton and then offer Alton what Allied thinks represents Alton's share of the settlement as allocable in turn to Alton's economic loss above the no-fault limits. Assume in this regard that Allied settles with Baker for $18,000 and then offers Alton $8,000 as representing the amount of the settlement in excess of no-fault limits ($10,000) due to Alton. Alton can either accept the $8,000 or demand a separate arbitration between Beneficial and Allied over the fair evaluation of his claim for more. Such an arbitration proceeding would be very similar to those normally held under uninsured motorist coverage where a first-party insurer and its insured arbitrate the value of the insured's tort claim against a third party (the uninsured motorist allegedly negligently injuring the insured), with the first-party insurer in effect assuming the role of the third party's tort liability insurer. The main difference would be that only a portion of the insured's economic loss due from the third party, not his entire economic and noneconomic loss, would be assessable against the first-party insurer. Note again that Alton (as

with uninsured motorist coverage) must pay his own lawyer if he wishes to retain one in such a proceeding.[3] Note too that any amounts payable by Allied to Alton in excess of no-fault limits, whether payable pursuant to arbitration or not, could be payable periodically as losses accrue, as with the no-fault benefits.

3. Allied can litigate against Baker (either pursuant to arbitration or otherwise), with either Alton or Allied able to insist that Alton join the litigation, in which event Alton will be bound by the findings as to his losses. Alton will have a choice in such a proceeding against Baker of either being represented by a lawyer of his own choosing (whom Alton will be under an obligation to pay himself) or relying on Allied's lawyer. In this proceeding, whether by arbitration or otherwise, Alton and Allied will request that the judge or jury, in a special verdict, separate economic from noneconomic damages.[4]

Note that by virtue of standing to gain to the extent there is a finding of economic loss in excess of no-fault limits, Alton's interests coincide with Allied's. This is especially so because the finding of Alton's noneconomic loss (which accrues to Allied) will normally vary directly with the finding of economic loss, and never, as a practical matter, inversely. This coincidence of interest between Alton and Allied will make it less necessary for Alton to retain and pay his own lawyer in litigation against Baker.

Note also that in such a proceeding there is nothing to flag to the tribunal—whether judge, juror, or arbitrator—that to any abnormal extent Allied is a party-in-interest. In other words, the case will be tried exactly like a case where Alton is claiming for both his economic and his noneconomic loss and Allied is subrogated to the extent of any first-party payment to Alton. But there is no reason why, if necessary, steps could not be taken to shield a jury from knowing of Allied's interest as plaintiff, just as a jury is normally shielded from knowing of an insurance company's role as defendant or as subrogee.[5]

Allied will retain control of the handling of the claim against Baker throughout the case, including the right to settle at any point (even once the trial or hearing has begun or during appeal), subject once again to Alton's right to arbitration of the amount due him from Allied based on his tort claim for his economic loss above no-fault limits.

Assume that Alton (who, it will be recalled, has purchased $10,000 of no-fault coverage) has a total claim against Baker which is arbitrated to a decision under which the finding is that Baker is liable to Alton for $30,000 in economic loss and $25,000 in noneco-nomic loss. The arrangement could be structured so that: (1) The en-tire verdict is payable to Allied, with Allied then under an obligation to continue to pay Alton benefits periodically as losses accrue until the $30,000 limit is reached. (2) As another possibility, Allied could be obliged to pay over the $20,000 representing Alton's economic loss above the no-fault limits directly to Alton in lump sum, thereby ending any further obligation except to continue periodic payment of no-fault benefits until the $10,000 limit is reached. (3) Finally, Al-lied could pay Alton in lump sum the entire amount of Alton's eco-nomic loss above amounts already paid in no-fault benefits. The first arrangement strikes me as preferable.

Notes

Chapter 1: BLIND MAN'S BUFF *(pp.3–7)*

1. Learned Hand, address, Association of the Bar of the City of New York, November 17, 1921, reprinted in 3 *Ass'n Bar City of New York Lectures on Legal Topics* 87 (1926).
2. *Washington Post*, July 30, 1976, p. A–1.
3. *New York Times*, March 27, 1975, pp. 1, 29.
4. Ibid., p. 29.
5. The discussion of the history of research on RLF is closely based on a perceptive piece by Lawrence Altman, "A Dilemma for Doctors, Patients and the Courts, *New York Times*, April 27, 1975, pp. 1, 42.
6. Joseph Leaser, M.D., letter to the editor, *Newsweek*, May 12, 1975, pp. 4–6, quoted in R. Epstein, *Medical Malpractice: The Case for Contract*, 1976 Am. Bar Foundation Res. J. at 87, 114–15 n. 54.
7. *Washington Post*, July 30, 1976, p. A–1.

Chapter 2: THE UNDERWORLD OF TORT *(pp. 8–28)*

1. U.S. Dep't of Transportation, *Economic Consequences of Automobile Accident Injuries* (1970), 1:37–38; A. Conard, J. Morgan, R. Pratt, C. Votz, and R. Bombaugh, *Automobile Accident Costs and Payments: Studies in the Economics of Injury Reparation* (1964), p. 186 (45 per-

cent of the seriously injuried get no damage recovery through the tort law system).

2. *E.g.*, Nat'l Comm'n on Product Safety, *Final Report* (1970), p. 74.

3. *E.g.*, J. O'Connell, *Ending Insult to Injury: No-Fault Insurance for Products and Services* (1975), p. 41.

4. "Righting the Liability Balance," Report of California Citizens' Commission on Tort Reform (1977), p. 111.

5. U.S. Dep't of Transportation, *Economic Consequences of Automobile Accident Injuries*, 1:52.

6. N.Y. Insurance Department, "Automobile Insurance . . . For Whose Benefit?" A Report to Governor Nelson A. Rockefeller, (1970), p. 19, *n.* 26.

7. L. Meyer, "And a Doctor Explains How He Does It," *Washington Post* News Service, week of June 12, 1977.

8. M. Mayer, *The Lawyers* (1966), p. 263.

9. *New York Times*, May 9, 1973, p. 45; also referred to in O'Connell, *Ending Insult to Injury*, pp. 52–53.

10. As quoted in M. Bloom, *The Trouble with Lawyers* (1968), p. 130.

11. J. O'Connell and R. Simon, *Payment for Pain and Suffering: Who Wants What When and Why?* (1972), p. 19; also printed in 1971 *U. Ill. L. F.* 1, 19.

12. J. O'Connell, *The Injury Industry* (1971), p. 65.

13. *Gunn* v. *Washek*, 405 Pa. 521, 176 A. 2d 635 (1961).

14. Bloom, *Trouble with Lawyers*, p. 131, referred to in O'Connell, *Injury Industry*, p. 57.

15. *Philadelphia Sunday Bulletin*, Feb. 21, 1971, p. 11; also referred to in O'Connell, *Injury Industry*, p. 57.

16. *Standards for No-Fault Motor Vehicle Accident Benefits Act: Hearings on S. 1381 Before the Senate Comm. on Commerce, Science, and Transportation,* 95th Cong., 1st Sess. (1977), p. 208.

17. Ibid.

18. J. Carlin, *Lawyers on Their Own* (1962), pp. 87–88; also referred to in O'Connell, *Injury Industry*, pp. 57–58.

19. "Comment: Settlement of Personal Injury Cases in the Chicago Area," 47 *N.W.U.L. Rev.* (1953): 895, 899; R. Yoder, "How an Ambulance Chaser Works," *Saturday Evening Post*, March 23, 1957, pp. 19, 96; also referred to in O'Connell, *Injury Industry*, p. 59.

20. R. Harris, "Gambling Lawyer," *Wall Street Journal*, May 22, 1978, p. 1.

21. Carlin, *Lawyers on Their Own*, p. 90; also referred to in O'Connell, *Injury Industry*, p. 59.

22. Carlin, *Lawyers on Their Own*, pp. 84–85; also referred to in O'Connell, *Injury Industry*, pp. 59–60.

23. J. G. Dunne, *True Confessions* (1977), pp. 212-13.
24. Ibid., p. 218.
25. *Congressional Record*, 117 (Feb. 24, 1971): S1851; also referred to in O'Connell, *Injury Industry*, p. 60.
26. *Wall Street Journal*, Aug. 28, 1964, p. 1. A confession from a ring member broke the case. Anderson received a five-year sentence.
27. *Malpractice Lifeline*, vol. 3, no. 10, May 22, 1978.
28. *Newsweek*, April 7, 1975, p. 49.
29. H. Lancaster, "Faked Out," *Wall Street Journal*, Dec. 23, 1974, pp. 1, 13.
30. *Newsweek*, April 7, 1975, p. 49.
31. Ibid.
32. Taken from a private letter, dated May 4, 1964; also referred to in O'Connell, *Injury Industry*, pp. 18-19.
33. R. Dudnik and J. Leonard, "Instructions to Clients," in *Anatomy of a Personal Injury Law Suit: A Handbook of Basic Trial Advocacy* (published by the American Trial Lawyers Association, now renamed the Association of Trial Lawyers of America, 1968), pp. 20-21.
34. Private letter, note 32 *supra*.
35. As quoted in *State No-Fault Automobile Insurance Experiences: Hearings Before the House Subcomm. on Interstate and Foreign Commerce*, 95th Cong., 1st Sess. (1977), p. 716.
36. A. Conard, "Book Review," *UCLA L. Rev.*, 13 (1966): 1432, 1433; also referred to in O'Connell, *Injury Industry*, p. 17.
37. U.S. Railroad Retirement Board, *Work Injuries in the Railroad Industry 1938-40*, (1947), p. 176; quoted in F. Harper and H. James, *The Law of Torts*, 2 (1956): 1303-4. Harper and James say in their torts treatise, "this conclusion is particularly significant in view of the stable and conservative character of railroad employees. We know of no other study on this question." Ibid., 2:1304, n. 3.
38. U.S. Dep't Transp., *State No-Fault Automobile Insurance Experience, 1971-77* (1977), p. 60.
39. Although the studies concerned consumer products, as opposed to capital goods, the results seem significantly applicable to both.
40. W. Whitford, "Products Liability," *Supplemental Studies to Final Report, National Commission on Product Safety*, 3 (1970): 221, 228.
41. Statement of H. Denenberg, *Hearing of the National Commission on Product Safety*, 9A (1970): 311, 312.
42. Ibid., 9A: 314-17.
43. O'Connell, *An Alternative to Abandoning Tort Liability*, Minn. L. Rev., 60 (1976): pp. 551-53; P. Atiyah, *Accidents Compensation and the Law*, 2d ed. (1975), pp. 550-51; Accident Prevention and Variable Premium Rates for Work-connected Accidents, *Industrial L.J.*, 4

(1975): 1–5; *Report of the National Commission on State Workmen's Compensation Laws* 97, (1972): fig. 5.5; W. Blum and H. Kalven, "Ceilings, Costs, and Compulsion in Auto Compensation Legislation," 1973 *Utah L. Rev.*, pp. 341, 380, n. 44.

On the other hand, keep in mind that largely through workers' compensation insurance, more has probably been done by way of deterrence for industrial accidents than for any other kind. Harper and James, *Law of Torts*, p. 757, § 12.4.

44. Interagency Task Force on Product Liability (undated), *Final Report*, p. IV–11.
45. Ibid., p. V–14.
46. Special Advisory Panel on Medical Malpractice, State of New York, *Report* (1976), p. 19.
47. E. Bernzweig, *Defensive Medicine*, in U.S. Dep't of Health, Education and Welfare, *Report of the Secretary's Commission on Medical Malpractice* (1973), Appendix, pp. 38–40 citing "Child Head X-Ray: Value Doubted After a Study of 570 Cases," *Medical Tribune*, 11, no. 54 (Oct. 26. 1970): 1 ff. Also referred to in O'Connell, *Ending Insult to Injury*, n. 3 *supra*, p. 43.
48. *Business Insurance*, Sept. 10, 1973, p. 3. Also referred to in O'Connell, *Ending Insult*, p. 43.
49. Special Advisory Panel, *Report*, p. 161.
50. R. Gambino, "The Genesis of Medical Error: Three Case Histories," *New York Times*, March 20, 1976, p. 27.
51. T. Davis, "President's Page," *Trial*, 14 (June 1978): 4; also Interagency Task Force, *Final Report*, p. VII–77.
52. "BNA," *Product Safety and Liability Reporter*, 5, no. 12 (March 15, 1977): 227.
53. R. Keeton, *Basic Text on Insurance Law* (1971), § 7.8.
54. N.Y. Ins. Dep't., n. 6 *supra*, p. 38.
55. D. Moynihan, "Next: A New Auto Insurance Policy," *New York Times Magazine*, Aug. 27, 1967, p. 76.

Chapter 3: The Tricks—and the Tragedies . . . of the Trade *(pp. 29–61)*

1. J. Laing, "For the Plaintiff," *Wall Street Journal*, Aug. 2, 1972, p. 1; also referred to in J. O'Connell, *Ending Insult to Injury: No-Fault Insurance for Products and Services* 4 (1975), p. 4.
2. Laing, "For the Defense," *Wall Street Journal*, July 5, 1973, p. 1; also referred to in O'Connell, *Ending Insult*.

3. J. Star, "The Million-Dollar Attorney for the Maimed," *Chicago Tribune Magazine*, April 3, 1977, pp. 24, 25.
4. Ibid., pp. 25–26.
5. Laing, "For the Plaintiff," p. 13.
6. Ibid.
7. Star, "Million-Dollar Attorney," p. 30.
8. Laing, "For the Defense," p. 10.
9. Star, "Million-Dollar Attorney," p. 28.
10. Laing, "For the Defense," p. 10.
11. Ibid.
12. Star, "Million-Dollar Attorney," p. 28.
13. Ibid.
14. Laing, "For the Defense," p. 10.
15. Star, "Million-Dollar Attorney," p. 28.
16. Ibid., p. 30.
17. Ibid., p. 25.
18. Laing, "For the Defense, p. 10.
19. Ibid.
20. O'Connell, *Ending Insult*, note 1 *supra*, pp. 6–7.
21. J. Goulden, *The Million-Dollar Lawyers* (1978), p. 72.
22. Ibid., p. 285.
23. Laing, "For the Defense," p. 10.
24. Ibid.
25. "The Doctor in Court," *Medical Trial Technique Quarterly* (1974), pp. 283, 288.
26. Ibid., pp. 287–88.
27. Ibid., p. 288.
28. Ibid., p. 289.
29. Ibid.
30. Ibid., p. 290.
31. Ibid., p. 297.
32. Ibid., pp. 300–301.
33. *Gilborges* v. *Wallace*, 153 N.J. Super. 121, 379 A2d 269 (App. Div. 1977).
34. *Richardson* v. *Employers Liability Assurance Corp.*, 102 Cal. Rptr. 547, 25 Cal. App. 3d 232 (1972).
35. Institute of Continuing Legal Education, University of Michigan, *Liability: Trial Demonstrations and Lectures*, ed. J. Reed (1967), p. 244.
36. Goulden, *Million-Dollar Lawyers*, note 21 *supra*, p. 71.
37. *New York Times*, Feb. 19, 1976, p. 28. But for a discussion of a contention on behalf of Miss Hearst of Bailey's inadequate representa-

tion of her by virtue of his seeking headlines through "flamboyance" and "showing off" and by virtue of appearing tired and shaky in court and consuming "what might have been medicine for a hangover", see *New York Times*, Aug. 4, 1978, p. B-2. For Mr. Bailey's answer see *New York Times*, Aug. 8, 1978, p. A-10.

38. *Cecil* v. *Gibson*, 37 Ill. App. 3d 710, 346 N.E.2d 448 (1976).
39. Goulden, *Million-Dollar Lawyers*, pp. 84–85.
40. Institute of Continuing Legal Education, *Liability*, pp. 456–59.
41. Ibid., pp. 505–7.
42. J. Sanders, "Two Judges Help 'King of Torts' Chalk Up $6.8-Million Settlement," *Nat'l L.J.*, Nov. 6, 1978, p. 9.
43. L. Nizer, *My Life in Court* (1961), pp. 347–79. For quotes see pp. 360–62, 363–64, 366, 373, 374, 376, 377, 378, 379.
44. Ibid., pp. 380–425. For quotes see pp. 418, 422–24.

Chapter 4: MORE ON LAWYERS' FEATS AND CLIENTS' DEFEATS *(pp. 62–83)*

1. J. Star, "The Million-Dollar Attorney for the Maimed," *Chicago Tribune Magazine*, April 3, 1977, pp. 24–25.
2. Ibid., p. 25.
3. Ibid., p. 26.
4. M. O'Connor, "Making It Clear," *Champaign–Urbana News-Gazette*, Feb. 23, 1976, p. A-3.
5. Star, "Million-Dollar Attorney," p. 26.
6. M. Mayer, *The Lawyers* (1966), p. 266.
7. S. Shellenbarger, "He Helps Lawyers Get Into the Act," Associated Press release, week of May 15, 1978.
8. *New York Times*, June 28, 1978. p. A-15.
9. *Preston* v. *Carr*, Y & J 175, 179 (1826), as quoted in J. Wigmore, *Evidence*, 6, § 1845 (rev. by J. Chadboun, 1976): 488.
10. Ibid., p. 489.
11. F. Pollock and F. Maitland, *History of the English Law* (1st. ed., 1895), p. 667, as quoted in Wigmore, *Evidence*, 6:489.
12. Wigmore, *Evidence*, 6:490.
13. *New York Times*, June 28, 1978, p. A-15.
14. Ibid.
15. *Washington Post*, Aug. 21, 1978, pp. C-1–C-2.
16. *New York Times*, June 28, 1978, p. A-15.
17. *New York Times*, July 24, 1978, p. D-4.

18. *Wall Street Journal*, April 11, 1978, pp. 1, 17. Perkins was sentenced to a month in prison. *Wall Street Journal*, Oct. 18, 1978, p. 7.
19. *Buehler* v. *Whalen*, 70 Ill. 2d 51, 64 (1978).
20. Brief of Defendant-Appellant, Debra Whalen, p. 18; 70 Ill. 2d at 65.
21. Brief of Whalen, p. 18.
22. Ibid., p. 19.
23. Letter to author from Ray H. Freeark, Jr., January 30, 1979; 70 Ill. 2d at 66.
24. 70 Ill. 2d at 65.
25. Conversation with Richard C. Hodson, Attorney for Marie Buehler, December 1978.
26. 70 Ill. 2d at 65.
27. Conversation with Hodson.
28. Brief of Plaintiffs-Appellees, Marie Buehler, *et al.*, p. 14.
29. 70 Ill. 2d at 65–66.
30. 70. Ill. 2d at 67. The Illinois Supreme Court in the Buehler case was confronted with an appeal from the trial court's denial of defendant Whalen's motion for entry of a default judgment against Ford. Whalen claimed that Ford's abuse of discovery procedures entitled her to a default judgment as a means of punishing Ford. Instead of granting Whalen's motion, the trial judge held a hearing in order to determine whether Ford should be held in contempt of court. The court decided that Ford was not guilty of contempt "because of the technical language of the various requests made to Ford to produce information." In other words, Ford was technically free of contempt because plaintiff's request for discovery had not been sufficiently precise. 70 Ill. 2d at 66.

    The Supreme Court denied that there had been any such "technical language," implying that if the Supreme Court had held the contempt hearing Ford would not have been acquitted. Indeed, the court went further and said that "the trial court would have been justified" if it had stricken Ford's answer and submitted only the question of damages to the jury. 70 Ill. 2d at 67. However, the Supreme Court's language technically does not have the effect of reversing the trial court's decisions that Ford was neither in contempt nor subject to the default penalty. Thus, in a highly technical sense, Ford was found, after the fact, to have violated no rule warranting a penalty. Nonetheless, the Illinois Supreme Court castigated Ford's abuse of discovery.
31. J. O'Connell and A. Myers, *Safety Last: An Indictment of the Auto Industry* (1966), p. 180; *see* People *ex rel.* Gen. Motors Corp. *v.* Bua, 37 Ill. 2d 180 (1967).
32. J. Goulden, *The Million-Dollar Lawyers* (1978), pp. 297–98; O'Connell and Myers, *Safety Last*, pp. 181–82.

33. Goulden, pp. 296–97, 305.

34. *New York Times*, note 8 *supra*.

35. R. Erwin, "Defense of Persons Accused of Driving While Under the Influence of Alcohol," *The Practical Lawyer* 11 (1965): 73, 80–84, 89–90.

36. B. Nissen, "For the Defense," *Wall Street Journal*, Oct. 31, 1978, pp. 1, 33.

37. In point of fact, trial judges will often "send the case to the jury" even if they think only one side should win, that is, even if they think there should be a directed verdict. They do this in order to lessen the chance of a reversal by an appellate court. It works this way: If the judge does not give the case to the jury but directs a judgment for, say, the defendant, and the appellate court thinks the case should have gone to the jury, the appellate court will have to reverse the trial judge's decision. But if the trial judge thinks the defendant should have a directed verdict but nonetheless gives the case to the jury, and then the jury finds for the defendant, there is no harm done. The defendant certainly won't complain by appealing (since all he cares about is that he won) and the plaintiff has no complaint (unless he maintains the extreme proposition that on these facts that *he* should have had a directed verdict). On the other hand, if the jury finds for the plaintiff where the trial judge knows the defendant should have had a directed verdict, the trial judge will simply overrule the jury and award what is called a "judgment notwithstanding the verdict." As a result, sending the case to the jury makes it much less likely the case will be successfully appealed.

Chapter 5: THE CIVIL JURY *(pp. 84–106)*

1. California Citizens' Comm'n on Tort Reform, "Report: Righting the Liability Balance" (1977), p. 53.

2. C. Desmond, "Should It Take 34 Months for a Trial?" *New York Times Magazine*, Dec. 8, 1963, pp. 29, 82.

3. *Chicago Tribune*, April 22, 1978 p. 8.

4. *Wall Street Journal*, Nov. 29, 1977, p. 40.

5. *Wall Street Journal*, June 12, 1975, p. 10.

6. H. Kalven, "Juries and Personal Injury Cases: Their Functions and Methods," in W. Curran and N. Chayet, eds., *Trauma and the Automobile* (1966), pp. 335, 339.

7. J. Bishop, book review, *Yale L.J.*, 69 (1960): 925, 927.

8. "Sudden Riches for the Casualty Insurers," *Business Week*, May 1, 1978. pp. 66, 71.

9. F. James and S. Law, "Compensation for Auto Accident Victims: A Story of Too Little and Too Late," *Conn. B.J.*, 26 (1952): 70, 78–79.

10. *Sheldon v. River Lines*, 91 Cal. App. 2d 478, 205 P.2d 37 (1949).

11. L. Green, *Traffic Victims* (1958), p. 78.

12. *Time*, Feb. 20, 1978, p. 65.

13. For a report on a preliminary ruling upholding the lawyers' contention and for ancillary proceedings before an insurance commissioner in Kansas, see *ATLA Law Rep.*, 21 (October 1978): 368–69.

14. H. Kalven and H. Zeisel, *The American Jury* (1966), pp. 8–9.

15. Ibid., p. 9.

16. M. Mayer, *The Lawyers* (1966), p. 252.

17. As quoted in A. Strick, "Trial by Battle," *Center Magazine*, May–June 1978, pp. 51, 56.

18. Kalven, "Juries and Personal Injury," note 6 *supra*, p. 336.

19. M. Rosenberg, "Contemporary Litigation in the United States," in H. Jones, ed. *Legal Institutions Today: English and American Approaches Compared* (1977), pp. 152, 177–78.

20. C. McCormick, "Jury Verdicts upon Special Questions in Civil Cases," *FRD*, 1 (1941): 176–77; also quoted in R. Charrow and V. Charrow, *The Comprehension of Standard Jury Instructions: A Psycholinguistic Approach* (1978), p. 10, n. 13 (Preliminary Report).

21. Charrow and Charrow, *Comprehension*, pp. 7–8.

22. Ibid., pp. 8–9.

23. J. Swain, "Common Sense in Jury Trials," *Cal. S. B. J.*, 30 (1955): 405, 412; also quoted in Charrow and Charrow, *Comprehension*, p. 10.

24. *Skidmore v. Baltimore & O. R. Co.*, 167 F.2d 54, 64 (2d Circ. 1948); also quoted in Charrow and Charrow, *Comprehension*, p. 10.

25. 347 F. Supp. 995 (N.D. Ill. 1972); also cited in Charrow and Charrow, *Comprehension*, p. 3, n. 4.

26. Ibid., p. 39.

27. Ibid., p. 44, n.6.

28. p. 24.

29. Cal. Jury Instructions, Civil § 3.75 (6th ed. 1977).

30. Charrow, and Charrow, *Comprehension*, p. 99.

31. Ibid., p. 43.

32. Ill. Pattern Jury Instructions, Civil § 34.02 (2d ed. 1971).

33. 282 F.2d 34 (2d Cir. 1960), *cert. denied*, 364 U.S. 870, 81 S.Ct. 115 (1960). *But see Burlington Northern, Inc.* v. *Boxberger*, 529 S.2d 284 (9th Cir. 1976).

34. R. Nordstrom, "Income Taxes and Personal Injury Awards, *Ohio St. L.J.*, 19 (1958), pp. 212, 227.

35. *U.S.* v. *English*, 521 F.2d 63, 75 (9th Circ. 1975).

36. *Johnson* v. *Penrod Drilling Co.*, 510 F.2d 234 (5th Cir. 1975). For a

Federal decision actually reversing a charge instructing the jury *not* to consider future inflation, see *Bach* v. *Penn Central Transp. Co.,* 502 F.2d 1117 (6th Cir. 1974).

37. E.g., *U.S.* v. *English,* 521 F.2d 63 (9th Cir. 1975).
38. *Bach* v. *Penn Central Transp. Co.,* 502 F.2d 1117 (6th Cir. 1974).
39. *Johnson* v. *Serra,* 521 F.2d 1289, 1294 (8th Circ. 1975).
40. Much of the above discussion on inflation is based on J. Fleming, "The Impact of Inflation on Tort Compensation," *Am. J. Comp. L.,* 26 (1977): 51.
41. L. Green, *Judge and Jury* (1930), p. 398; also cited in Charrow and Charrow, *Comprehension,* p. 9.
42. Charrow and Charrow, *Comprehension,* pp. 25–26.
43. *Investment Service Co.* v. *Allied Equities Corp.,* 519 F.2d 508, 510 (9th Cir. 1975).
44. C. Bok, *I Too, Nicodemus* (1946), pp. 261–62.
45. E. Griswold, "1962–63 Harvard Law School Dean's Report," pp. 5–6.
46. *New York Times,* April 26, 1978, pp. 1, 40.
47. J. O'Connell, "Jury Trials in Civil Cases?" *Ill. B.J.,* 58 (1970): 796; G. Braden and R. Cohn, *The Illinois Constitution: An Annotated and Comparative Analysis,* (1969), pp. 24–27.
48. Rosenberg, "Contemporary Litigation," note 19 *supra,* p. 176–77.
49. Kalven and Zeisel, *American Jury,* note 14 *supra,* pp. vi–vii.
50. Kalven, "Juries and Personal Injury," note 6 *supra,* pp. 345–47.
51. Kalven and Zeisel, *American Jury,* p. 466.
52. Kalven, "Juries and Personal Injury," p. 348.
53. Ibid., p. 349.
54. *New York Times,* April 10, 1978 p. B–1.
55. *New York Times,* April 18, 1978, p. 18.
56. W. Martin, "An Interview with Richard 'Racehorse' Haynes," *Trial,* 14 (April 1978): 26, 31.
57. E. Solender and E. Solender, "Minimizing the Effect of the Unattractive Client on the Jury: A Study of the Interaction of Physical Appearance with Assertions and Self-Experience References," *Human Rights,* (1976): 201, 206.
58. Kalven and Zeisel, *American Jury,* p. 149.
59. Kalven, "Juries and Personal Injury," p. 343.
60. Ibid., pp. 343–44.
61. H. Kalven, "The Dignity of the Civil Jury," *Va. L. Rev.,* 50 (1964): 1055, 1062.
62. Ibid.
63. Concerning attempts to make jury duty more palatable, see *Wall Street Journal,* Nov. 29, 1977, p. 40.

64. Rosenberg, "Contemporary Litigation," note 19 *supra*, p. 179.
65. Charrow and Charrow, *Comprehension*, note 20 *supra*, p. 3.
66. Concerning New York's experience, see *New York Times*, April 19, 1978, p. 43. Concerning New Jersey's experience, see *Nat'l L.J.*, Nov. 27, 1978, p. 16.
67. *New York Times*, April 26, 1978, pp. 1, 40.
68. *New York Times*, July 21, 1975, pp. 1, 10.
69. *New York Times*, April 26, 1978, pp. 1, 40.

Chapter 6: THE JUDGE *(pp. 107-29)*

1. *Time*, Aug. 20, 1979, p. 50
2. M. Mayer, *The Lawyers* (1966), p. 495.
3. Ibid., p. 499.
4. According to the study of the 162 judges on the Cook County Circuit Court (the main trial bench), 139 are Democrats, 20 are Republicans, and 3 assert their political independence. Of the 139 Democrats, all but 19 have been active in the regular Democratic organization as precinct captains, ward or township party officers, candidates for public office, or as lawyers in agencies or offices usually under the patronage system. Press release, statement by F. Greenberg, Committee on Courts and Justice, April 23, 1978. See *Chicago Sun-Times*, April 23, 1978, p. 6.
5. W. Sayre and H. Kaufman, *Governing New York City* (1960), as quoted in M. Kempton, "Below the Bench," *New York Review of Books*, May 6, 1971, pp. 31, 32.
6. Kempton, "Below the Bench," p. 32.
7. M. Tolchin and S. Tolchin, *To the Victor: Political Patronage from the Clubhouse to the White House* (1971), as referred to in Kempton, "Below the Bench," p. 32.
8. Kempton, "Below the Bench," p. 32.
9. "The Gilt-Edged Profession," *Forbes*, Sept. 15, 1971, pp. 30, 33.
10. H. James, *Crisis in the Courts* (1967), p. 11.
11. *New York Times*, Oct. 13, 1971, p. 50.
12. Mayer, *The Lawyers*, p. 488.
13. J. Goulden, *The Benchwarmers* (1974), pp. 12-13.
14. Ibid., pp. 7-8.
15. *New York Times*, Sept. 5, 1968, p. 30.
16. Mayer, *The Lawyers*, p. 496.
17. Goulden, *Benchwarmers*, p. 13.
18. James, *Crisis in the Courts*, pp. 24-25.
19. As quoted in Mayer, *The Lawyers*, p. 49.

20. Private communication, Dec. 17, 1963.
21. J. Carlin, *Lawyers on Their Own* (1962), pp. 134–35.
22. Private communication, Dec. 17, 1963.
23. Mayer, *The Lawyers*, p. 499.
24. "Report: The Cook County Judicial Monopoly: A Study for the Committee on Courts and Justice" (April 1978), p. 8; quoted in *Chicago Sun-Times*, April 24, 1978, p. 68.
25. Mayer, *The Lawyers*, p. 495.
26. James, *Crisis in the Courts*, p. 12.
27. M. Royko, "Short Course in Legal Ethics," *Chicago Daily News*, Jan. 3, 1968, p. 3.
28. J. Mills, "I Have Nothing to Do with Justice," *LIFE*, March 12, 1971, pp. 57, 66.
29. *New York Times*, May 23, 1978, p. B-2.
30. Goulden, *Benchwarmers*, note 13 *supra*, p. 18.
31. *Washington Post*, April 23, 1978, p. D-1.
32. F. Greenberg, "The Illinois 'Two Tier' Judicial Disciplinary System: Five Years and Counting," *Chi.-Kent L. Rev.*, 54 (1978): 69, 70.
33. *New York Times*, April 30, 1978, p. E-6.
34. *Time*, Aug. 20, 1979, pp. 50, 54.
35. *See New York Times*, July 27, 1979, p. B-5.
36. For a discussion of the case, see R. Cohn, "Judicial Discipline in Illinois: A Commentary on the Judge Elward Decision," *Chic. B. Rec.* 59 (January–February 1978): 200, 218. For an able attempt by Elward's lawyers—ultimately, in this writer's view unsuccessful—to defend the Court's Commission decision, see D. Reuben and L. Ring, "Judges Have Rights Too," *Chi. B. Rec.*, 59: 220. But for a more generalized contention by a law review commentator that "only when there exists a reasonable probability that litigants' rights stand to be adversely affected by untoward judicial biases can it be said that the community suffers the kind of loss of respect for the judiciary which should be addressed by a judicial disciplinary system," see "Comment: Toward a Disciplined Approach to Judicial Discipline," *Northwestern U.L. Rev.*, 73 (1978): 503, 528. According to that author, Elward's conduct did not justify disciplinary action under this test. For a citation to the recent literature on judicial discipline, see loc. cit., p. 503, n. 4. For a further contention by a lawyer who has "observed and been subjected to incompetent, arbitrary and prejudiced judges" that nonetheless the independence of the judiciary requires that "not much . . . be done . . . about judges who violate their professional obligations," see M. Freedman, "Judicial Tenure Bill: A Threat to the Independence of Judges," *Nat'l. L.J.*, Dec. 25, 1978, p. 23.
37. *Peoria Journal-Star*, Jan. 5, 1977, p. 1, as quoted in Greenberg, "Illinois 'Two Tier' System," p. 92.

38. Although both the Courts Commission and the Appellate Court found a haircut order was not related to the offense charged, because the Courts Commission also found the order unrelated to rehabilitation and unduly restrictive of personal liberties, the court decision could not serve to validate that of the Courts Commission. *People ex rel. Harrod* v. *Illinois Courts Comm'n*, 69 Ill. 2d 445, 456 (1978). Presumably, if the Courts Commission had just stopped with ruling that the haircut order was not related to the offense charged, it might have been upheld by the Illinois Supreme Court. (But, given the manner in which Supreme Court strained to invalidate the Courts Commission decision, who knows?)

39. Greenberg, "Illinois 'Two Tier' System," p. 109.

40. *People ex rel. Harrod* v. *Illinois Courts Comm'n*, 69 Ill. 2d 445, 456 (1978).

41. Press release, Illinois Judicial Inquiry Board, re Supreme Court Decision in *Harrod* Case, March 30, 1978, p. 4.

42. Greenberg, "Illinois 'Two Tier' System," p. 112. Although more than 75 percent of the judges brought before the Courts Commission have been found guilty of misconduct, with punishment ranging from reprimand, censor, or suspension to removal from the bench (*Chicago Tribune*, Sept. 24, 1978, p. 18), these figures are misleading in that the Judicial Inquiry Board presents only cases of relatively clear misconduct to the Courts Commission, with many more cases being dropped by the Judicial Inquiry Board for lack of such a level of evidence as is likely to convince the Courts Commission of the necessity of disciplinary action.

43. *Judicial Administration Newsletter*, 8 (May 1978): 4.

44. *Stump* v. *Sparkman*, 98 S. Ct. 51, 712 (1978).

45. *Wall Street Journal*, May 18, 1978, p. 24. The Texas experience highlights the comment of comic writer Robert Orben: "America now has legalized gambling in three separate places—Las Vegas, Atlantic City and voting booths." *Wall Street Journal*, Dec. 6, 1978, p. 18.

46. E. Costikyan, *Behind Closed Doors* (1966), p. 179.

47. Ibid., p. 180.

48. See *New York Times*, Feb. 12, 1976, p. 25. E. Miller, "Global Watchdog," *Harv. L. Bull.*, 29 (1978): 24, 26–27.

49. Costikyan, *Behind Closed Doors*, p. 203.

50. K. Minogue, book review of J. Griffith, *The Politics of The Judiciary* (1977) in *Times* (London) *Literary Supplement*, Jan. 6, 1978, p. 11.

51. Levin, *Urban Politics and the Criminal Courts*, 16 *The Judges' Journal* (Summer 1977): 16, 20, 21; for the editorial summarizing the findings, see *Wall Street Journal*, Aug. 15, 1977, p. 12.

52. For a similar statement made anonymously about an anonymous judge, but obviously talking about Wyzanski, see Mayer, *The Lawyers*, note 2, *supra*, p. 498.

53. F. Frankfurter and H. Phillips, *Felix Frankfurter Reminisces* (1960), pp. 102–3.
54. M. Howe, ed., *Holmes–Laski Letters* (1953), 1:165.
55. Mayer, *The Lawyers*, pp. 494–95.
56. Private communication, Dec. 17, 1963, note 20 *supra*.
57. Mayer, *The Lawyers*, p. 499.
58. James, *Crisis in the Courts*, note 10 *supra*, p. 25.

Chapter 7: THE PERSONAL INJURY LAWYER *(pp. 130–53)*

1. *Black's Law Dictionary*, 4th ed. (1951), p. 1246.
2. H. Lea, *Superstition and Force: Essays on the Wager of Law—The Wager of Battle—The Ordeal Torture* (1866), pp. 199, 201–2.
3. Ibid., p. 88, n. 2.
4. Ibid., p. 120.
5. Ibid., pp. 121, 139.
6. Ibid., p. 121.
7. *E.g.* F. Wellman, *The Art of Cross-Examination* (1931), p. 19; J. Ehrlich, *The Lost Art of Cross-Examination* (1970), pp. 8, 9, 17, 18, 27.
8. Ehrlich, *Lost Art*, p. 17; K. Rosengern, "Can the Adversary System Survive?" *ABA Journal*, 55 (1969): 1157, 1158.
9. N. Savay, *The Art of the Trial* (1929), p. 21.
10. C. Curtis, *It's Your Law* (1954), p. 18.
11. H. Goitein, *Primitive Ordeal and Modern Law* (1923), p. 71.
12. J. Seligman, *The High Citadel: The Influence of Harvard Law School* (1978), p. 153.
13. A. Stone, "Legal Education on the Couch," *Harv. L. Rev.*, 85 (1971): 392, 415–16; also quoted in Seligman, *High Citadel*, p. 8.
14. M. Rosenberg, "The Adversary Proceeding in the Year 2000," *Case and Comment*, 74 (1969): 3, 9.
15. T. Arnold, *The Symbols of Government* (1962), pp. 183–85.
16. F. James, *Civil Procedure* (1965), p. 7.
17. Wellman, *Art of Cross-Examination*, pp. 22, 123.
18. A. Cornelius, *Cross-Examination of Witnesses* (1929), p. 31.
19. L. Lake, *How to Cross-Examine Witnesses Successfully* (1957), p. 3.
20. M. Freedman, "Professional Responsibility of the Criminal Defense Lawyer: The Three Hardest Questions," *Mich. L. Rev.*, 64 (1966): 1469, 1475; also appearing in M. Freedman, *Lawyer's Ethics in an Adversary System* (1975), p. 43.

21. M. Freedman, "The Professional Responsibility of the Prosecuting Attorney," *Geo. L. J.*, 55 (1967): 1030, 1046.
22. Ehrlich, *Lost Art*, note 7 *supra*, p. 49.
23. C. Curtis, "The Ethics of Advocacy," Stan. L. Rev., 4 (1951): 3, 9, 18. Concerning the material in the text accompanying notes 1–11, 5–23, see also A. Strick, *Injustice for All* (1977), chs. 2, 3, 5, 11, 12.
24. *New York Times*, May 16, 1977. p. 35.
25. J. Goulden, *The Million-Dollar Lawyers* (1978), pp. 64–65.
26. M. Bloom, *The Trouble with Lawyers* (1968), p. 143.
27. "The Workshop Sessions: Summary Report, *U. Ill. L.F.*, 1967, pp. 618, 622; also printed in R. Keeton, J. O'Connell, and J. McCord, eds., *Crisis in Car Insurance* (1968), pp. 258, 262.
28. J. K. Galbraith, *The Affluent Society*, 2d ed. (1969), p. 104.
29. R. Coles, book review of S. Rosenfeld, *The Time of Their Dying, Book World, Washington Post*, April 10, 1977, p. E–7.
30. Address of Geoffrey Palmer, University of Illinois College of Law, Oct. 20, 1977.
31. F. Mackinnon, *Contingent Fees for Legal Services* (1964), p. 198.
32. As quoted in Bloom, *Trouble with Lawyers*, p. 139.
33. Ibid., pp. 139–40.
34. Testimony of M. T. Bloom, *Hearings on S.1381 Before the Senate Committee on Commerce Science and Transportation*, 95th Cong., 1st sess. (1977), p. 209.
35. Ibid., p. 208.
36. Bloom, *Trouble with Lawyers*, p. 153.
37. Testimony of M. T. Bloom, p. 203.
38. Bloom, *Trouble with Lawyers*, p. 144.
39. W. Burger, "The Special Skills of Advocacy: Are Specialized Training and Certification of Advocates Essential to Our System of Justice?" *Fordham L. Rev.*, 42 (1973): 227; but see *New York Times* Feb. 11, 1978, p. 1.
43. Private conversation with the author.
44. Testimony of M. T. Bloom, p. 209.
45. J. Star, "The Million-Dollar Attorney for the Maimed" *Chicago Tribune Magazine*, p. 34.
46. See M. Franklin, R. Chanin, and I. Mark, "Accidents, Money and The Law: A Study of the Economics of Personal Injury Litigation," Col. L. Rev., 61 (1961): 1, 14, 30; H. L. Ross, *Settled Out of Court* (1962), pp. 193–98.
47. See U.S. Department of Transportation, *Automobile Personal Injury Claims*, 1 (1970): 64–65, 115; J. O'Connell and R. Simon, *Payment for Pain and Suffering* (1972), p. 17; also printed in *U. Ill. L.F.* (1972), p. 17.

48. A. Ehrenzweig, *"Full Aid" Insurance for the Traffic Victim: A Voluntary Compensation Plan* (1954), p. 6. For a slightly revised version of the book, see the same title by the same author in *U. Calif. L. Rev.*, 43 (1955): 1–10.

49. M. Mayer, *The Lawyers* (1966), p. 267.

50. Private conversation with the author.

51. Mayer, *The Lawyers*, p. 266.

52. N. Sheresky, *On Trial* (1977), p. 188.

53. *New York Times*, Aug. 7, 1966, p. E–5.

54. J. Q. Wilson, "Don't Blame the Adversary System," *Fortune*, July 31, 1978, pp. 131–32.

55. L. Loevinger, "Preface," in J. Marshall, *Law and Psychology in Conflict* (1966), p. viii.

56. L. Powers, Interprofessional Education and Medical Legal Conflict Seen from the Other Side, *Ann. J. Med. Educ.*, 40 (1965): 233 ff.; quoted in W. Curran and D. Shapiro, *Law, Medicine and Forensic Science*, 2d ed. (1970), pp. 3, 6, 8.

57. *See* Wilson, "Don't Blame Adversary System," p. 131.

58. Ibid., p. 132.

59. J. O'Connell, *The Injury Industry: And The Remedy of No-Fault Insurance* (1971), p. 154.

Chapter 8: No-Fault Auto Insurance as a Solution
(pp. 157–75)

1. *Chicago Tribune*, Oct. 6, 1976, p. 1.

2. *Washington Post*, Aug. 2, 1978, p. A–12.

3. Common Cause, "Trial Lawyers Group Contributes Almost Quarter of a Million Dollars to 1976 Congressional Candidates," press release, Feb. 28, 1978.

4. Committee for Consumers No-Fault, "Trial Lawyer Opponents of No-Fault Raise and Spend $1 Million in Political Fund," press release, Nov. 5, 1978.

5. Demkovich, "It's Time for Another Battle on No-Fault Insurance," *Nat'l J.*, Oct. 8, 1977, pp. 1572–73.

6. See Chapter 2, note 1, *supra*.

7. *See generally* J. O'Connell, *The Injury Industry and the Remedy of No-Fault Insurance* (1971), pp. 94–154, and J. O'Connell and R. Henderson, *Tort Law, No-Fault and Beyond: Teaching Materials on Compensation for Accidents and Ailments in Modern Society* (1975), pp. 223–46.

8. *U.S. Dep't of Transportation, Economic Consequences of Automobile Accident Injuries* (1970), 1: 37–38; A. Conard, J. Morgan, R. Pratt, C. Votz, and R. Bombaugh, *Automobile Accident Costs and Payments: Studies in the Economics of Injury Reparation* (1964), p. 186 (45 percent of the seriously injured get no damage recovery through the tort law system).

9. Conard, "Testimony Before the New York Joint Legislative Committee on Insurance Rates and Regulation," *U. Mich. L. Quadrangle Notes* (Fall 1970), p. 14.

10. U.S. Dep't of Transportation, *Economic Consequences*, 1:52.

11. *Lawyer Reform News*, 1 (April/May 1971): 4.

12. U.S. Dep't of Transportation, *Automobile Personal Injury Claims* (1970), 1:78. The Department of Transportation study lists the figures for nineteen states. In 1970, the national average was about 47 percent.

13. *E.g.*, P. Keeton and R. Keeton, *Torts: Cases and Materials* (1971), p. 514. The Keetons' figures were later cited and independently confirmed in N.Y. Insurance Dep't, *Automobile Insurance . . . For Whose Benefit? A Report to Governor Nelson A. Rockefeller* (1970), pp. 34–37.

14. O. Connell, *Injury Industry*, pp. 70–72; J. O'Connell and W. Wilson, *Car Insurance and Consumer Desires* (1969), p. 15.

15. For a description of modified no-fault plans see O'Connell and Henderson, *Tort Law*, pp. 281–82. (Nevada repealed its law in 1979.)

16. For a citation to the statutes see J. O'Connell, "Operation of No-Fault Auto Laws: A Survey of the Surveys," *Neb. L. Rev.*, 56 (1977): 23, 26–27, nn. 17–30, 32–39; reprinted in *Ins. L. J.*, 1977, pp. 152, 155, nn. 17–30, 32–39; O'Connell and Henderson, *Tort Law*, pp. 279–81. For a discussion of plans approaching pure no-fault see O'Connell and Henderson, *Tort Law*, pp. 283–84. *Mich. Compl. Laws Ann* (Supp. 1976), §§ 500.3101–.3179. Under the Michigan law, wage-loss is tied to inflation. Originally pegged at $1,000 per month, the maximum payment for lost wages is now more than $1,300. See *Mich. Comp. Laws Ann.* (Supp. 1976), § 500.3107(b). See also *Minn. Stat. Ann.* (Supp. 1978), §§ 65B.14,-.41-.71; N.Y. Ins. Law §§ (McKinney Supp. 1978), 670–678; S. 1381 and H.R. 6601, 95th Cong., 1st sess. (1977).

17. L. Ring, "The Fault with 'No-Fault' " *Notre Dame Lawyer*, 49 (1974): 796, 826.

18. See O'Connell, "Operation of No-Fault," pp. 29, 157.

19. See U.S. Dep't of Transportation, *State No-Fault Automobile Insurance Experience, 1971–1977* (June 1977), p. 64.

20. *New York Times*, July 25, 1976, p. 1.

21. *Wall Street Journal*, Jan. 21, 1976, pp. 1, 12.

22. *New York Times*, July 25, 1976, p. 1.

23. *New York Times*, April 18, 1976, p. 1.

24. *Fla. Stat. Ann.* (Supp. 1978), § 627.7375.

25. *N.Y. Ins. Law* (McKinney Supp. 1978), § 678.

26. *Wall Street Journal*, Jan. 21, 1976, p. 1.

27. *New York Times*, July 25, 1976, p. 34.

28. Insurance Institute for Highway Safety, *Status Report*, 11, no. 4 (March 3, 1976): 9.

29. O'Connell, *Injury Industry*, note 7 *supra*, pp. 109–110.

30. DOT, *State No-Fault*, note 19 *supra*, p. 70. A New Jersey report indicates that only 21 percent of the premium applies to bodily injury coverage. Legislative Study Commission, *No-Fault Automobile Insurance Reform in New Jersey* (1977), p. 71.

31. 1977 New Jersey Report, p. 72.

32. Note, "No-Fault Automobile Insurance: An Evaluative Survey," *Rut. L. Rev.*, 30 (1977): 909, 953–54.

33. Ibid., pp. 960, 964, 966, 970.

34. Ibid., pp. 975–78.

35. Insurance Bureau, Michigan Dep't of Commerce, *No-Fault Insurance in Michigan: Consumer Attitudes and Performance* (1978), p. 35.

36. 1977 New Jersey Report, p. 71.

37. *Money*, November 1976, p. 75.

38. 1977 New Jersey Report, pp. 50–51.

39. See DOT, *Economic Consequences*, note 8 *supra*, 1: 277–78, Table 31. FS. They also received from other sources than fault-finding claims, such as health insurance, only $17,899, for a total of $21,641. Ibid.

40. See O'Connell, "Operation of No-Fault," note 16 *supra*, p. 41, n. 80; reprint, p. 166.

41. Ibid., at n. 81.

42. Ibid., at n. 83.

43. Ibid., p. 42, n. 84; reprint, p. 167.

44. The basic reason for this maldistribution of payment is that when the claim from an auto accident is for a small amount, it will cost the insurance company so much to defend itself, compared to what is at stake, that it is often cheaper to pay even an inflated amount for the claim, to be rid of it. But when auto accident victims' losses are large, the cost of adjusters' and lawyers' time in defending the claim is so small compared to what is at stake that payment is stoutly resisted. O'Connell, *Injury Industry*, note 7 *supra*, pp. 34–35.

45. 1978 Michigan Report, p. 34.

46. Ibid.

47. A. Widiss, "A Survey of the No-Fault Personal Injury Experience in Massachusetts," in Council on Law-Related Studies, *No-Fault Automobile Insurance in Action* (1977), p. 211, Table 30.

48. Ibid., p. 209, Table 28.
49. DOT, *State No-Fault*, note 19 *supra*, p. 32, Table III–7. The figures are from 1969.
50. Ibid., p. 36.
51. A. Widiss, "Massachusetts No-Fault Automobile Insurance: Its Impact on the Legal Profession," *B.U.L. Rev.*, 56 (1976): 323; also printed in Council on Law-Related Studies, *No-Fault Automobile Insurance in Action*, p. 102.
52. Ibid., p. 336; reprint, p. 100.
53. Little, "No-Fault Auto Reparation in Florida: An Empirical Examination of Some of Its Effects," *Mich. J.L. Reform*, 9 (1975): 1, 25; also printed in Council on Law-Related Studies, *No-Fault Auto Insurance in Action*, p. 289.
54. Widiss, "Massachusetts No-Fault," p. 337; reprint, p. 101.
55. Widiss, "Survey of No-Fault," p. 222.
56. R. Bovbjerg, "The Impact of No-Fault Auto Insurance on Massachusetts Courts," *New England L. Rev.*, 11 (1976): 325, 339; also printed in Council on Law-Related Studies, *No-Fault Automobile Insurance in Action*, p. 141.
57. DOT, *State No-Fault*, pp. 55–57.
58. O'Connell, "Operation of No-Fault," note 16 *supra*, p. 44, n. 94; reprint, p. 168.
59. Widiss, "Massachusetts No-Fault," pp. 355, 347; reprint pp. 119, 111.
60. Ibid., p. 346 and p. 110; *New York Times*, Jan. 25, 1976, p. 1.
61. O'Connell, "Operation of No-Faults, p. 44, n. 97; reprint p. 169.
62. A. Widiss, "Accident Victims Under No-Fault Automobile Insurance: A Massachusetts Survey," *Iowa L. Rev.*, 61 (1975): 1, 64–65; also printed in Council on Law-Related Studies, *No-Fault Automobile Insurance in Action*, pp. 78–79.
63. Ibid., pp. 50–51; reprint, pp. 64–65.
64. 1978 Michigan Report, note 35 *supra*, pp. 15–18. The report notes that the wording of this question as presented to the public did not indicate the savings in premiums that would probably result from elimination of duplicated benefits. Thus, the report continues, the question was worded so as to reflect a lower distaste for duplication of benefits than that which probably would be indicated if more information had been supplied.
65. Ibid., p. 17.
66. Ibid., p. 23.
67. Ibid., pp. 24–25. The main problems identified were high cost of insurance, the insurance industry's rating and pricing systems, and the availability of insurance. Ibid., pp. 24–27.

68. Ibid.
69. Ibid., p. i.
70. See *Kluger* v. *White*, 281 So. 2d 1 (Fla. 1972). Act of Aug. 4, 1976, ch. 266, § 7, 1976 Mass. Adv. Legis. Serv. (amending Mass. Ann. Laws ch. 90, § 34 0 [Law Co-op. 1975]). The Act of Aug. 4, 1976, is codified at Mass. Ann. Laws ch. 90, § 34 0 (Law Co-op Supp. 1977). *Shavers* v. *Kelley*, 402 Mich. 554, 267 N.W. 2d 72 (1978).
71. As quoted in O'Connell, "Operation of No-Fault," p. 45, n. 103; reprint, p. 169.
72. The 1978 Michigan Report indicates that between 1973 and 1976 the price of providing property damage benefits has increased substantially and is a major factor in overall rate increases. 1978 Michigan Report, p. 47.
73. J. Little, "No-Fault Auto Reparation," note 61 *supra*, pp. 61, 325.
74. DOT, *State No-Fault*, note 19 *supra*, p. 80.

Chapter 9: WHAT TO DO NEXT? *(pp. 176–85)*

1. National Comm'n on Product Safety, *Final Report* (1970), p. 73 (hereinafter cited as *Final Report*).
2. G. Bushnell, "Defendant's Trial Techniques in Products Liability," in S. Schreiber and P. Rheingold, eds., *Law, Practice, Science* (1967), pp. 13–47.
3. Main, "What Happens if You Sue the Bastards," *Money*, Nov. 1978, pp. 85, 92.
4. J. O'Connell, *Ending Insult to Injury: No-Fault Insurance for Products and Services* (1975), p. 1.
5. *Final Report*, p. 73.
6. U.S. Dep't of Commerce, Interagency Task Force on Product Liability, *Briefing Report* (1977), p. iii (hereinafter cited as Task Force).
7. *Final Report*, pp. 73–74.
8. *See* First World Congress on Product Liability, *Proceedings*, (1977), p. 177 (remarks of M. Belli).
9. Insurance Services Office, *Product Liability Closed Claim Survey: A Technical Analysis of Survey Results* (1977), p. 98 (hereinafter cited as ISO Study).
10. Ibid., p. 79.
11. Ibid., p. 90. "In fact, over 1% of all claims involved [defense costs] greater than $50,000, averaging, nearly $140,000." Ibid., p. 92.

12. See also J. O'Connell, "An Alternative to Abandoning Tort Liability: Elective No-Fault Insurance for Many Kinds of Injuries," *U. Minn. L. Rev.*, 60 (1976): 501, 511.
13. Task Force, pp. 8–9.
14. Ibid., pp. ii, 6.
15. O'Connell, *Ending Insult*, note 4 *supra*, p. 29.
16. Center for the Study of Democratic Institutions, "Medical Malpractice: A Discussion of Alternative Compensation and Quality Control Systems," A Center Occasional Paper, D. McDonald, ed. (1971), p. 17.
17. O'Connell, "Alternative," pp. 506–9.
18. American Insurance Association, *Product Liability Legislative Package: Statutes Designed to Improve the Fairness and Administration of Product Liability Law* (revised March 1977), pp. 3, 14–22.
19. Ibid., pp. 32–33; for an explanation of this provision, see ibid., pp. 3–4.
20. Ibid., pp. 4–5, 34–63.
21. Ibid., pp. 78–96. An addendum was added to the publication based on action adopted by the American Insurance Association, Sept. 6, 1977. Another proposal was added in the revision of March 1977.
22. See J. O'Connell and R. Henderson, *Tort Law, No-Fault and Beyond: Teaching Materials on Compensation for Accidents and Ailments in Modern Society* (1975), pp. 761–62; O'Connell, *Alternative*, note 15 *supra*, pp. 513–14.
23. American Bar Association, *Interim Report of the Commission on Medical Professional Liability* (1976), p. 17.
24. R. Begam, "Products Liability 'Crisis' Disproven," *Trial*, Feb. 1977, p. 2.
25. This language appears in a typical workers' compensation statute. A. Larson, *Workmen's Compensation Law* vol. 1 (1972), § 6.00 *et seq.*
26. R. Keeton and J. O'Connell, *Basic Protection for the Traffic Victim* (1965), p. 303.
27. Secretary's Comm'n on Medical Malpractice, *Medical Malpractice: Report*, U.S. Dep't of Health, Education, and Welfare Pub. No. (OS) 73–88 (1973), pp. 131–33 (statement of Richard M. Markus).
28. Accident Compensation Act, 1972, No. 43, 1 N.Z. Stat. 521. See O'Connell, "Transferring Injured Victims' Tort Rights to No-Fault Insurers," *U. Ill. L.F.*, 1977, pp. 749, 781–84.
29. National Committee of Inquiry, *Report: Compensation and Rehabilitation in Australia* (1974); for a discussion of the Australian proposal, see Palmer, "Accidents, Sickness and Compensation: The Direction of Social Welfare in Australia," in O'Connell and Henderson, *Tort Law*, p. 696.

30. Report of the Royal Commission on Civil Liability and Compensation for Personal Injury (1978), Cmnd. 7054 (known as the "Pearson Commission" after its Chairman, Lord Pearson). See A. Ogus, P. Corfield, and D. Harris, "Pearson: Principled Reform or Political Compromise?" *Indus. L.J.*, 1978, p. 143

31. R. Lyons, "Rx for Health Care: The Cost Is Staggering," *New York Times*, Dec. 17, 1978, p. E-4.

32. O'Connell, "Transferring," p. 759, n. 41.

33. Lyons, "Rx for Health Care." For a lucid discussion of the high costs but often inadequate coverage under U.S. Social Security covering disability see R. Ball, Social Secuirty Today and Tomorrow ch. 7 (1978).

34. F. Harper and F. James, *The Law of Torts* (Supp. 1968), 2:4-5. See also O'Connell, "Transferring," pp. 760-61.

35. O'Connell, "Transferring," p. 782, n. 107.

Chapter 10: HARNESSING THE LAWSUIT LOTTERY *(pp. 176-85)*

1. J. O'Connell, "Transferring Injured Victim's Torts Rights to No-Fault Insurers: New "Sole Remedy" Approaches to Cure Liability Insurance Ills," *U. Ill. L.F.*, 1977, pp. 749, 775-6.

2. Concerning the fear of many insurers of unlimited coverage or even coverage with extremely high dollar limits, see ibid., p. 786; O'Connell, "Financing First-Party No-Fault Insurance by Assignment by Third-Party Tort Claims," *Ins. L.J.*, 1978, pp. 207, 217. For a discussion of both caps and deductibles as a means of controlling costs, see pp. 786-89 of "Transferring" and pp. 217-18 of "Financing."

3. It would also be possible for the insurer to offer optional first-party no-fault benefits for "pain and inconvenience," in scheduled amounts to avoid problems of evaluation. See J. O'Connell, "Harnessing the Lawsuit Lottery: ELective No-Fault Insurance for All Kinds of Accidents," *Wash. U. L.Q.*, 1978, p. 698, n. 27.

4. For more on the mechanics of handling the claim between the no-fault insured and its insured such as to eliminate any conflict of interest as to the amount due from any fault-finding claim from a third party, see Appendix to this volume, adapted from O'Connell, "Harnessing," pp. 698-702.

5. Ibid., at p. 703, n. 37.

6. For an indication that when employees have an election, they never choose to preserve their tort rights as opposed to accepting no-fault coverage under workmen's compensation acts, see S. Horovitz and J.

Bear, "Would a Compulsory Workman's Compensation Act Without Trial by Jury Be Constitutional in Massachusetts?" *B. U. L. Rev.*, 18 (1938): 1, 35–36.

7. O'Connell, "Transferring," p. 792, n. 140; O'Connell, "Financing," p. 209, n. 5.

8. See Appendix to this volume, adapted from O'Connell, "Harnessing," pp. 698–702.

9. For more extensive discussions of the arguable inapplicability of rules against transfer of personal injury claims to my proposal for first-party no-fault insurance, see O'Connell, "Transferring," pp. 804–9; "Financing," pp. 221–25; "Harnessing," pp. 707–08, 711–12, n. 55.

10. See also O'Connell, "Transferring," pp. 807–9; "Financing," pp. 224–25; J. O'Connell, "Supplementing Workers' Compensation Benefits in Return for an Assignment of Third-Party Tort Claims—Without an Enabling Statute," *Tex. L. Rev.*, 56 (1978): 537, 552; "Harnessing," pp. 707–08, 711–12, n. 55.

11. M. Reder, "Contingent Fees in Litigation with Special Reference to Medical Malpractice," in S. Rottenberg, ed., *The Economics of Medical Malpractice* (1978), pp. 211, 224–29, 231.

12. J. O'Connell, "The Interlocking Death and Rebirth of Contract and Tort," *Mich. L. Rev.*, 75 (1972): 659, 681–83; reprinted in abridged form in *Ins. L.J.*, 1977, pp. 734, 745–47.

13. Nat'l Comm'n on State Workmen's Compensation Laws, *Compendium on Workmen's Compensation*, M. Rosenblum, ed. (1973), pp. 16–18.

14. See W. Blum and H. Kalven, *Public Law Perspectives on a Private Law Problem: Auto Compensation Plans* (1965); first published in *U. Chi. L. Rev.*, 31 (1964): 641.

15. O'Connell, "Transferring," pp. 780–81, nn. 104, 105.

16. *Couch* v. *Central Maloney Transformer Corp.*, No. 75871 (King County, Washington Superior Court, Apr. 24, 1974) (transcript on file at the law offices of Philip H. Corboy and Associates, 33 N. Dearborn St., Chicago, Ill. 60602); noted in P. Corboy, "The Expanding Universe of Jeffrey O'Connell: Backing into a Brave New World," *U. Ill. L.F.*, 1976, p. 100, n. 63.

17. J. O'Connell and R. Simon, *Payment for Pain and Suffering: Who Wants What, When and Why?* (1972), pp. 29–34; also printed in *U. Ill. L.F.*, 1972, pp. 1, 29–34.

18. Ibid., p. 21, Table 3.2.

19. But see *Wall Street Journal*, Oct. 20, 1978, p. 1.

20. O'Connell and Simon, *Payment*, pp. 25–28.

21. *Wall Street Journal*, Oct. 20, 1978, p. 1.

22. E.g., L. Lander, *Defective Medicine: Risk, Anger, and the Malpractice Crisis* (1978), pp. 32–33.

23. *Wall Street Journal*, March 27, 1972. p. 1.

24. O'Connell and Simon, *Payment*, p. 53, quoting A. Conard *et al.*, *Automobile Accident Costs and Payments: Studies in the Economics of Injury Reparation* (1964), pp. 9, 280–81.

25. L. Burchard, "Newsletter: Social Science," *Intellectual Digest*, Sept. 1973, p. 38, quoting *Psychiatric News*, 8, no. 1: 6; J. O'Connell, *Ending Insult to Injury* (1975), pp. 113–15.

26. See e.g., *Tunkl* v. *Regents of University of California*, 60 Cal. 2d 92, 383 P.2d 441, 32 Cal. Rptr. 33 (1963); *Hunter* v. *American Rentals, Inc.*, 189 Kan. 615, 371 P.2d 131 (1962).

27. Note 9 *supra*.

28. E.g., *Wheeler* v. *Rudek*, 397 Ill. 438, 74 N.E. 2d. 601 (1947).

29. H. Kalven, *The Dignity of the Civil Jury*, Va. L. Rev., 50 (1964): 1055, 1065, 1972.

30. Letter to the author from James Strnad, dated May 26, 1978.

31. L. Ross, *Settled Out of Court: The Social Process of Insurance Claims Adjustment* (1970), p. 145.

32. *Business Week*, Sept. 6, 1976, pp. 46, 48. But, for an alternative proposal that first-party no-fault insurance be written under government (i.e., social security) auspices, see O'Connell, "Transferring," note 1 *supra*, pp. 799–802.

33. "Sue! Sue!" *Forbes*, Sept. 1, 1975, pp. 63–64. On the other hand, enabling legislation could be passed authorizing the coverage. But for a description of the problems attendant on passing legislation, see O'Connell, "Transferring," p. 764, n. 54. Concerning some technical matters of implementing the proposal, see Appendix to this volume. Concerning binding members of the insured's family, other adults in the family could voluntarily become first-party insured. Arguably, adults could bind minor members of their families. See O'Connell, "Transferring," pp. 790–91, n. 136; and O'Connell, "Financing," p. 220, n. 36. As to the out-of-state validity of first-party no-fault insurance contracts in return for assignment of the payees' entire tort claim, see O'Connell, "Harnessing," p. 707, n. 51.

   Granted, implementation of my proposal may be thwarted by fear as to the propriety and/or legality of having insurers actually prosecute others' personal injury claims. In that event, the first-party no-fault insurer could contract for the right to waive—but not actually prosecute—its insureds' third-party tort claims. O'Connell, "Harnessing," pp. 708–11.

34. For a discussion of the legality of such an arrangement under workers' compensation laws, see O'Connell, "Supplementing, note 12 *supra*, pp. 559–66.

35. Concerning related collective bargaining matters, see O'Connell, "Supplementing," pp. 548–49.

36. See J. O'Connell, *The Injury Industry: And the Remedy of No-Fault Insurance* (1971), p. 95.

37. L. Silberman, "Will Lawyering Strangle Democratic Capitalism?" *Regulation*, March/April 1978, pp. 15, 20.

38. M. Green, "Disorder in the Court," *Washington Post, Book World* section, May 21, 1978, p. E-1.

39. W. Shakespeare, *Henry VI, Part Two*, IV, ii.

40. Silberman, "Will Lawyering," p. 15.

41. Ibid., pp. 19, 44.

42. Ibid., p. 44.

43. *Wall Street Journal*, April 3, 1978, pp. 1, 32.

44. *The Washington Monthly*, Sept. 1977, p. 7.

Chapter 11: SOME MORE DOUBTS—AND HOPES *(pp. 206–21)*

1. *New York Times Magazine*, Dec. 2, 1973. p. 6.

2. *New York Times Magazine*, Jan. 6, 1974, p. 6.

3. *New York Times*, June 21, 1970, p. 7.

4. *New York Times*, Jan. 3, 1974, p. 37.

5. *Wall Street Journal*, Jan. 23, 1975, p. 10.

6. *New York Times*, Dec. 27, 1973, p. 29.

7. *Hearings on S.J, Res. 129 Before the Consumer Subcom. of the Senate Comm. on Commerce,* 90th Cong., 2d Sess. (1968), p. 54.

8. D. Moynihan, "Next: A New Auto Insurance Policy," *New York Times Magazine*, Aug. 27, 1967, pp. 26, 78.

9. M. Dukakis, "Legislators Look at Proposed Changes," in R. Keeton, J. O'Connell, and J. McCord, eds. *Crisis in Car Insurance* (1968), pp. 222, 225.

10. *New York Times*, June 2, 1968, section 3 (Business and Finance), p. 1.

11. P. Hellman, "Your Policy Is Hereby Cancelled," *New York Times Magazine*, Nov. 8, 1970, pp. 32, 126.

12. *New York Times*, Dec. 28, 1973, p. 25.

13. *New York Times*, June 2, 1968, section 3 (Business and Finance), p. 1.

14. *Wall Street Journal*, Feb. 1, 1972, p. 18.

15. J. O'Connell, "Transferring Injured Victims' Tort Rights to No-Fault Insurers: New 'Sole Remedy' Approaches to Cure Liability Insurance Ills," *U. Ill. L.F.* 1977, pp. 749, 801–2, n. 166.

16. M. Hunt, "Damage Suits: A Primrose Path to Immorality," *Harper's*, Jan. 1957, pp. 67, 68.

17. L. Ross, *Settled Out of Court* (1970), pp. 27, 29, 32–33, 35, 37, 40, 44–45.

18. R. Churchill, *Winston S. Churchill*, Vol. 2: *Young Statesman, 1901–1914* (1967), p. 294.

19. N. Bliven, book review of J. K. Galbraith, *Economics and the Public Purpose* (1973), in *The New Yorker*, Dec. 31, 1973, pp. 57–58.

20. D. Moynihan, *Coping* (1974), p. 23.

21. Ibid., p. 4.

22. *Nat'l Underwriter* (prop. & cas. ed.), Dec. 6, 1968, p. 1.

23. For citations to discussions pro and con concerning my proposal for third-party no-fault insurance, see O'Connell, "Transferring," pp. 761–64, 794–97; J. O'Connell, "Financing First-Party No-Fault Insurance by Assignment of Third-Party Tort Claims," *Ins. L.J.* 1978, pp. 207, 214 n. 11a.

24. Concerning such rules, see R. Keeton, *Basic Text on Insurance Law* (1971), § 3.11 pp. 170–73. For a discussion of the interraction of first- and third-party no-fault, see O'Connell, "Transferring," pp. 795–96. As one workable device, combining first-party and third-party no-fault, whereby insurance premiums currently being largely misspent on product liability insurance could be used by car manufacturers to cover their customers and simultaneously eliminate product liability claims against themselves, car manufacturers could sell no-fault insurance to those purchasing their cars in return for all their customers' tort claims arising from auto accidents. The coverage would be most valuable in states without or with very inadequate no-fault auto statutes. But even under relatively generous no-fault laws, the car manufacturer's supplement to statutory benefits would be of great value, given the often limited nature of even generous statutory benefits, especially for wage loss. Thus, even in such states a guarantee of payment of losses above statutory no-fault limits would be very valuable to the most needy auto accident victims. And it could be provided at relatively modest cost, if benefits would be payable only in rare instances where all other sources—including the relatively generous no-fault statutory benefits—are exhausted.

25. S.F. No. 2000, Minn. Legislature (1976).

26. O'Connell, "Transferring," p. 766.

27. *Wall Street Journal*, Feb. 25, 1974, p. 1.

28. O'Connell, "Transferring," p. 767.

29. Ibid., p. 772. This "sole remedy" legislation for industrial accidents is more thoroughly discussed generally at ibid., pp. 764–74.

30. D. Moynihan, "Foreword" to J. O'Connell, *Ending Insult to Injury* (1975), pp. xi, xviii–xx.

31. Moynihan, "Next," note 8 *supra*, pp. 26, 82.

32. Moynihan, "Foreword," p. xx.

33. L. Cooperrider, "Book Review," *Wayne L. Rev.*, 22 (1975): 189, 194–95, reviewing O'Connell, *Ending Insult*.

Appendix: MAKING IT WORK *(pp. 223–27)*

1. For a discussion minimizing the conflicts of interest between insurer and insured, see O'Connell, "Harnessing the Law Suit Lottery: Elective No-Fault Insurance Financed by Third-Party Tort Claims, *U. Wash. L.Q.*, 1978, pp. 693, 699, n. 30.
2. See ibid., p. 700, n. 31.
3. Ibid., p. 701, n. 32.
4. Ibid., p. 701, n. 33.
5. Ibid., pp. 701–02, n. 34.

Index

Death benefits, 169
DeKalb, Ill., 64
Defense Lawyers, xi, 141, 204
Delaware add-on no-fault auto law,
    161, 162, 172
Delay in resolution of fault claims, 9,
    19, 22, 23, 38, 41, 70-75, 82,
    160, 164, 171, 178, 192, 195,
    197, 205, 216
Delay, lessening of, under no-fault,
    170-71, 192, 197
Denenberg, Herbert, 24, 210
Desmond, Chief Justice Charles, 84
Deterrence of unsafe conduct, 23-27,
    283-85; *see also* Market deter-
    rence
  auto accidents, 23
  medical malpractice, 25-27
  products liability, 23-25
Detroit Lawyer, The, 141
Devil's Advocate, 151
Disability insurance, 200, 221
Disclaimers of liability, 197
Discounting to present value, 94
Discovery procedures, 66-77
District of Columbia, 117
Doctors, 25, 151, 163, 164, 201, 215
  as defendants, 3-7, 49-57, 195
  as expert witnesses, 19, 32, 34-36
  role in claims against others,
    10-11, 16-19
Dodd, Lester P., 141-42
Dog, seeing-eye, in court, 32
Donelon family, 57-61
Donovan, Leisure, Newton and Ir-
    vine, 70
Dooley, Justice James, 74
"Dooley, Mr.," 113
DOT: *see* United States Department
    of Transportation
Double payment, 9, 12, 18, 173, 214
  elimination of, 173, 187, 192
Drama lessons for lawyers, 66
Drunken driving, 77-83, 201
Dukakis, Michael, 209
Dunne, John Gregory, 15
Duty to warn, 180

Economic loss, from accidents, 8, 9,
    12, 16, 21, 157, 159-60, 162,
    163, 166, 167, 168, 169, 170,
    173, 182, 187, 188, 189, 191,
    194, 198, 214, 216, 220, 223-27;
    see also Medical expense; Wage
    losses; Property damage
Economists, 105, 183
Egan, Michael, 207-08
Ehrenzweig, Albert, 145-46
Elective first-party insurance,
    187-205, 206, 216, 219-21,
    223-27; *see also* First-party in-
    surance
  adverse selection, avoidance of,
    188
  arbitration under, 224-27
  conflict of interest under, 224-27
  double payments, elimination of,
    187, 192
  economic loss, all paid under, 188
  fault claims, transfer of, under
    187-88, 189-91
  legal barriers to, 190
  implemation, ways of, 200
  litigation, effect on, 198-99
  periodic payment under, 187
  settlement of claims when, 188
Elective third-party no-fault insur-
    ance, 214-16, 219-21
Elevator accident, 31, 33, 34
Elias, Mr. and Mrs. Antonio, 11
Elward, Judge Paul, 118-19
Employers Liability Insurance Corp.,
    38-39
Engineers, 24, 42-43, 62, 105, 177
England, 67, 68, 107-08, 109, 110,
    125, 131, 136, 138, 151, 168,
    183, 213
Erdmann, Martin, 116
Erlich, Jake, 134
Erwin, Richard, 78-82
Essex County, N.J., 135
Ethics: *see* Canons of ethics
Eton, 125
Europe, 152
European products liability law, 138